SCIENCE
AND
MATHS
FOR
CURIOUS KIDS

A world of knowledge—from
atoms to zoology!

ARCTURUS

What is STEM?

STEM is a world-wide initiative that aims to cultivate an interest in Science, Technology, Engineering, and Mathematics, in an effort to promote these disciplines to as wide a variety of students as possible.

ARCTURUS

This edition published in 2022 by Arcturus Publishing Limited
26/27 Bickels Yard, 151–153 Bermondsey Street,
London SE1 3HA

Authors: Laura Baker and Lynn Huggins-Cooper
Illustrator: Alex Foster
Consultant: Anne Rooney
Designers: Jeanette Ryall and Mark Golden
Packaged by: Lucy Doncaster

ISBN: 978-1-3988-0698-6
CH008785US
Supplier 26, Date 0322, Print run 12249

Printed in China

CONTENTS

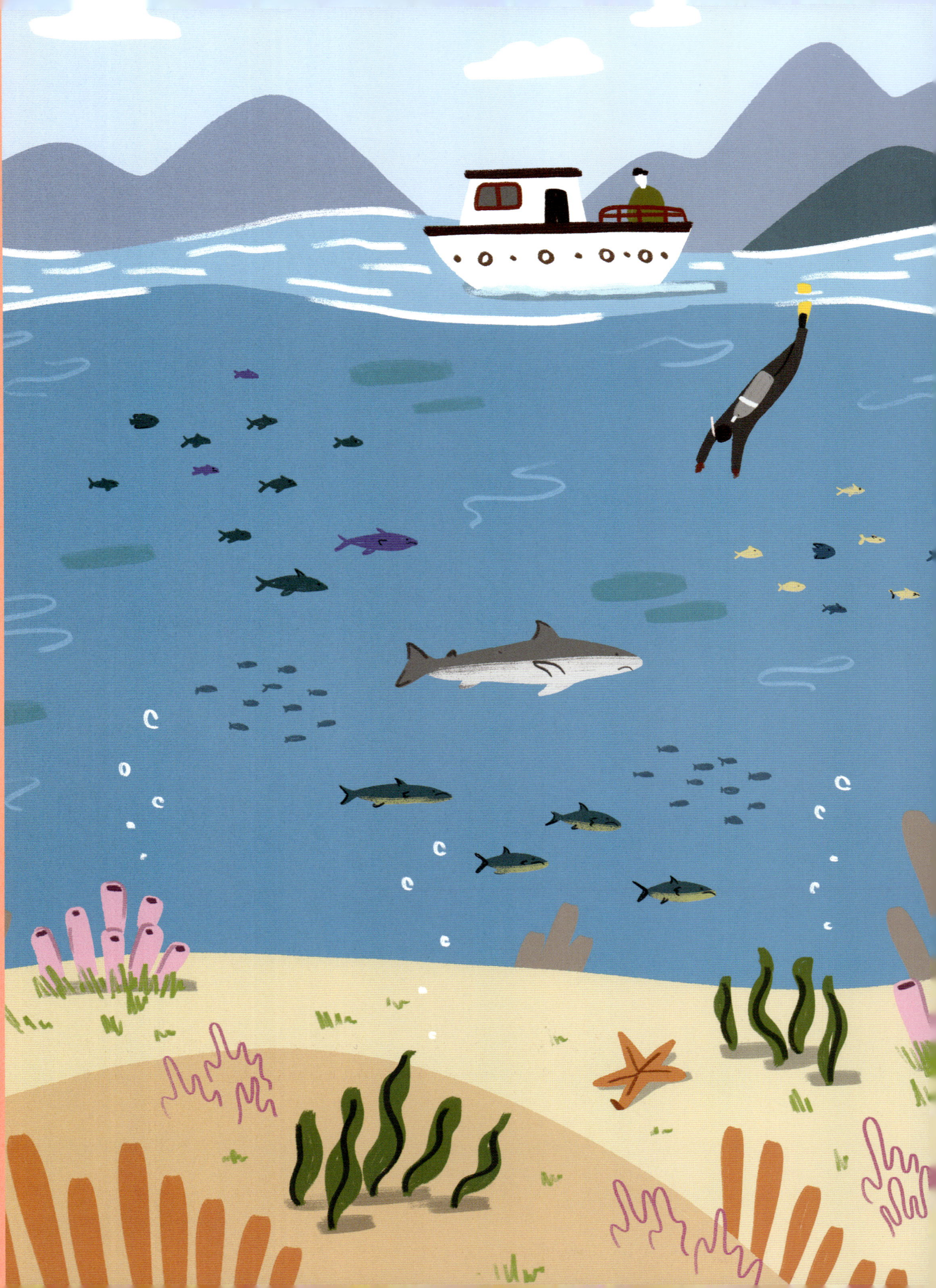

WELCOME TO THE WORLD OF SCIENCE AND MATHEMATICS

Have you ever wondered why the sky is blue, how our bodies work, what makes the planets go round the Sun, or how life first began? Yes? Then you're in the right place.

We're going to delve deep into each of the three sciences—biology, chemistry, and physics—as well as taking a look at some of the key principles of mathematics. All of these subjects work together to increase our understanding of the world and the wider Universe, from the tiniest microorganisms to the most massive stars and galaxies.

To help you understand, there are lots of illustrations and diagrams, as well as a glossary at the back of the book, which explains what some of the key words mean.

So, whether you're a budding biologist, a keen chemist, a fan of physics, or a mighty mathematician, get comfortable, read on, and prepare to be amazed by what you will learn.

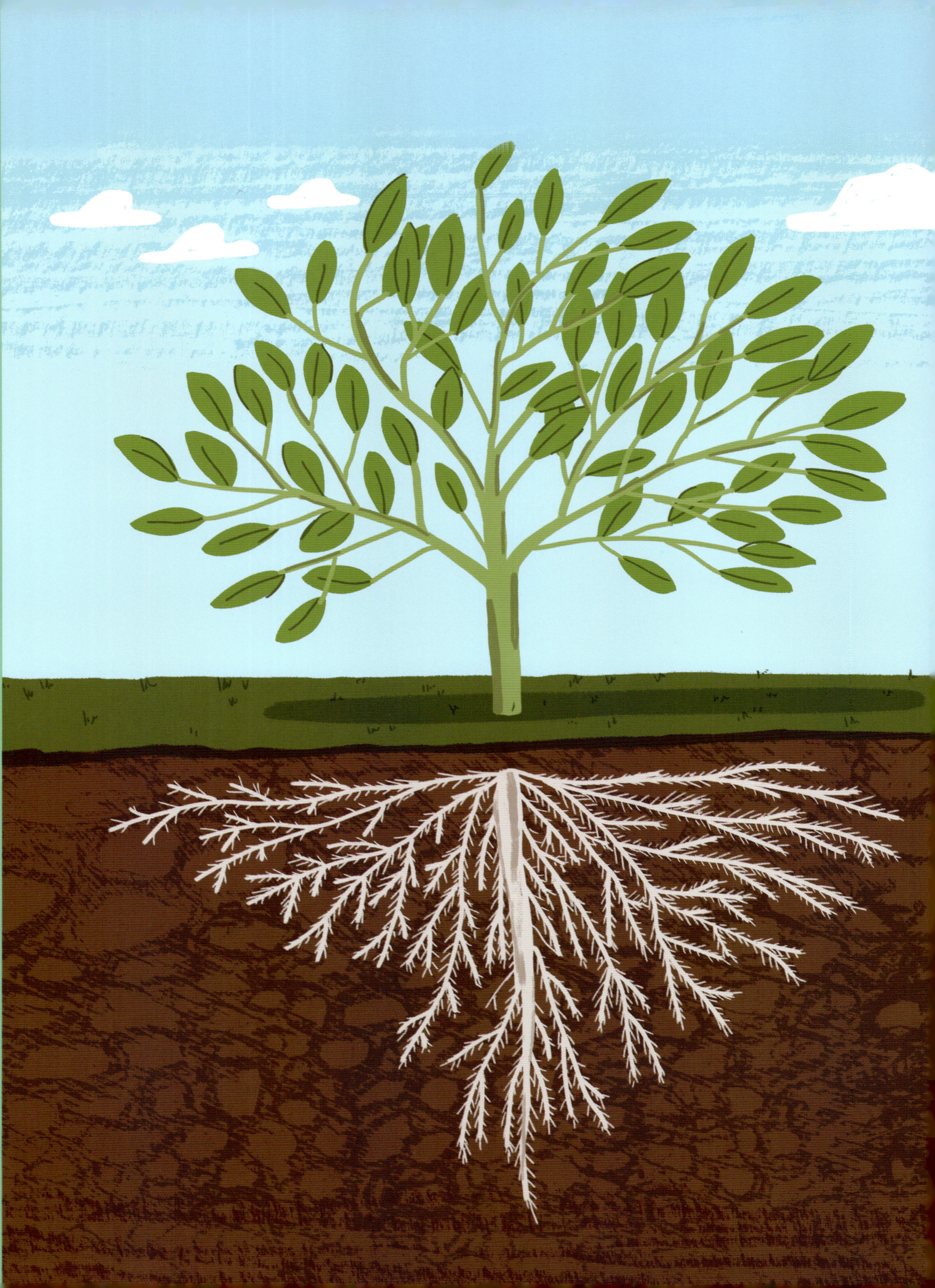

SECTION 1: BRILLIANT BIOLOGY

Biology is the study of all **living organisms**, big or small, old or new, animal or plant, and more (also called **biodiversity**). Studying biology can tell us about what our planet used to look like, how life began, and where it might go next.

Biology is broken down into many different areas of study. Some people study plants and their importance to humans and other living things. Others dive into the animal kingdom and wonder at the millions of **species** there are to discover. Others look at the human body, from bones to brains to blood! And some scientists like to go microscopic, studying the tiniest organisms that we know.

The people who study biology are called **biologists**. Whatever their field, they all have one major thing in common: they are interested in finding answers to questions about life.

Become a biologist yourself as you journey through these pages and uncover some of the mysteries of our incredible living world.

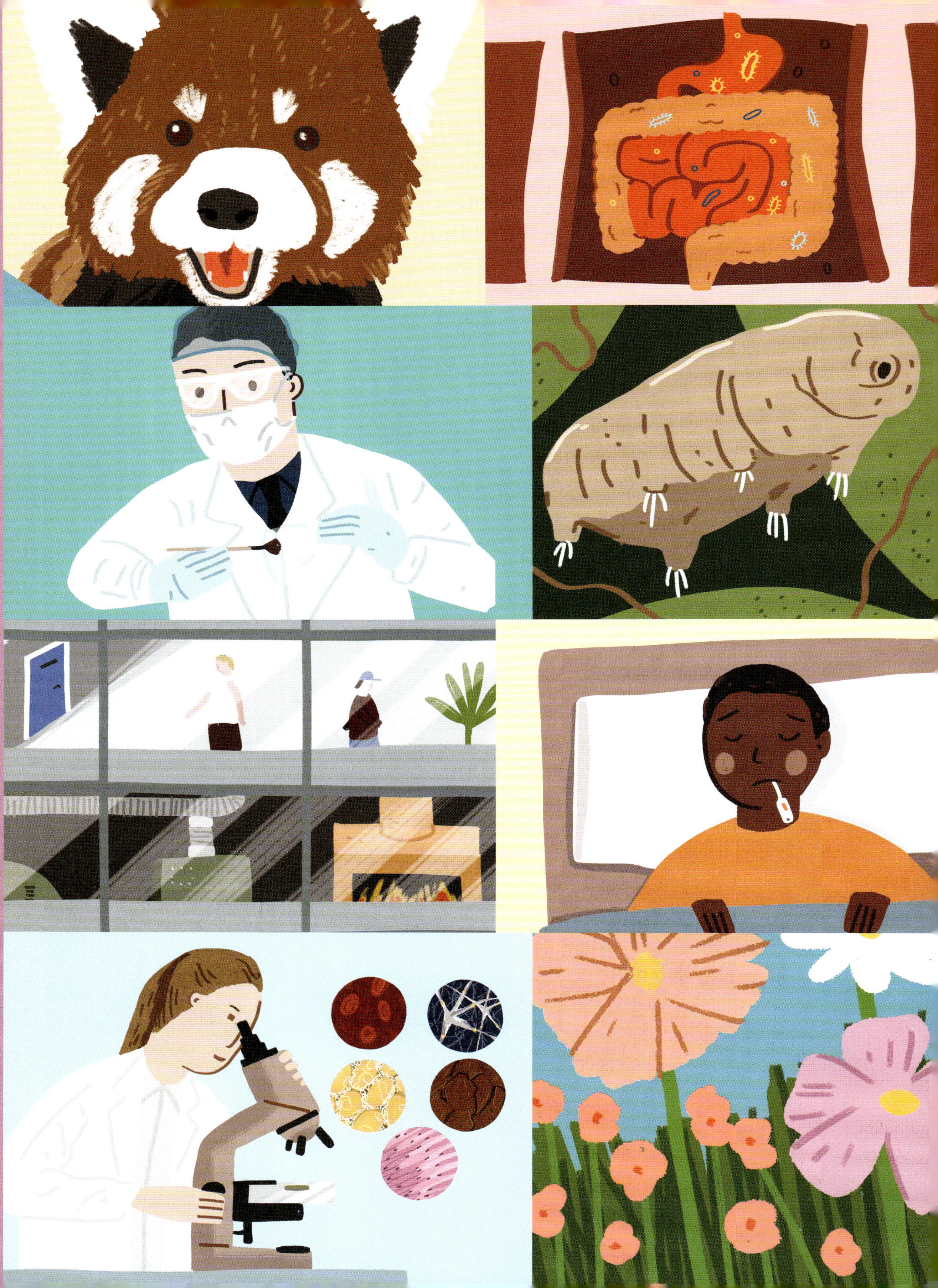

CHAPTER 1

MICROBIOLOGY: THE BUILDING BLOCKS OF LIFE

Whether it's a blue whale, the largest animal on Earth, or the tiniest of **bacteria,** each living **organism** is made up of **cells**. Some creatures are complete with just a single cell, while others are made of millions or more. The human body is formed of trillions of cells!

Microbiology is the study of **microorganisms**—the living things so small that you need a microscope to see them. In this chapter we'll look at the chemical building blocks of life and peer through the microscope to see cells at work.

BUILDING LIFE

Biology and chemistry collide when we begin to talk about the building blocks of life. From chemistry we know that there are over a hundred natural **elements** that make up everything in the Universe. A small selection of these elements is what allows life to exist on Earth. Without them, life simply could not be.

IN YOUR ELEMENT

BREAK IT DOWN

An element is something that cannot be broken down into a simpler substance. Some are metallic, such as gold and silver. Some are gas at Earth's usual surface temperatures, while others are solid or liquid. Each element is made of a different type of atom. Everything on the planet is made up of one or more elements.

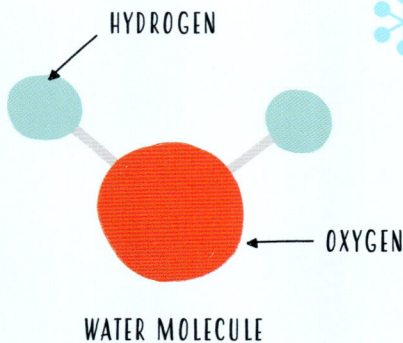

OXYGEN AND HYDROGEN

HYDROGEN

OXYGEN

WATER MOLECULE

Hydrogen is the most abundant element in the Universe, meaning there is more of it than any other element. It is also the lightest. Hydrogen atoms often bond with oxygen atoms to create water molecules. A molecule is a group of atoms that are bonded together. Separately, oxygen also exists as the part of the air that many organisms need to breathe to survive.

NITROGEN

Nitrogen makes up nearly 80% of Earth's atmosphere. It is also found within organisms as a part of large molecules called proteins, along with other elements such as oxygen, hydrogen, and carbon. Every cell in your body contains proteins.

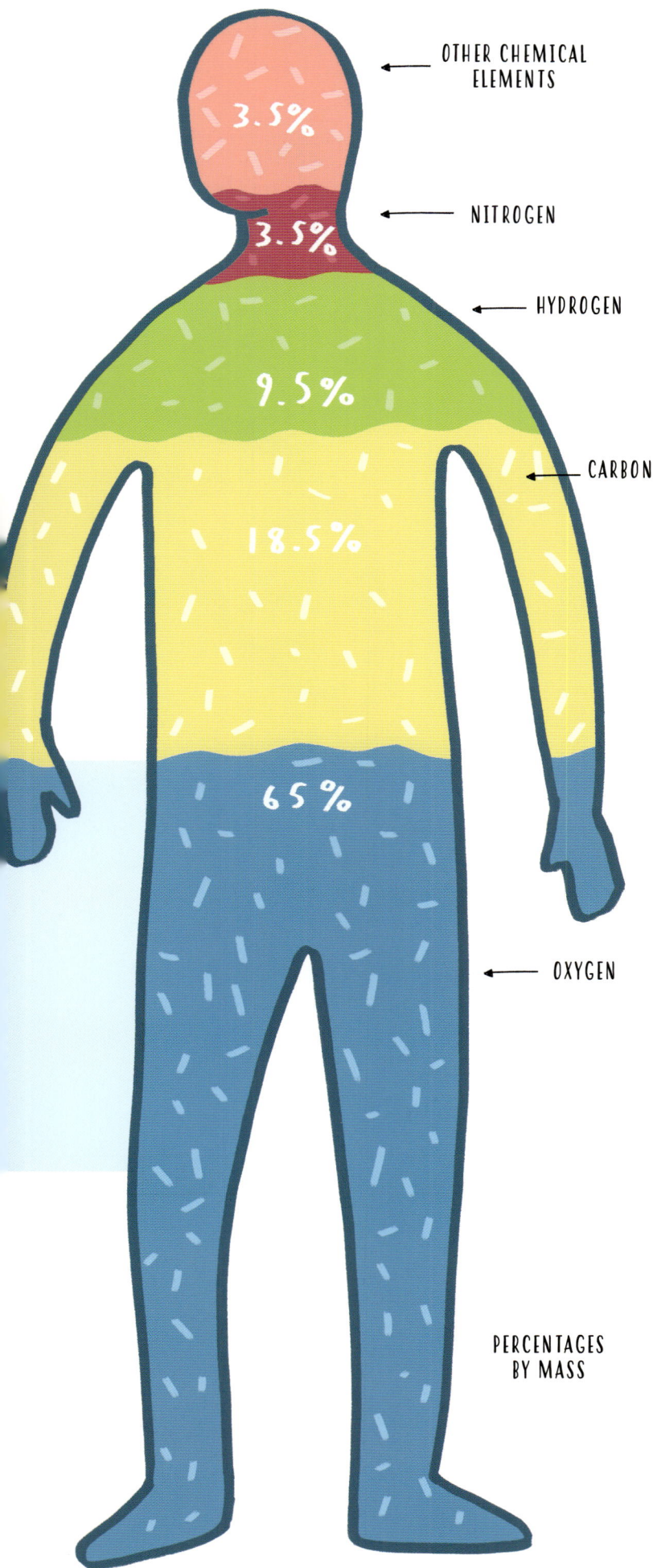

OTHER CHEMICAL ELEMENTS

3.5%

NITROGEN

3.5%

HYDROGEN

9.5%

CARBON

18.5%

65%

OXYGEN

PERCENTAGES BY MASS

✳ CARBON

Carbon is the most important element in creating and sustaining all life on Earth. It is especially good at bonding in different ways with other elements, forming **organic compounds**. Variations of carbon-based compounds are found in millions of living things. These are grouped into four main types:

1. Carbohydrates: These molecules are formed of carbon, hydrogen, and oxygen. They include sugars and starches and provide energy to living cells.

2. Lipids: These are greasy or waxy substances such as fats and oils. They can store energy for an organism and form cell membranes (the outer layer).

3. Proteins: These are large and important molecules that play a vital part in life. They build cells, speed up chemical reactions (changes in molecules), and carry messages and materials through organisms.

4. Nucleic acids: These carry instructions to make proteins as well as information on cell functions and reproduction. For example, nearly every cell in the human body holds **DNA** (deoxyribonucleic acid), which is like a coded instruction manual for reproducing and taking care of our cells.

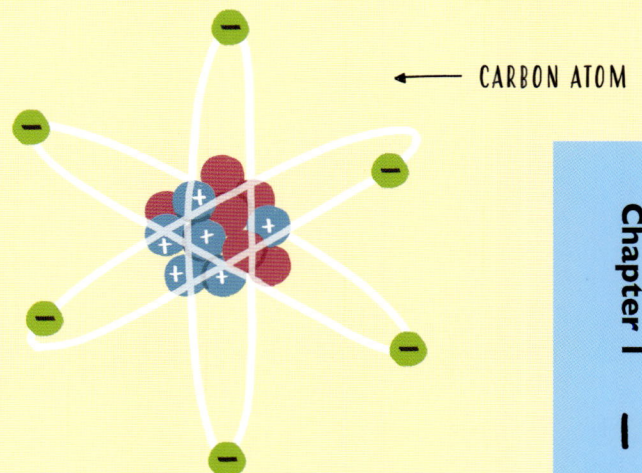

CARBON ATOM

CODING LIFE

Every living thing carries a code that determines how the organism will look and function. These instructions are held on strands of DNA, or **deoxyribonucleic acid**, found in nearly all living cells. DNA is what makes you uniquely YOU.

LADDER OF LIFE

DNA is a long, stringy **molecule** (group of atoms bonded together) made of two strands with links between them. These are twisted into a spiral ladder structure, called a **double helix**. The ladder has rungs made of four chemical bases—adenine, cytosine, thymine, and guanine.

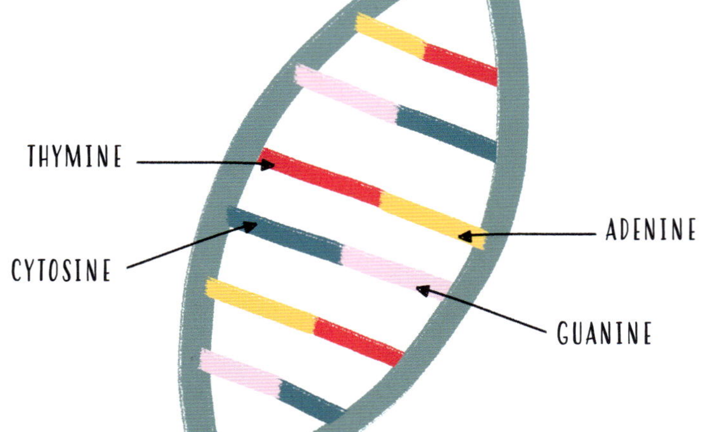

THYMINE

CYTOSINE

ADENINE

GUANINE

The bases always appear in pairs. This is an extremely clever feature of DNA. It means that when a cell needs to reproduce, for example to help the organism grow or heal, the DNA splits itself down the middle of the ladder to create two new strands. These are easily completed by matching pairs to create exact copies of the original chain.

CHROMOSOMES

GENES →

DEEP IN DNA

DNA holds the secret recipe for an individual organism. Within a molecule of DNA are short sections called **genes**. Each gene carries a different piece of information. The pieces of information control characteristics such as eye shade, height, and nose shape.

Genes are held within **chromosomes**. These are coiled strands of DNA found within a cell's **nucleus**. Humans have 46 chromosomes holding over 20,000 genes across them. We inherit half our chromosomes from each parent (23 from each). This is how you can have some of your father's features and some of your mother's. Other organisms have different numbers of chromosomes. Fruit flies, for example, have just eight, while a red king crab has 208!

DETECTIVE DNA

Since each person's DNA is unique (unless you are an identical twin), it can be used as a way to identify us. This makes DNA the perfect tool for solving a crime. People called **forensic scientists**—experts who use science in criminal investigations—gather DNA from a crime scene in cells such as hair or saliva. They analyze the cells to create a **DNA profile**. This is a picture of part of the suspect's DNA. They can then use this to try to find a DNA match, and the culprit.

?

OUT OF CURIOSITY

We share about half of our genes with a banana! That's because most genes just control how an organism works: how it carries out chemical reactions to grow and use energy. All organisms do that in much the same way because they have all evolved from the simple single-celled organisms that appeared billions of years ago.

BACK TO BASICS

Cells are only small, but they play a big part in life. Every living thing—plant, animal, or other—is made of cells. Most are too tiny to see without a microscope. But all have their own important role. There are millions of different types of cells, giving us the basic units of life.

INSIDE A CELL

Within a cell are various structures that help perform that cell's particular function. Every animal cell has several main elements. The nucleus holds DNA and controls what goes on. The **cell membrane** surrounds the cell and allows **nutrients** to pass in and out. The **cytoplasm** is a jelly-like substance where chemical reactions happen, changing one molecule to another. **Mitochondria** give life to the cell, releasing energy from nutrients through chemical reactions.

ANIMAL CELL

CELL MEMBRANE

NUCLEUS

VACUOLE

CYTOPLASM

MITOCHONDRION

PLANT CELL

NUCLEUS

CYTOPLASM

CELL WALL AND MEMBRANE

MITOCHONDRION

CHLOROPLASTS

VACUOLE

ANIMAL OR PLANT

Both animal and plant cells have a nucleus, cell membrane, cytoplasm, and mitochondria. A plant cell has some extra features, too, to maintain its unique life. Outside the cell membrane is a stiff **cell wall** to support the cell. Within the cytoplasm are green **chloroplasts**, which create nutrients for the plant. Finally, both plant and animal cells have **vacuoles**: spaces that store material to help control conditions in the cell, such as how floppy or firm it is.

MAKING MORE CELLS

Living organisms grow, heal, and reproduce by making new cells. There are two main ways that a cell can replicate (copy) itself.

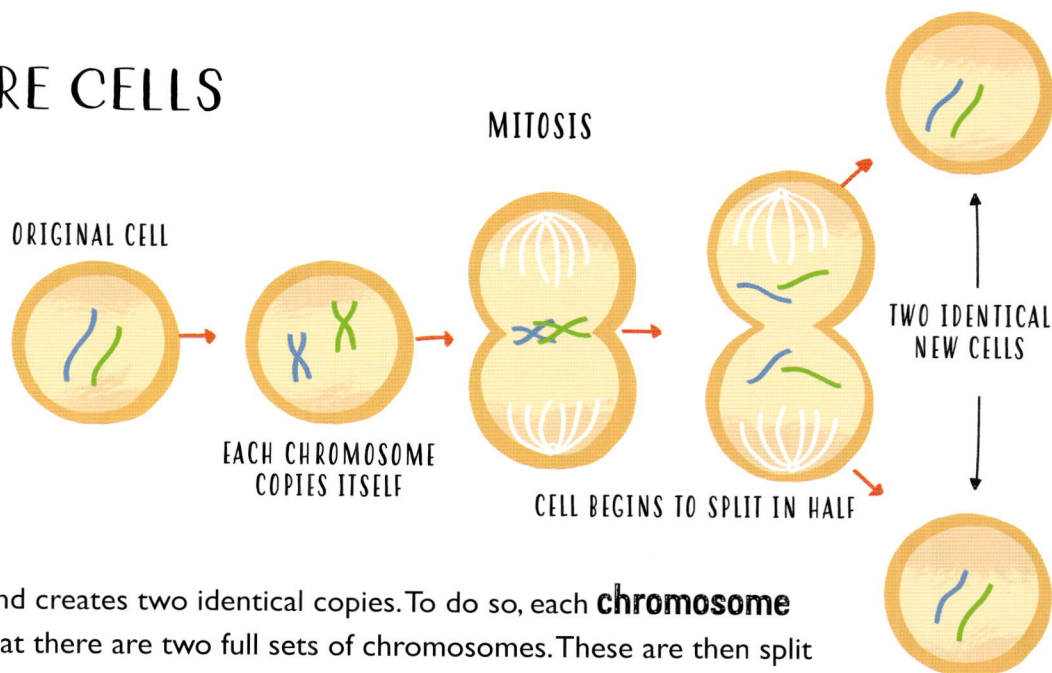

MITOSIS

ORIGINAL CELL

EACH CHROMOSOME COPIES ITSELF

CELL BEGINS TO SPLIT IN HALF

TWO IDENTICAL NEW CELLS

1 In **mitosis**, a cell divides and creates two identical copies. To do so, each **chromosome** makes a copy of itself so that there are two full sets of chromosomes. These are then split evenly, with one set moving to each end of the original cell as it begins to divide into two. This process is carried out so accurately that each new cell carries the same genetic make-up as the first. These identical cells are the means by which the organism grows and heals.

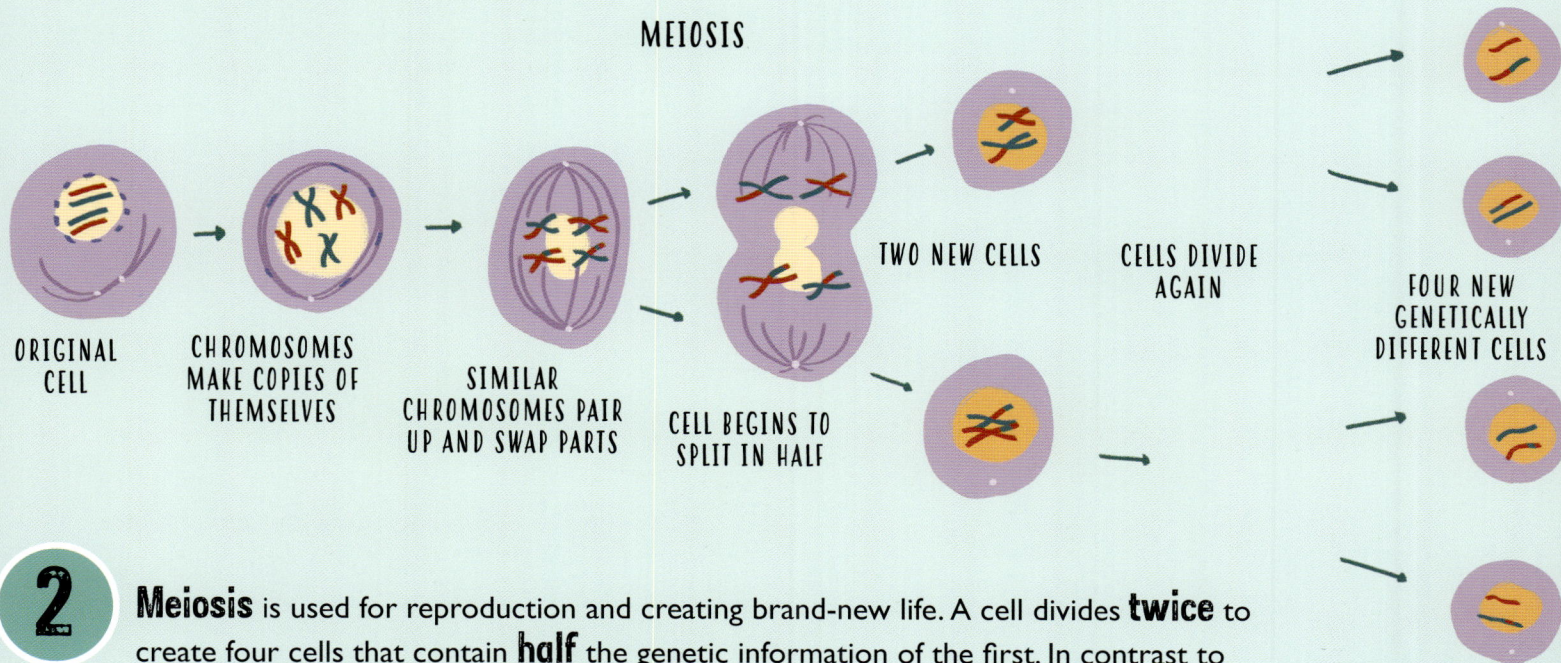

MEIOSIS

ORIGINAL CELL

CHROMOSOMES MAKE COPIES OF THEMSELVES

SIMILAR CHROMOSOMES PAIR UP AND SWAP PARTS

CELL BEGINS TO SPLIT IN HALF

TWO NEW CELLS

CELLS DIVIDE AGAIN

FOUR NEW GENETICALLY DIFFERENT CELLS

2 **Meiosis** is used for reproduction and creating brand-new life. A cell divides **twice** to create four cells that contain **half** the genetic information of the first. In contrast to mitosis, similar chromosomes pair up and swap chunks between them. When the cell splits in half, each new cell has a different mixture of genes. The two new cells then divide again, so that there are now four cells genetically different from the original and each with half the number of chromosomes. When one of these cells from each parent comes together to make a baby, they each bring half the chromosomes the baby needs.

CELL FACTORY

Each cell inside your body—and inside every living organism—is buzzing with activity. Some cells carry oxygen, some help you think, some store energy, and some protect you. Inside your body are trillions of little factories working hard to keep you alive.

NUCLEUS

If the cell is a factory, the **nucleus** is the control and command desk, or the boss. It tells the cell how to grow, replicate, and work. Inside the nucleus are the **chromosomes** that hold the DNA. They keep the blueprints to show how the factory's products should look.

RIBOSOMES

Ribosomes are busy workers on the factory floor. They make proteins, reading the code in the DNA to find out how to make each one. Proteins control all functions in the body.

WORKING IN A PLANT CELL

NUCLEUS

CHROMOSOMES

CELL MEMBRANE

RIBOSOMES

CHLOROPLASTS

MITOCHONDRIA

CELL MEMBRANE

The **cell membrane** is the shipping and receiving department. It allows useful materials to enter the cell and sends out products and waste that the cell has made.

ENERGY

Both the **mitochondria** and **chloroplasts** (in a plant) are the factory's power source. Between them, they manage at a cellular level the energy the organism needs.

CELL SPECIALTIES

One organism can be made of many different types of cells. These work together to make the organism and keep it working.

For example, the human body has about 200 different types of cells that perform different functions. Each has a different shape and inner structure to perform its function perfectly.

MICRO POWER!

NERVE CELLS

Nerve cells transmit nerve signals between the brain and different parts of the body and within the brain.

RED BLOOD CELLS

Red blood cells carry oxygen through the body.

SKIN CELLS

Skin cells protect everything inside the body.

FAT CELLS

Fat cells store energy as fat.

MUSCLE CELLS

Muscle cells enable your body to move.

GOING MICROSCOPIC

At the microscopic level, a whole other world exists. Tiny cells invisible to the naked eye are busy with their own lives. These are microorganisms, or microbes. Some help us, some can be harmful—and some have no effect on us at all!

MICROORGANISMS

A microorganism is exactly that: an organism that is "micro," or microscopic. They can only be seen using a **microscope**. **Viruses** are too small to be seen with a normal microscope.

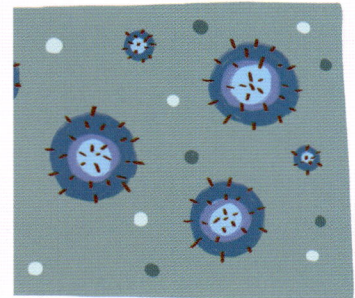

VIRUSES

Some microorganisms have only one cell. Others are tiny plants and animals, such as tardigrades, with many cells.

ARCHAEA

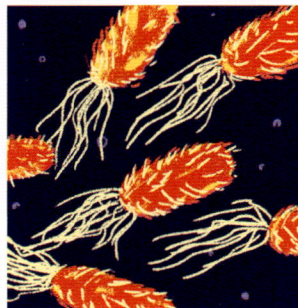

TARDIGRADE

?

OUT OF CURIOSITY

When the microscope was invented in the early 17th century, people discovered the astonishing world of microorganisms. Since then, microscopes have been getting more and more powerful.

Today, we can **magnify** things up to 500,000 times their size!

SINGLE CELLS

Most microorganisms are just one cell. These are called **single-celled organisms**. These were the very first life forms on planet Earth, around 4 billion years ago, emerging in the oceans. These earliest cells were **prokaryotic** cells, which are simpler than plant and animal cells, known as **eukaryotes**. In a **prokaryote**, DNA floats freely, rather than in a nucleus. Today's **bacteria** and **archaea** (see page 23) are prokaryotes, while all other living things are made of eukaryotic cells.

Fungi are eukaryotes that can be single-celled or many-celled. They feed on animal and plant matter and are important in decomposing natural waste. Yeast is a fungus that turns sugar into carbon dioxide gas, so it is used to make bread fluffy. Some fungi cause diseases, but others are used in medicines.

PROTOZOA

Protozoa are single-celled eukaryotes. Some have tails, hair, or even foot-like pseudopods. They feed on bacteria, algae, and micro-fungi.

Plankton are tiny living things that drift and float in oceans and fresh water, where they are eaten by fish and other living things. Plankton can be bacteria, plant-like algae, protozoa—or even little animals and plants.

Helpful microbes

We often hear bad things about bacteria, fungi, and other tiny organisms, but some can be helpful to humans. For example, bacteria called *Rhizobium* are found in soil and provide nutrients to plants. In the food industry, bacteria such as *Lactobacillus* can change milk into cheese and yogurt.

THE GOOD, BAD, AND UGLY

Bacteria and viruses are well known for making us sick, but although this is true, many bacteria don't deserve this reputation. Many help plants and animals with important survival mechanisms.

BACTERIA

A **bacterium** is a single-celled organism. Bacteria cells have a cell wall, but no nucleus. Instead, DNA floats in the cytoplasm. There are millions of different types of bacteria, each with its own shape and structure. Some have tails to move around. Some have outer slime to protect themselves.

DIGESTIVE SYSTEM

BAD BACTERIA

Some bacteria can make people and animals ill. They can cause **diseases** such as food poisoning or meningitis. Once inside the body, the bacteria cells reproduce quickly. The body tries to eject or kill these intruders with strategies such as sneezing, fever, and vomiting.

There are medicines that can kill bacteria. In 1928, scientist Sir Alexander Fleming discovered **penicillin**, a substance produced by a fungus that works as a medicine called an **antibiotic**. Antibiotics attack the bacteria that cause infections in humans and animals and are now used all over the world to save lives.

GOOD BACTERIA

There are billions of bacteria cells within your body that help to keep you healthy. Some live on the skin, others in the nose, and others even in the mouth. In the digestive system alone, millions of bacteria help break down and digest food. Many of the good bacteria in your body work to fight off bad bacteria!

VIRUSES

Unfortunately, viruses are not as helpful as good bacteria. These sneaky things make animals, plants, and other living things sick. In humans, they cause colds, flus, measles, and other diseases, such as COVID-19. Viruses are not made of cells: their DNA is wrapped simply in a **protein** coat. Scientists do not agree on whether we can call them "living things" or not. Viruses can only reproduce by entering the cell of a living thing, then using the machinery of the cell to make copies of themselves.

MEASLES VIRUS

The body's **immune system** works hard to fight viruses once they are inside. Viruses can't be treated by antibiotics, so the best thing to do is to avoid them getting in your body in the first place by washing your hands and wearing a mask when appropriate.

OUT OF CURIOSITY

Some deep-sea fish have bacteria that can produce light to lure in prey in the deep dark sea.

KINGDOMS OF LIFE

Every creature, big or small, is **classified** into a kingdom of life. These group life forms by features they share. In the 1700s, organisms were divided into two categories—plant or animal. Now, with more advanced science and super-strong microscopes that can detect the tiniest speck, many scientists agree on **six kingdoms** of life.

ANIMALS

This kingdom includes millions of species (groups of similar-looking organisms that can reproduce or **breed** together). Animals range from simple organisms such as sea sponges, to huge whales and clever creatures such as humans. The life forms in this kingdom cannot produce their own food, so they eat other organisms.

PLANTS

From tiny floating duckweed to towering trees, plants can be found all over the world—even in the ocean! These multi-celled organisms produce their own food, by using the energy of sunlight and chemicals around them. This kingdom is crucial to supporting most life on Earth.

FUNGI

The fungus kingdom includes both single and multiple-celled organisms. These life forms were thought to be plants in the past, but scientists now know they are very different. Unlike plants, fungi do not produce their own food. Instead, they absorb (or soak up) nutrients from matter such as dead plants and animals.

BACTERIA

This group of prokaryotes (see page 19) is found all over the world, in all environments and nearly all conditions, including inside plants and animals. Bacteria get their energy from sunlight or by breaking down chemicals or dead organisms. Some can move using hair-like pilli or tail-like flagella.

ARCHAEA

These prokaryotes look like bacteria but many thrive in hostile conditions, such as volcanic vents in the ocean, hot springs, or highly salty seas. They were only recently discovered but are in fact thought to be among the oldest types of living organisms on Earth.

PROTISTS

In this kingdom are eukaryotic (see page 19) single-celled and many-celled organisms. The kingdom includes algae, protozoa, slime molds—and anything else that doesn't fit into the other categories! Protists can produce their own food or feed on other organisms.

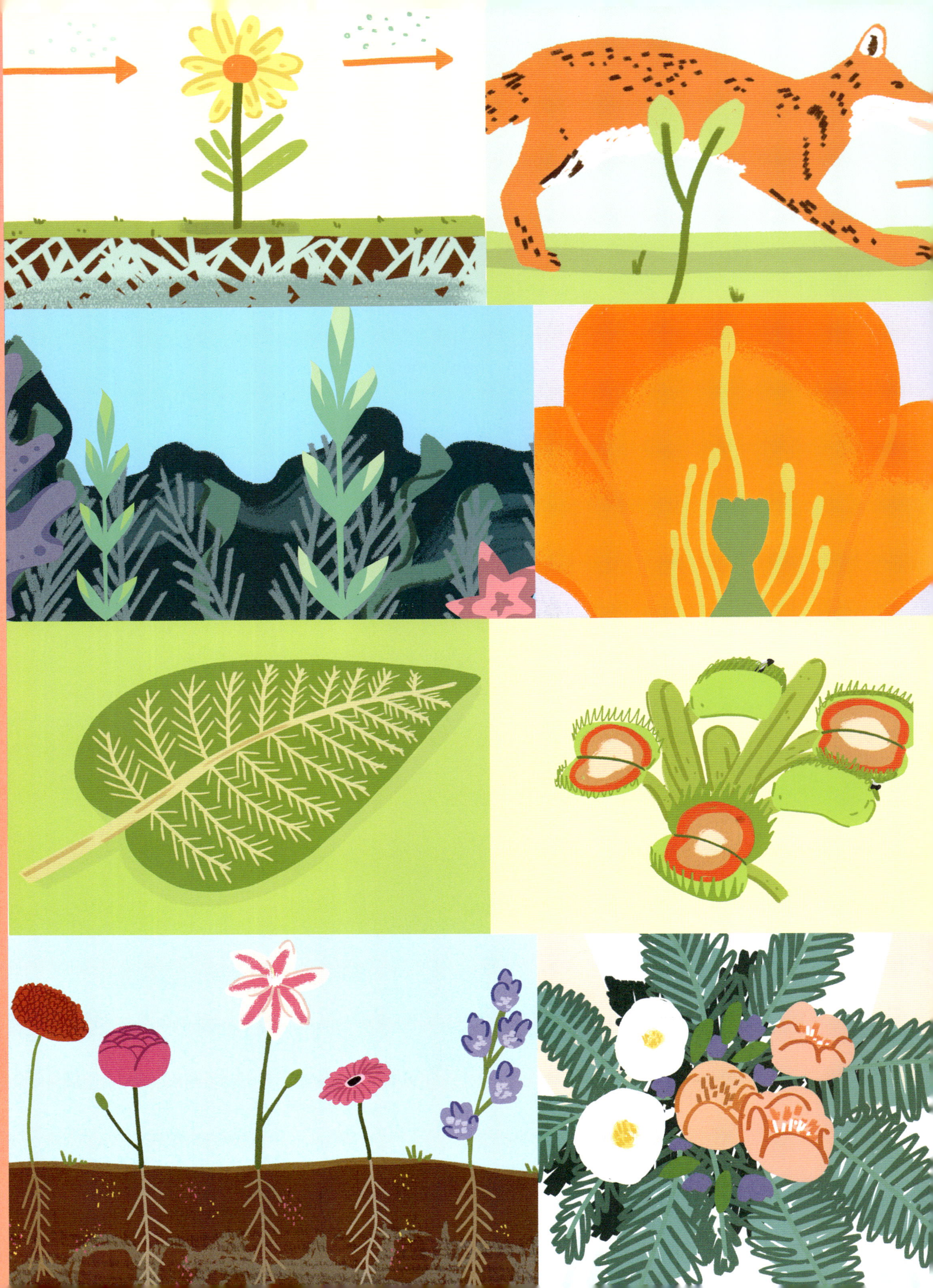

CHAPTER 2

BOTANY: THE WORLD OF PLANTS

Plants cover much of our planet's surface, from blades of grass to floating lily pads to towering trees. They provide us with food, materials, and even oxygen to breathe. There are hundreds of thousands of different species of plants—and **botanists** study all of them!

Botany is the study of plants and plant life. This includes the characteristics of plants, what plants need to survive and thrive, where you can find them across Planet Earth, and how plants can help us and our world. Let your curiosity blossom and your plant knowledge bloom as you travel through this botanical chapter.

THE POWER OF PLANTS

Plants provide us with beautiful scenery, shelter, materials, and food to eat. They transform the air we breathe. If plants weren't on Earth, people and other animals wouldn't be either.

CIRCLE OF LIFE

Plants absorb a gas called **carbon dioxide** from the air and give off **oxygen** in return. Humans need that oxygen to breathe, and if there was too much carbon dioxide in the air, we couldn't survive. In fact, people and other animals breathe out carbon dioxide— which plants then absorb! It's one of those extraordinary cycles that keep life going.

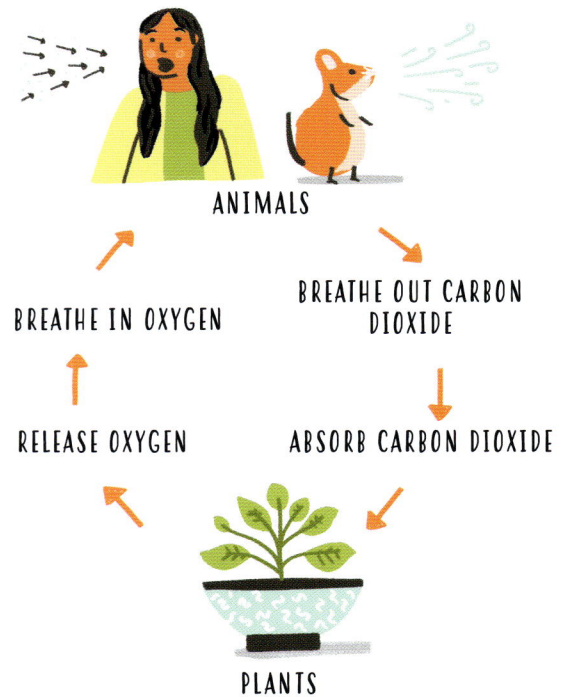

THANK YOU, PLANTS

ANIMALS

BREATHE IN OXYGEN

BREATHE OUT CARBON DIOXIDE

RELEASE OXYGEN

ABSORB CARBON DIOXIDE

PLANTS

FOOD AND SHELTER

Not only do plants give us oxygen, but they also give us food. They are at the bottom of most food chains, as many animals eat plants to survive. On top of that, plants provide homes and shelter for wildlife, from woodland birds in tall trees to tiny beetles in fallen leaves.

PHOTOSYNTHESIS

Photosynthesis is a process that happens inside green plants to produce food for them to survive. It is all about harnessing the power of the sun and storing it as **energy** that can be used by the plant.

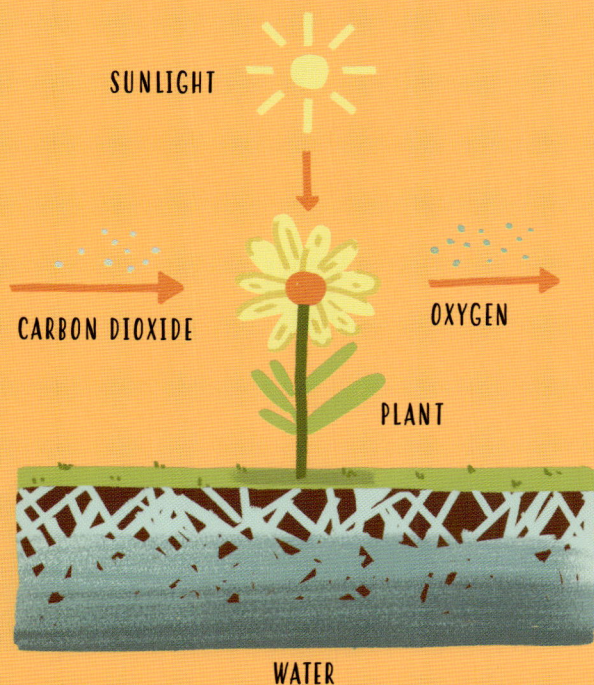

SUNLIGHT

CARBON DIOXIDE

OXYGEN

PLANT

WATER

1. The sun shines down on the plant. A green substance called **chlorophyll** in a plant's leaves absorbs the sun's energy.

2. A plant's roots soak up water from the ground, while a plant's leaves absorb carbon dioxide from the air.

3. Using energy from the sunlight, the plant combines the carbon dioxide and water to make a sugar called glucose.

4. A plant uses the glucose for energy. Oxygen is created in the process and is released into the air.

BABY PLANTS

Plants are living things, and just like animals, they have to reproduce. Different plants reproduce in different ways. Many plants produce **seeds**, which are tiny "baby" plants wrapped in a protective case, along with a food store. Seeds may form inside flowers (see page 29), inside cones (see page 32), or in fruit. Other plants, such as ferns, reproduce by releasing **spores**, which are simpler than seeds. If the seeds or spores land in the right spot and get the right amount of water and sunshine, they will grow into new plants, and the cycle begins again.

PARTS OF A WHOLE

Whether a plant is big or small, flowering or not, most plants have the same basic parts. These parts work together to help the plant function perfectly—carrying out photosynthesis and reproducing.

LEAVES

Photosynthesis happens in the leaves of plants. They have tiny holes that are used for gas exchange, taking in carbon dioxide and releasing oxygen, and for letting water out.

STEM

The stem helps support the plant, usually by keeping it standing upright. It carries water and nutrients from the roots toward leaves and flowers.
A tree's **trunk** is a hard, woody stem, made of tough cellulose and lignin.

ROOTS

A plant's roots hold it in place. Usually, roots reach into the ground, but some wrap around other plants or even reach into the air. Roots take in water and minerals to supply the plant with important **nutrients**.

FLOWERS

Not all plants grow flowers, but the ones that do rely on them to **reproduce**. Flowers are often bright or smelly to attract bees, butterflies, and other animals that carry pollen to the plant so it can make seeds (see page 36). Although most flowers smell nice, some smell like rotting flesh to attract flies!

TO EACH ITS OWN

Each plant is adapted to its environment, with different features to help it survive. Some plants, such as potatoes and carrots, store **food** in swollen underground stems or roots. This helps them survive winter.

Some plants, such as moss, don't have roots or stems. These are called **non-vascular** plants. They live in damp places so they can absorb moisture. These simple plants often grow low to the ground.

LEAVE IT TO THE LEAF

The leaf is where the magic happens, making food for the plant to survive. Just like plants themselves, leaves are many different shapes and sizes. However, most leaves share the same basic features.

The leaf's **veins** transport water and nutrients from the stem to different parts of the leaf. Once photosynthesis has taken place, the veins also transport the **glucose** that was created to the rest of the plant for energy.

The **petiole** connects the leaf to the plant's stem. It connects with the **midrib**, which provides support to the leaf, helping it to stand strong whatever the weather.

On the underside of the leaf are tiny **stomata**: little holes that allow carbon dioxide to go in and oxygen to flow out.

MIDRIB

VEINS

STOMATA

PETIOLE

SURVIVING AND THRIVING

Just like us, a plant needs certain things to thrive in the world. It requires food, drink, and a few other special ingredients for survival on Planet Earth.

SUNLIGHT

OUT OF CURIOSITY

While plants can't speak, some can in fact communicate with each other! They release chemicals to warn other plants if insects are attacking.

HAPPY, HEALTHY GREENS

How do you know if a plant is healthy? It can't smile or talk, but it does have other ways of telling us. Most plants show their strength by standing upright with bright green leaves open. If a plant starts to wilt, it may not be getting everything it needs. A healthy plant may turn itself toward the sun to take in more light, and its roots branch out in search of water and nutrients.

LIGHT AND WARMTH

A plant soaks up **sunlight** for energy to make its food. It needs **warmth**, which also helps its seeds to grow.

SPACE

Roots require enough **space** to spread out, grow deep, or even stretch upward away from soggy soil. With enough space, roots find the water and nutrients that plants need.

CARBON DIOXIDE

This gas is an essential ingredient used in photosynthesis, combining with water to create **glucose**. It is taken in through the **stomata** in the plant's leaves.

CARBON DIOXIDE

SPACE

WATER

MINERALS

WATER

Water is the other crucial component for photosynthesis. Plants drink it up through their roots and stem, like a straw. Some plants require lots of water to survive while others, such as a cactus in a desert, have adapted to need very little.

MINERALS

Plants need rich **soil** to provide them with important nutrients, including nitrogen, phosphorus, and potassium. Plants take these in through their roots.

PLENTIFUL PLANT TYPES

Although we may think of plants as green-leafed and blossoming, there are many that do not fit this form. With hundreds of thousands of species of plants across the world, there are countless variations.

GROUPED IN TWO

There are two main groups of plants: vascular and non-vascular.

1 **Vascular plants** have special vessels for moving water and nutrients around. This group includes most of the plants on the planet.

Vascular plants are further split into groups such as flowering plants, conifers, ferns, and horsetails. There are over 260,000 different species of **flowering plants** known so far. These include orchids, sunflowers, and even peas.

Conifers, such as pines and cedars, usually have leaves shaped like needles. They grow seeds in cones that eventually drop to the ground. Conifers are usually evergreen, which means they do not drop their leaves in winter. Deciduous trees lose their leaves in winter. They have thinner, softer leaves that can't survive winter cold.

Ferns are leafy plants that reproduce by releasing **spores** from structures on the underside of their leaves called sporangia.

FERN-TASTIC!

FERNS

2 Unlike vascular plants, **non-vascular plants** have no stems or roots, and sometimes not even true leaves. They often anchor themselves to the ground using hair-like structures called rhizoids. You might even find them on rocks or tree bark rather than in soil. These plants reproduce using spores. Non-vascular plants include mosses and green algae.

Mosses have small leaves and grow in carpets low to the ground, often in damp, shadowy places. There are over 12,000 species of moss worldwide.

Some **green algae** are tiny single cells, while other species grow to large seaweed size. They find water and grow wherever they can, whether it's in the sea or on ice.

MOSS

UNDERWATER SURVIVORS

We know there are plants living underwater, but how do they survive? Many aquatic plants stay close to the surface to take in sunlight. These plants, such as water lilies, often have large floating leaves. Plants deeper in the sea have adapted to require less sunlight, and they draw carbon dioxide from the water around them. No plant can live in the deep ocean, where sunlight cannot reach.

CARNIVORES

If a plant can't find what it needs in the traditional way, it might come up with creative solutions to fill in. For example, the **Venus flytrap** lives where the soil is lacking in rich nutrients. So instead, this hungry flower snatches insects and other small animals with its jaw-like leaves.

33

FLOWERS OF LIFE

Every living thing—plant, animal, fungus, even bacterium—has a life cycle. The life cycle of a flowering plant includes the stages of seed, plant, flower—then fruit and seeds.

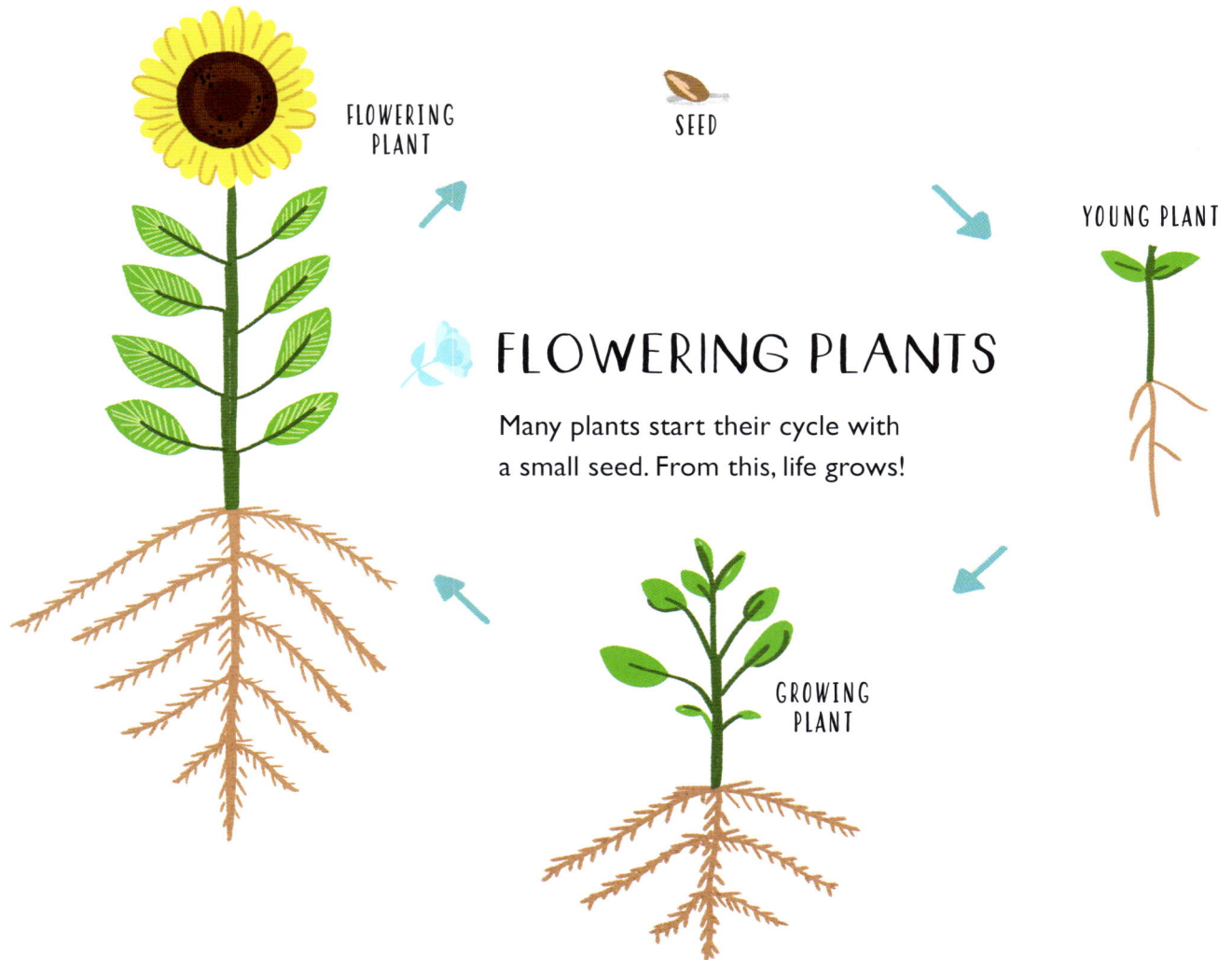

FLOWERING
PLANT

SEED

YOUNG PLANT

FLOWERING PLANTS

Many plants start their cycle with a small seed. From this, life grows!

GROWING
PLANT

1. A seed is dropped. It holds DNA and food that the new plant will need. This is where the plant's life begins.

2. The seed finds a home in the ground. When there is enough warmth and water, the outer case of the seed splits, and the plant starts to sprout. The roots dig into the soil and seek out nutrients. The stem pushes above the ground.

3. As the plant takes in more sunlight, water, and nutrients, leaves develop, and the plant grows taller and taller.

4. A flower grows. After the flower has been pollinated (see page 36), the seeds develop and ripen. The cycle is ready to start again.

INSIDE A FLOWER

Inside a flower are lots of little organs that help the plant live out its cycle. **Sepals** at the base protect the flower before it opens. Once it does, **petals** spread out. These are often bright to attract insects. The flower also has a **nectary**, which produces a sugary liquid called nectar, also used to attract animals. A **stamen** consists of a filament supporting an anther that holds pollen grains. A **stigma** collects grains of pollen, and an **ovary** contains **ovules** that eventually become seeds.

FRESH FRUIT

After **pollination**, a flower's ovules turn into seeds while its ovary turns into a fruit. Some fruits are fleshy, as in a peach, while others are hard, as in a walnut. Some fruits don't look like fruits at all! For example, dandelion fruits are feathery tufts that lift dandelion seeds on the wind. Some fruits, such as raspberries, are made of several ovaries. Not all fruits are edible (or eatable), because they are poisonous or dry. Edible fruits are very useful for spreading seeds over a large distance, as they are eaten—then pooped—by animals from birds to monkeys.

PETAL

STIGMA

STAMEN

OVARY

OVULE

NECTARY

SEPAL

INSIDE STORY!

POWER OF POLLEN

Flowering plants, from apple trees to wheat grass, are important to our world, so it's equally important that they are able to reproduce. There are two main ways that flowering plants create this miracle of new life: sexual and asexual reproduction.

1 MALE PLUS FEMALE

Most flowering plants make their babies by **sexual reproduction**. This requires both male and female parts, which can often be found inside the same flower. The stamens are **male** parts, where pollen is produced. The pollen then needs to transfer to the **female** stigma, ovary, and ovules, usually of a different plant.

CROSS-POLLINATION OF PLANTS

SELF-POLLINATION

POLLINATION

Pollinators—including insects, birds, bats, and monkeys—are attracted to a flower's sweet **nectar**. When they lap it up, they brush past the pollen, which sticks to their body. As they move onto another flower, the **pollen** brushes on to the new plant's female stigma. This is called pollination. Finally, the pollen works its way down to the ovules, where **fertilization** occurs, and a seed is born.

Pollination can also be carried out by the breeze. As the wind blows, it picks up pollen and scatters it onto other flowers. A few plants, usually those living in isolated places, self-pollinate. This means that a flower is fertilized by its own pollen.

SEED DISPERSAL

Once a new seed has been produced in a fruit, it must find its way to the ground to grow into a new plant. This is called **seed dispersal**. Some seeds travel by **wind**. This is the case with key-shaped, twirling sycamore seeds. Others hitch a ride on an **animal**, either by going through the animal's digestive system (see page 35) or by attaching to the animal's fur with hooks. And some seeds, such as those of the sandbox tree, are more dramatic, bursting out of their fruit with little plant explosions when they're ripe.

(see page 35)

2

GOING IT ALONE

The second type of reproduction is called **asexual reproduction**. The plant can grow new life by itself, without male and female parts or seeds. This often occurs when a human interferes, cutting off a section from the parent plant and rehoming it in rich soil, where an identical plant will grow. Some plants reproduce on their own, such as garlic or daffodils, which form large **bulbs** underground. These store food but can also split to make a new plant.

OUT OF CURIOSITY

All the tiny pollen grains floating in the wind are what cause some people to suffer from hay fever—it makes them sneeze!

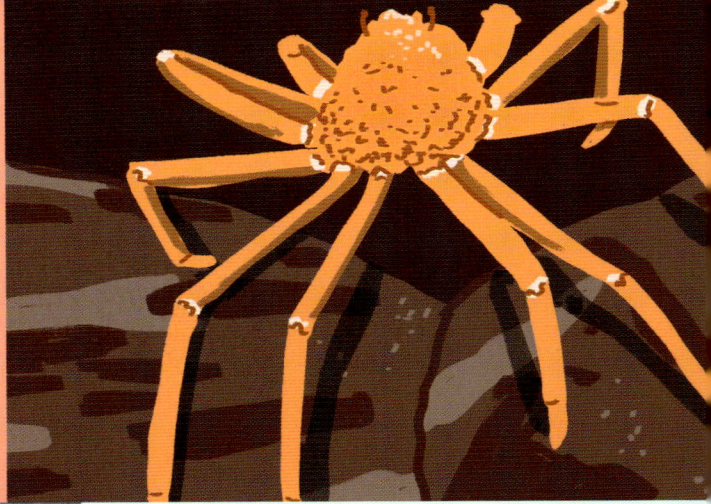

CHAPTER 3

ZOOLOGY: THE ANIMAL KINGDOM

As the largest kingdom of life on Earth, animals come in an incredible variety of shapes, sizes, and types. From fish, amphibians, and reptiles to mammals, birds, and inverterbrates, this kingdom is fascinating to explore.

Zoologists study animals: how they act, how they're grouped, and where you can find them. In this chapter, we'll go on a safari to observe the different types of animals, as well as taking a peek at their life cycles and the part they play in the food chain.

ANIMAL CLASSIFICATION

There are millions of species of animals living across the planet. A species, such as lions, is a group of animals that look similar and can make babies together. To better understand animals, scientists place species into larger groups, based on their similarities.

FAMILY TIES

All animals are related, but how closely? Classification allows scientists to group species into families and larger groups, such as orders and classes. Using features such as feathers and number of legs helps zoologists create the classifications for different animals. For example, two feathered birds are more closely related than a bird with two legs and a spider with eight! There are several groups of animals: mammals, birds, fish, reptiles, amphibians, and invertebrates. But animal similarities and differences can go even deeper than that, if you look closely.

LEOPARD VS. FENNEC FOX

FOR EXAMPLE

Let's look closely at a couple of examples to see how we can group and divide animal families:

	LEOPARD	FENNEC FOX
WARM-BLOODED?	YES	YES
HOW MANY LEGS?	FOUR	FOUR
LAYS EGGS?	NO	NO
FUR OR SCALES?	FUR	FUR
LONG MUZZLE?	NO	YES
CAN RETRACT ITS CLAWS?	YES	NO
FAMILY	CAT	DOG

The fennec fox and leopard have a lot in common, making them both mammals. However, their differences, such as the shape of their muzzle (nose and mouth) and the fact that the leopard can retract (pull back) its claws into its paws, put them in different families.

OUT OF CURIOSITY

The biggest animal ever to live on Earth is the blue whale. Its heart alone can weigh as much as a car. And yet, because both have lungs and warm blood, this massive creature can be grouped with the tiny bumblebee bat.

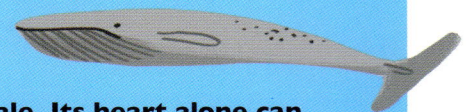

Classification Key Flowchart

DOES THE ANIMAL HAVE ANY HAIR?
- **YES** → **MAMMAL**
- **NO** → **DOES IT HAVE FEATHERS?**
  - **YES** → **BIRD**
  - **NO** → **DOES IT HAVE DRY SKIN?**
    - **YES** → **REPTILE**
    - **NO** → **DOES IT HAVE SCALES?**
      - **YES** → **FISH**
      - **NO** → **AMPHIBIAN**

KEY TO DISCOVERY

Next, let's look at a salamander and a hummingbird, using a **classification key**. This is a series of questions that helps identify an animal's grouping.

First, follow the key on this page for a salamander. A salamander has no hair, no feathers, no dry skin, and no scales, which leads you to the group **AMPHIBIAN**. Now follow the same key for a hummingbird. As it has no hair, but it does have feathers, you should arrive at **BIRD**. These animals belong to two very different groups.

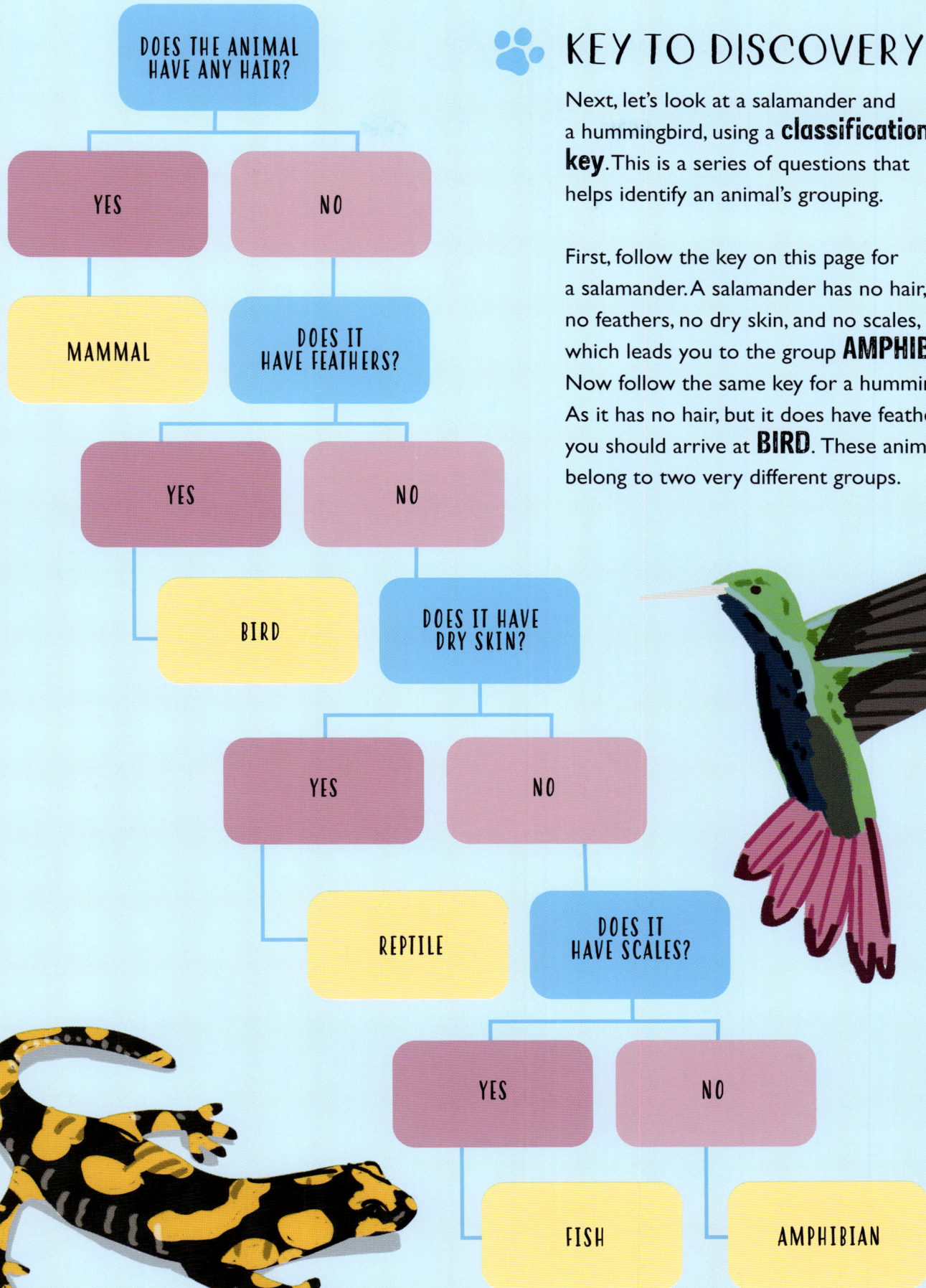

VARIOUS VERTEBRATES

The millions of animal species around the world are divided into two core groups based on one main feature: whether or not they have a backbone. Within each group, the animal species are further broken down.

SUN BEAR

BONE STRUCTURES

The first of the two main classifications for animals is **vertebrates**. Every animal in this group has a **backbone**: the series of bones that run down the back, from the base of the neck to the tailbone. The backbone protects the vital nerves of the **spinal cord** and gives the organism structure. The animals in this group are divided into five categories.

MAMMALS

The class of **mammals** has the smallest number of species, but the most diverse. It includes lions, dolphins, sun bears, rabbits—and humans! Mammals all have warm blood and hair or fur. Even dolphins and whales have whiskers. Mammals usually give birth to live young and feed their young on milk.

CHAMELEON

REPTILES

Reptiles are cold-blooded, so they take in heat from the sun and from their own muscles, and then seek out shade if they get too hot. Most reptiles lay eggs, although some, like certain snakes, give birth to live young. All reptiles have dry scales or bonier plates called scutes. They can have four legs or none at all. This group includes tortoises, chameleons, snakes, and crocodiles.

BIRDS

Birds are descended from a group of small, feathered dinosaurs, which were reptiles that lived millions of years ago. Birds have feathers and wings. Most birds can fly, although some use their wings to help them swim or balance on land instead. Birds lay hard-shelled eggs and are warm-blooded. This group includes sparrows, eagles, parrots, penguins, and the tall ostrich.

TOAD

SCARLET MACAW

AMPHIBIANS

Amphibians live on land and in water. Most have four legs, which they use to walk or swim. Most amphibians start their lives in a different form, called larvae, in water, taking in oxygen from the water using structures called gills. When amphibians grow into adults, they usually develop lungs and legs and live on land. They have moist skin, cold blood, and lay soft-shelled eggs. This group includes frogs, toads, salamanders, and newts.

CLOWNFISH

FISH

Finally, the largest group by far! **Fish** were the very first animals to develop a backbone, and there are now over 30,000 different species of fish across the world. They all live in water and use gills to take in oxygen from the water. Almost all fish have scales. Most fish lay soft eggs, while others, such as sharks, give birth to live young. This group includes goldfish, clownfish, eels, and the great white shark.

WORLD OF INVERTEBRATES

Around 97% of animals on Earth are **invertebrates**. They have no backbone and instead have completely soft bodies or hard outer casings. They are divided into more than 30 groups. Here are some common ones.

INSECTS

This group has a couple of claims to fame. First, it is the largest group of animals on Earth. And second, it was the first to fly! **Insects** have six legs, a three-part body, a pair of antennae (feelers), and a hard **exoskeleton** (skeleton on the outside of the body). Many also have wings. This group includes everything from beetles to butterflies to the ruthless praying mantis.

BUTTERFLY

CRUSTACEANS

Crustaceans are closely related to insects. They have hard shells and jointed legs. They live mostly in water, although some, such as woodlice, live on land. Many have claws, which they use to grip things or defend themselves. They range from little krill to the giant Japanese spider crab.

JAPANESE SPIDER CRAB

SPIDER

ARACHNIDS

Most **arachnids** have two body sections and eight legs. They live on land or in water. Arachnids have a hard outer shell, but, unlike insects, they have no antennae or wings. They are mostly predators and have several pairs of eyes to see prey. This group includes mites, ticks, spiders, and scorpions.

SEA ANEMONE

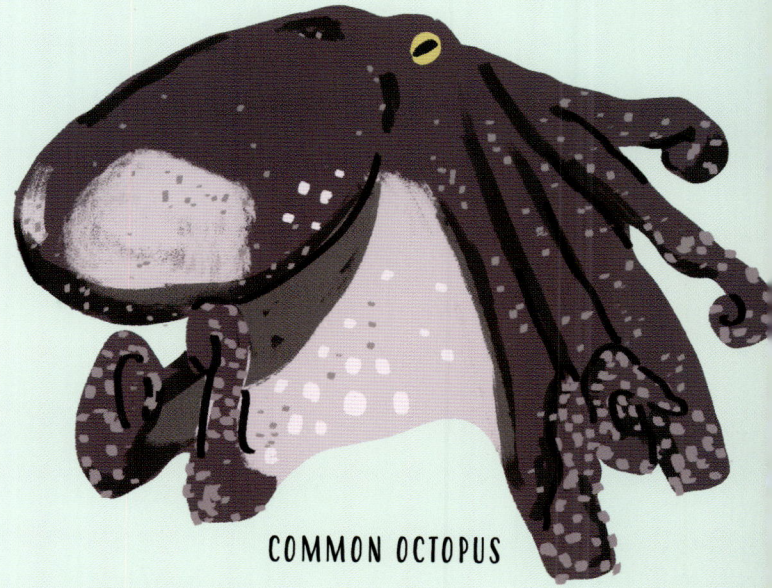

COMMON OCTOPUS

MOLLUSKS

Mollusks range greatly in size and shape. They include oysters, clams, octopus, snails, and the giant squid. All have a soft body, and many have a hard outer shell for protection. Most are found in water and swim around or crawl. Some animals in this group, such as slugs, do not have a central brain, while others, such as octopus, have quite large brains. Octopus can build dens from rocks and shells, hide from predators, and ambush their prey.

CNIDARIANS

Cnidarians can be found only in water. They spend part of their early life as a sessile (unmoving) cylinder-shaped polyp. As they reach adulthood, some cnidarians change body shape so they are able to swim. All cnidarians have stinging cells, which they can use to capture prey or defend themselves against predators. This group includes coral, sea anemones, and jellyfish.

LIFE CYCLES

Just like plants and other life forms, every animal goes through a life cycle. It is born, grows older and bigger, possibly has young of its own, and eventually dies. Its offspring might have their own offspring, and the cycle continues.

VARIETIES OF ANIMAL LIFE

Animals hatch from eggs or are born as live babies. Some animals look like their parents when they're born, while others go through a major change before they become adults. Each animal has its own unique life cycle.

NEWBORN CUB

YOUNG LION

ADULT LION

GROWING UP

Most mammals are born live from their mothers. They look similar to their parents when they emerge, but grow bigger as they age. Mammals provide milk for their young until they are able to find their own food. Humans take care of their babies for longer than any other species, in part because we are totally helpless at birth and then develop very slowly. Most mammals have shorter life cycles than humans. For example, a lion cub begins walking by 10 days old. By three or four years old it can have its own babies.

SPREADING WINGS

Many insects start their life as a **larva**—a newly hatched creature, which in insects often looks like a small worm. The larva fills up on food and grows bigger, sometimes shedding an outer skin as it does so. Once it is big enough, it becomes a **pupa**, or **chrysalis**. The insect spends the pupa stage sheltered in a cocoon or protected by a case, not moving while it changes shape.

EGG

CATERPILLAR
(LARVA)

EGG

CHICKEN

HATCHLING

🐾 BREAKING FREE

Birds begin life in eggs laid by their mothers. Fish, amphibians, and reptiles mostly lay eggs, too. Birds usually keep their eggs warm till they hatch, often by sitting on them. Inside an egg, a baby bird is growing. When it's ready, the baby breaks out, and a **hatchling** (or chick) appears. Over time, the little bird matures into an adult.

CHICK IT OUT!

CHICK

Inside, its body changes—a process called **metamorphosis**. Eventually the adult form emerges.

CHRYSALIS (PUPA)

BUTTERFLY

FOLLOWING FOOD CHAINS

Every animal needs to eat. Without food, it would have no energy, and without energy, it couldn't survive. Some organisms can make their own food, but animals can't. This is where food chains come in.

CHAIN OF COMMAND

A **food chain**, like those shown here and on pages 140—141, shows a series of organisms that depend on each other for food. Every food chain starts with a **producer**. These are the organisms that can produce their own food, such as plants. Everything that eats something else in the chain is called a **consumer**.

The first consumers in the chain are called the **primary consumers.** If they eat only plants, they are **herbivores.** The animals that eat the primary consumers are the **secondary consumers.** The animals next in line are the **tertiary consumers.** These animals that eat other animals are called **carnivores.** Some animals are happy to eat either meat or plants, and they are called **omnivores.**

ENERGY PYRAMID

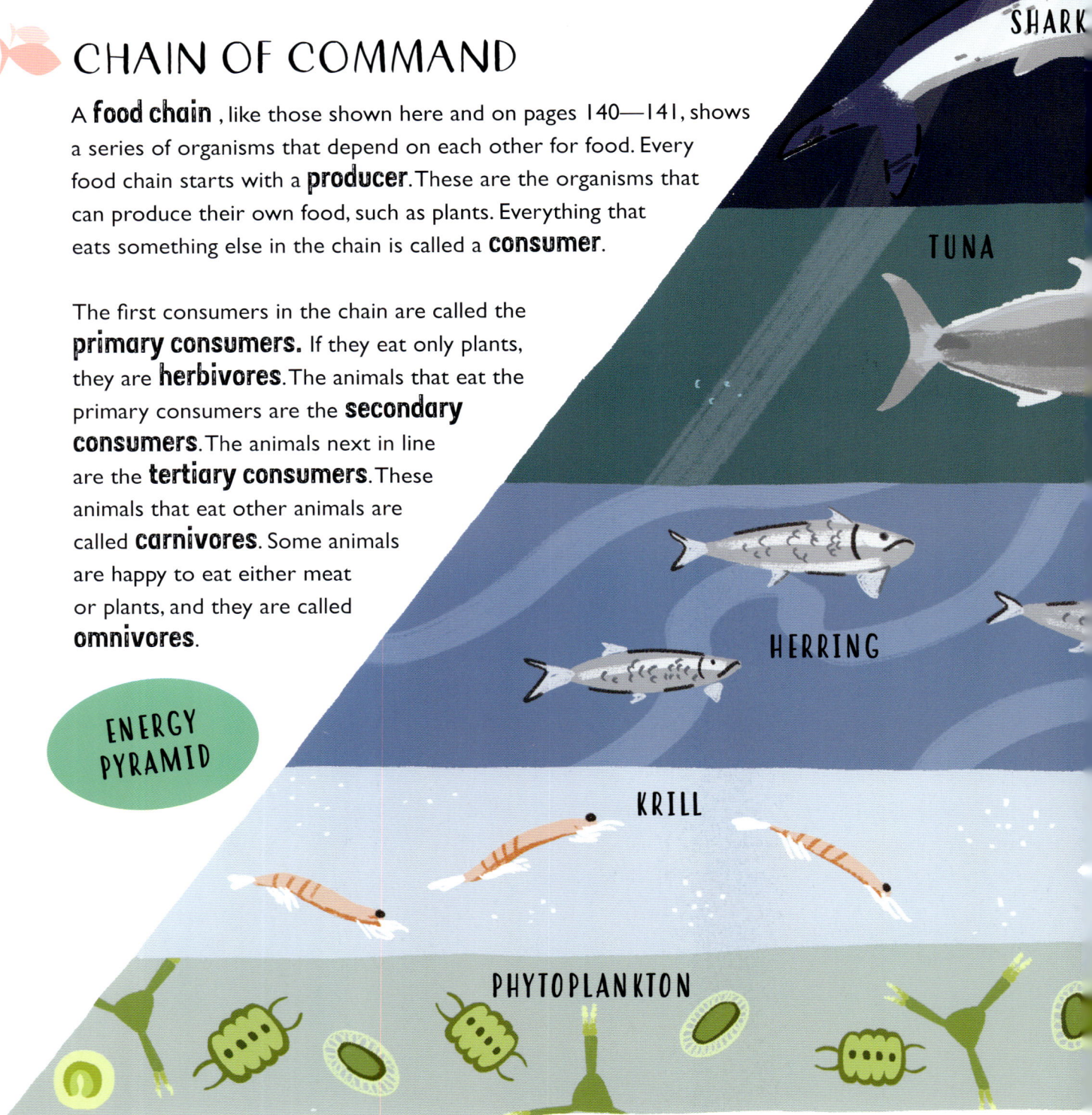

SHARK

TUNA

HERRING

KRILL

PHYTOPLANKTON

HUNTER OR HUNTED

In nature, animals must seek out their own food in whatever way they can to survive. Many animals hunt for their meals. They are **predators**. The animals that they hunt are their **prey**. If an owl eats a mouse, the owl is the predator and the mouse is its prey.

OAK TREE (PRODUCER) → INSECT (PRIMARY CONSUMER) → WOODPECKER (SECONDARY CONSUMER) → HAWK (TERTIARY CONSUMER)

ENERGY TRANSFER

Energy starts with the producer, which creates its own food, usually through the process of photosynthesis. The energy is then passed through each link in the chain, as one animal eats the next. The arrows in a food chain show the direction of the energy transfer—which way the nutrients are moving.

The energy decreases at each level of a food chain, forming an energy pyramid. Many producers are needed to support just one animal at the top of the pyramid, which is also the top of the food chain.

ENERGY DECREASING

CHAPTER 4

ECOLOGY: HABITATS AND CO-HABITATION

Across our planet, the weather and landscapes vary greatly. Ice and cold dominate the poles, while the regions around the equator have hot weather year round. Yet from poles to equator, mountaintops to deserts, living things make their homes. Different species have adapted over time to different temperatures and terrains.

Ecology is the study of how organisms relate to each other and their particular environment. This includes where creatures live, how the **climate** affects them, how they interact with others in the same space, and human effects on their home. As you travel through this chapter, think about the living things in your local habitats, whether they are city streets or farmland.

HABITATS AROUND THE WORLD

A **habitat** is the place where an animal, plant, or other living thing makes its home. A creature's habitat is where it finds food and shelter. Habitats range from deserts to ponds, rotting logs to rainforests.

🏠 HOME SWEET HOME

Each living thing is suited to the habitat where it lives. In its habitat, the organism can find its food, suitable shelter, and the right levels of sunlight and water.

African bush elephants, for example, move between African savanna and forest habitats. Their bodies are suited to eating the grass, leaves, and bark they find there. They are also suited to the climate, which has a rainy season and a dry season. **Climate** is a region's usual long-term weather pattern. In dry seasons, elephants use their tusks to dig up riverbeds and create new waterholes. Elephants also interact with the living things that share their habitat. Elephant dung spreads plant seeds—while dung beetles lay their eggs in it!

🏠 CLIMATE CONTROL

In each habitat, the food and shelter—from trees to grasses—are dependent on the climate and the wider **environment**. If the climate changes, food and shelter might become less readily available. Diseases, natural disasters, and human activities might also affect a creature's access to resources. Eventually, creatures may need to find a new habitat if their habitat changes too much or too fast.

FEELING AT HOME!

WATER CYCLE

Habitats vary across the world depending on how much sunlight and **water** they get. Areas with plenty of rain, such as rainforests, are full of plant and animal life. Dry deserts have fewer residents, which are all adapted to live with the limited water. The water on Earth is constantly moving and recycled in what is called the **water cycle**.

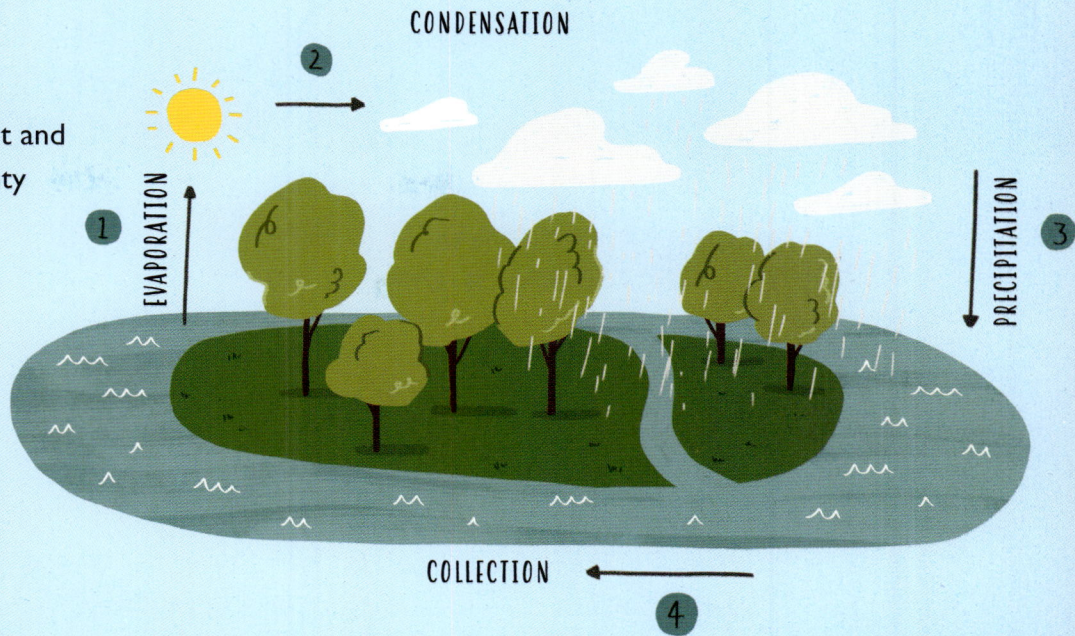

CONDENSATION

EVAPORATION

PRECIPITATION

1

2

3

4

COLLECTION

1. The sun **evaporates** water in lakes, rivers, and oceans. The water turns to vapor and rises into the air.

2. Water vapor in the sky cools down and **condenses** into little water droplets, which we see as clouds.

3. The droplets in the cloud get heavy, so the water drops back to Earth as rain or snow. This is called **precipitation**.

4. The rain runs across the land and into rivers, which carry it back to the ocean. This is **collection**, and the cycle begins again.

BIOMES

From deserts to grasslands, oceans to forests, Planet Earth has a wide range of **biomes**. A biome is a large community of life that is suited to a geographic region and climate.

BEAUTIFUL BIOMES

Similar biomes are found in different regions across the world. For example, the temperate forest biome is found in Europe, North America, and many other places. A biome can contain lots of different habitats. Habitats in a temperate forest include fallen leaves and tree branches.

Scientists divide Earth into anywhere between five and twenty biomes. These are some of the common ones.

BIOME TO BIOME

Polar biome: With the slippery ice and extreme cold, not just any creature can live in polar regions. In fact, some animals **migrate** to warmer climates when the **temperature** drops in winter. Others, including penguins and polar bears, thrive in these harsh lands at the top and bottom of the world.

Tropical forest: This warm, wet habitat is home to more species than any other biome. Trees stretch to the sky for sunlight, creating sunny habitats in their canopy and shadowy habitats below. Rainforests teem with animal, plant, and fungus life.

Temperate forest: This biome is full of trees, both with broad, flat leaves (deciduous trees) and with needle-like leaves (evergreen trees). The region has four seasons a year, and the leaves of deciduous trees follow, growing, changing, and falling in an endless cycle. Many animals eat the seeds, nuts, leaves, and berries provided by the trees.

Mountains: Within the mountains, there can be several habitats. The valleys host woodlands, while the slopes are covered by evergreens. On tall mountaintops, the climate is cold and windy. Very few plants live on the peaks—only those lower to the ground, such as mosses, can survive.

Desert: In the driest biome, animals and plants, such as cacti, have special features to store water for long periods of time. Deserts may be hot or cold, depending on their distance from the equator. In hot deserts, many animals hide under rocks or in burrows to escape the daytime heat, then come out in the cooler night to feast.

Grassland: With more rainfall than deserts but less than forests, grasslands are mainly covered in grasses. Grasses need less rain than tall trees. Grass provides food for herds of herbivores, who in turn are the perfect prey for carnivores such as lions. Grasslands are found across the world, with different names such as savannas, prairies, or pampas.

Water: Biomes are also found in the water that covers two-thirds of our planet. These biomes can be fresh water or salty oceans. At least one million animal species live in the oceans, ranging from tiny plankton to large whales. Habitats in the ocean biome range from sunlit coral reefs to the dark seafloor.

WORKING TOGETHER

No living thing can survive on its own.
It takes a whole team of plants and animals—as well as
many non-living elements—to keep the community thriving.

ROCK POOL ECOSYSTEM

ECOSYSTEM EFFORT

The interaction between the living and non-living things in a habitat is called an **ecosystem**. Energy, nutrients, and other materials travel through an ecosystem. An ecosystem needs every element to be in perfect balance. An ecosystem can exist in a single tree trunk, a rock pool, or a vast forest. Every part of the ecosystem affects others, from a single animal species to the carbon dioxide in the air.

TREE-MENDOUS TEAMWORK

Each organism within an ecosystem has its own habitat. But organisms cannot exist on their own—they all interact with others in the community. For example, insects living in a tree use the leaves as food, while birds use the branches for shelter.

REUSE AND RECYCLE

Alongside the life in an ecosystem are resources such as air, water, and soil. A key element in ecosystems is **recycling**. Nutrients, energy, and water all go through processes to be reused to continue supporting the community. For example, when an animal dies, its body decays into the soil, leaving nutrients that help plants grow.

Sunlight shines down on plants.

Carbon dioxide (CO₂)

Fossil fuels are **burned** for energy by factories and cars, releasing carbon dioxide into the air. This activity risks destroying the balance of the cycle.

Plants absorb carbon dioxide from the air. They use the energy in sunlight to turn CO₂ into food through **photosynthesis**.

Animals **breathe out** carbon dioxide, releasing it into the atmosphere.

Plant and animal waste put carbon back into the **soil**.

Microbes and decomposers break down the waste and release the carbon.

CARBON CYCLE

One of the key essential elements in all ecosystems is **carbon**. It is constantly used and **recycled** through plants, animals, and air to support life on Earth. The **carbon cycle** is carefully balanced naturally, but by burning fossil fuels humans are disrupting it.

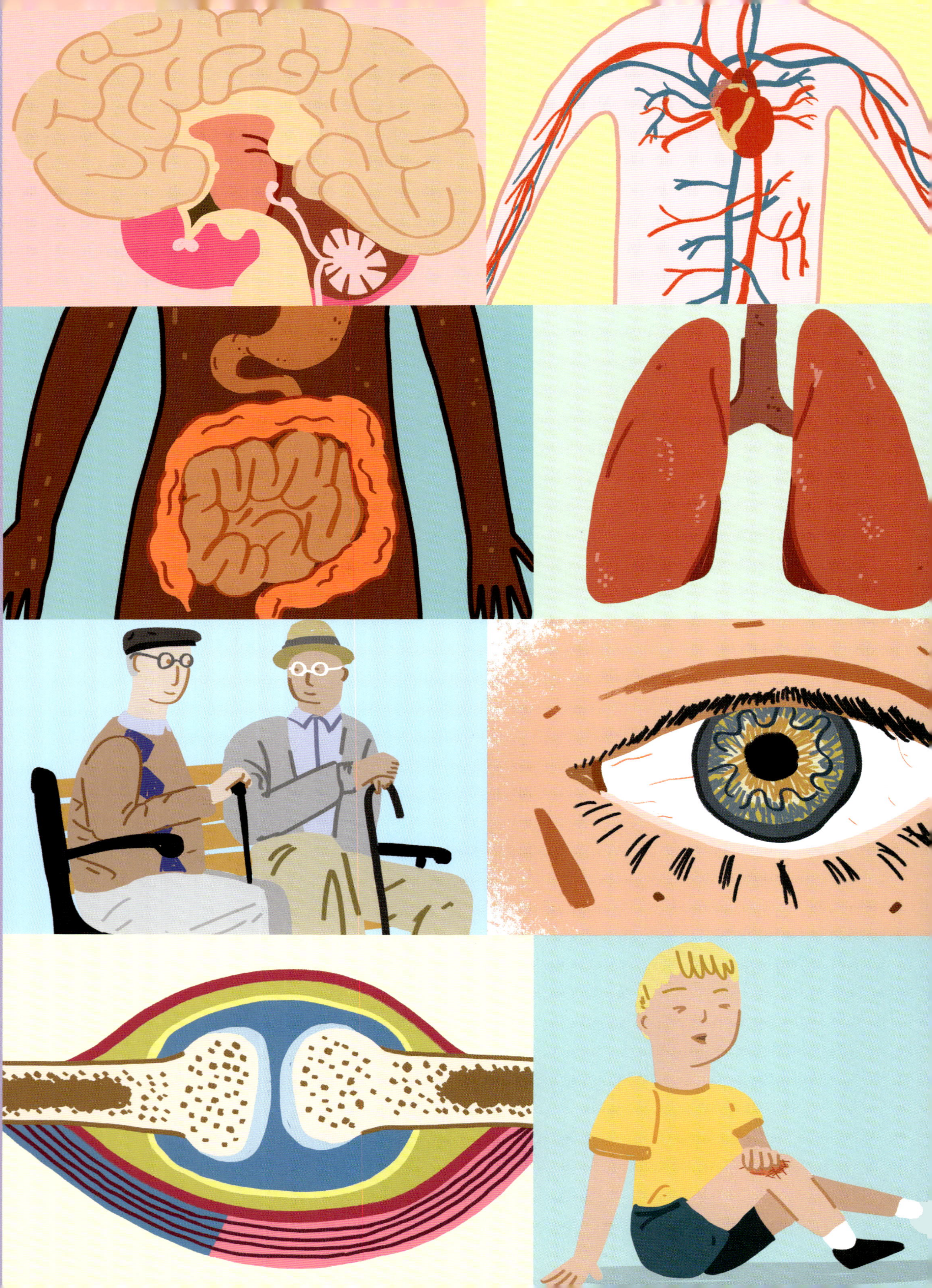

CHAPTER 5

ANATOMY: THE HUMAN BODY

The human body is like a well-oiled machine. A magnificent, miraculous machine. Many parts work together to create a living, breathing, thinking being. Amazingly, we all have these parts in common, and yet we are all individuals.

Human anatomy is the study of the structure of the body and how the various parts work. These include bones and muscles, the stomach and nerves, the heart and the brain, and how they all change as we age. Throughout this chapter, take a close look at yourself as we explore the fascinating body that makes you YOU.

IN YOUR BONES

The spectacular human skeleton gives us shape and structure.
It protects our delicate organs, such as the heart and brain.
Our bones also make blood cells and even help us hear!

STRUCTURING YOU

The human body has many delicate parts inside, such as the brain, heart, and lungs. The **skeleton** is what protects all of these. The human skeleton is made up of more than 200 bones, some quite big and some very small. Each hand has 27 bones while each foot is made up of 26. The **skull** protects the brain, and the **ribcage** surrounds the heart and lungs. Our skeleton also provides the body with support, helping us stand up straight.

OUT OF CURIOSITY

The smallest bone in the body, the stapes, is inside the ear. It is just 3 mm (0.12 in) long. The stapes helps carry sounds to the inner ear.

BONES

Connecting bones are muscles and joints that help the body move. Bones contain lots of calcium and other minerals, which make them strong. They can even repair themselves if they get broken. Bones are **living tissues** that grow as we do. Tissues are collections of similar cells, which are the body's smallest building blocks. In this case, bones are made of tiny bone cells.

IN THE BONE FACTORY

Bones have a protective layer of hard, tightly packed bone on the outside. Inside, there is a sponge-like structure that makes them light. Bones are slightly flexible, but become more rigid as you age. Inside many bones is **bone marrow**, where blood cells (see page 68) are made, around 500 billion of them every day.

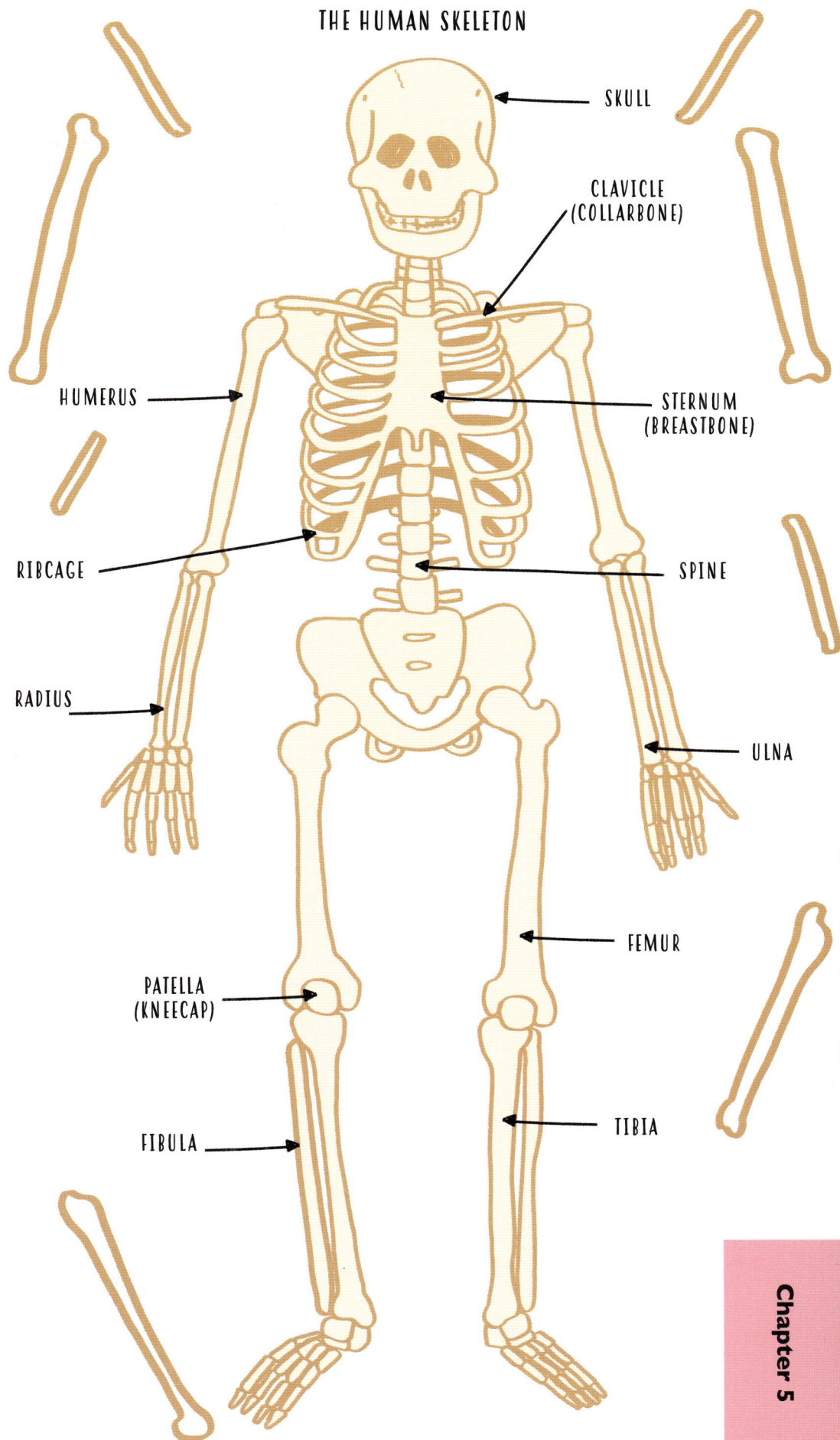

THE HUMAN SKELETON

SKULL

CLAVICLE (COLLARBONE)

HUMERUS

STERNUM (BREASTBONE)

RIBCAGE

SPINE

RADIUS

ULNA

FEMUR

PATELLA (KNEECAP)

FIBULA

TIBIA

MOVING AND GROOVING

The skeleton holds up the body, but how do the hundreds of bones work together to allow us to walk, run, grip, and stretch? That's where muscles and joints come in. Without them, we would be just a pile of bones!

JOINTS

Some bones are joined firmly together, such as in the skull. Others are connected with joints. **Synovial joints** connect bones that give us a large range of motion, such as in our arms and legs. They ensure that the ends of bones don't rub against each other and wear down when moving. Inside these joints, several parts work together. At the end of the bone is a smooth **tissue** called **cartilage**. It sits in a slippery liquid called **synovial fluid**. A **ligament** connects the bones in the joint to keep it all together.

BONE

CARTILAGE

LIGAMENT

SYNOVIAL FLUID

MUSCLES

To be able to move, bones and joints also need **muscles**. These are like stretchy cords that attach to bones using **tendons**.

Muscles work by **contracting**. This means that they shorten and tighten, pulling on the bone as they do so. If the bone has a joint, it can then move. But muscles can only **pull**. If they pull an arm up, the same muscle is unable to push it down again. The clever human body solves this problem by having each muscle work with another, in groups of two called **antagonistic muscles**. Each muscle is part of a pair that works in two directions.

For example, to bend the elbow, the arm has both a **biceps** on the front of the arm and a **triceps** on the back. Each one can contract to pull the arm up or down. To pull the arm up, the biceps contracts while the triceps relaxes. Then, to push the arm down again, the biceps relaxes while the triceps contracts.

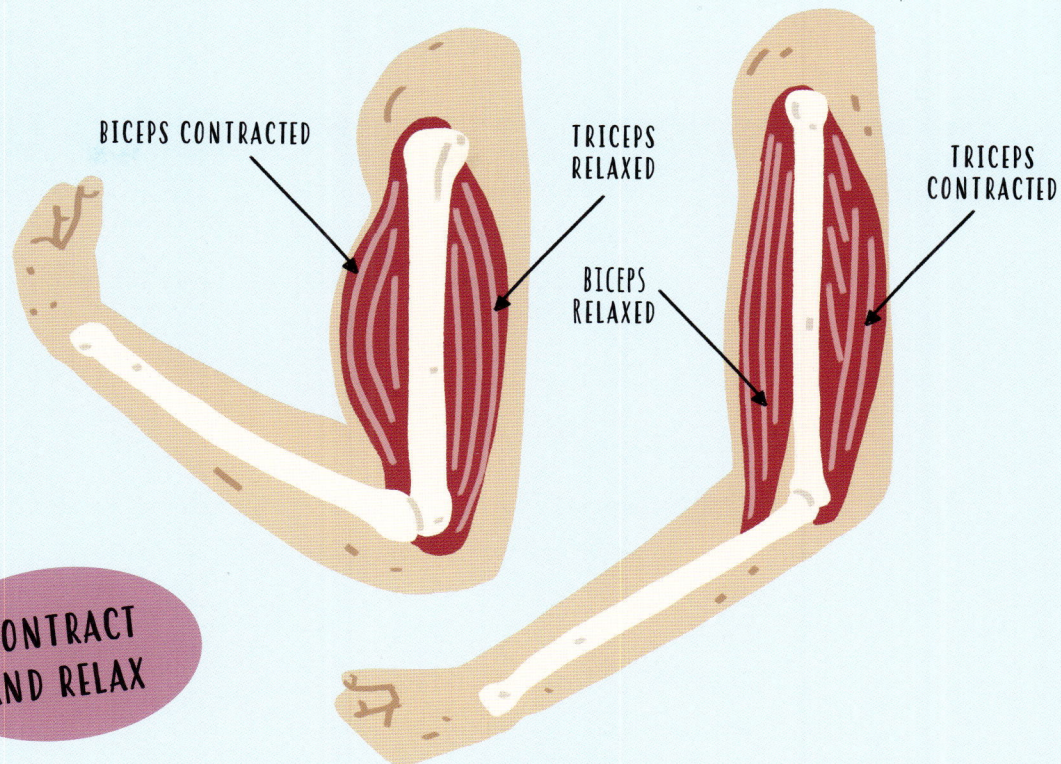

CONTRACT AND RELAX

BICEPS CONTRACTED

TRICEPS RELAXED

BICEPS RELAXED

TRICEPS CONTRACTED

WORKING TOGETHER

Many muscles work together when your body wants to move. Your body has more than 600 of them, after all! Wiggling your fingers takes several muscles at once. A runner needs to use both arm and leg muscles to pump their arms while they bend their legs and run. If you're dancing, you might use pairs of muscles all over to really groove with your whole body. Even a smile uses at least ten muscles to move your mouth.

ORGANS AT WORK

Even while you're sleeping, the organs in your body are working hard. They have many different functions but one thing in common. They all help you live!

♥ ORGANS

An **organ** is a group of tissues that work together to do a specific and important job. These are some of the main organs in the human body.

Lungs: When you breathe in, air travels down to the lungs. They take the oxygen from the air and put it in your bloodstream. They also remove carbon dioxide from your blood and breathe it out.

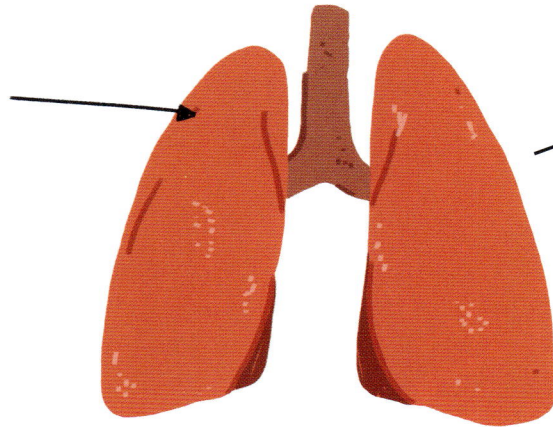

Kidneys: The two bean-shaped kidneys work as a filter for the blood. They clean out waste and extra water, to keep the body perfectly balanced. The waste is sent on to the bladder and leaves the body as urine.

Stomach and intestines: These organs are part of the **digestive system**. The stomach breaks down food into mush. The food then travels through the intestines, which absorb the water and nutrients.

BRAIN

LUNGS

HEART

STOMACH

INTESTINES

Brain: The brain sends signals to the rest of the body to tell various parts what they need to do, and it processes information that it receives. It controls other organs. It also holds thoughts, memories, and emotions.

Heart: The heart continuously pumps blood around your body, delivering oxygen and nutrients to every part.

Liver: The multi-purpose liver has more than 500 jobs. It cleans the blood, removing harmful toxins. It absorbs nutrients for the body, produces bile to help digest fatty foods, and can even store energy for you.

Bladder: The bladder stores urine, which is waste products from the bloodstream. The liquid stays there until the bladder gets too full—then it leaves the body, straight into the toilet!

Skin: Skin covers the body to protect and hold everything inside, including other organs. It gives you a sense of touch. It is the largest organ of all.

BRAIN CONTROL

While some animals, such as slugs, can live without a brain, humans wouldn't be who they are if they didn't have one. The brain helps us move, think, feel, talk, remember, and so much more.

WHAT DO YOU THINK?

The brain is a complex and busy organ. It is made up of billions of brain cells and uses 20% of the body's energy to keep us going. It is in charge of many different functions. Some of these help the body work, such as keeping your heart beating or your muscles moving, while others control your thoughts, emotions, and senses. Different parts of the brain help control different functions.

CEREBRUM

HYPOTHALAMUS

BRAINSTEM

CEREBELLUM

Cerebrum: The largest part of the brain is the cerebrum. It is the outer portion of the brain, with a deeply folded surface. This is where complex thinking and understanding happen. The cerebrum controls your personality and speech, processes sight and touch, helps you make sense of emotions and the space around you, and directs the rest of your brain and body when you decide to move.

BRAIN POWER!

Cerebellum: The cerebellum sits at the back of the skull. It helps control your muscles and movement, by assisting with balance and coordinating your body so that you move smoothly.

Brainstem: At the bottom of the brain and the top of the spinal cord is the brainstem. It helps with the things that you don't normally "think" about to make your body work, such as keeping your heart beating and your lungs breathing.

Hypothalamus: The hypothalamus may be only the size of a pea, but it plays a big part in regulating your body. The hypothalamus regulates a lot of hormones, which are the chemical messengers that control many aspects of how the body works, grows, and responds (including sleep, thirst, and hunger).

LEFT AND RIGHT

The brain is split into two sides, or **hemispheres**. The **left side** controls the actions of the right side of the body. The **right side** of the brain controls the left side of the body.

SPINAL CORD

NERVOUS SYSTEM

The brain is part of the body's **nervous system**. This system also includes nerves and the spinal cord. The spinal cord is a nerve "highway," a key part of the network of nerves all through the body that carries signals and messages to and from the brain. The spinal cord can even handle some nerve messages itself, without sending them to the brain. The instinct that makes you move your hand away from a flame is triggered just by the spinal cord so it can be started super quickly.

Chapter 5

THE JOURNEY OF BLOOD

Blood flows through the body in blood vessels, transporting vital materials and waste. From the powerful beating heart to tiny capillaries, each element works together as part of the circulatory system.

CIRCULATORY SYSTEM

The job of the **circulatory system**, or **cardiovascular system**, is to take blood around the body, delivering oxygen and nutrients and clearing out waste. It is made up of the heart, blood vessels, and the blood itself.

PUMPING LIFE

ARTERIES

VEINS

BUSY BLOOD

The red substance you might see if you cut yourself is a very important delivery system for the body. It transports different types of cells, which each have a particular job. **Red blood cells** bring oxygen to every part of the body and take away carbon dioxide. **White blood cells** fight any intruders that might cause disease. **Blood platelets** help the blood clot, or clump together, to fix cuts and stop blood from leaving the body.

HUMAN CIRCULATORY SYSTEM

BEATING HEART

The heart is a powerful **muscle**, about the size of your fist. When the right side of the heart contracts, it pumps blood that has returned to the heart from the lungs out into the body. When the left side contracts, it takes blood from the lungs and pumps it to the body. Each **heartbeat** is the muscle contracting. The heart can beat more than 100,000 times in a single day—that's over 35 million times in a year! The average person's heart will beat more than 2.5 billion times in their lifetime.

HUMAN HEART

BLOOD VESSELS

The blood vessels are like a network of roads that travel all through your body, allowing the blood to travel from one place to another. **Arteries** take blood away from the heart, delivering oxygen and nutrients to the body. **Capillaries** are smaller tubes that branch out and take the blood from the arteries to specific areas. **Veins** then take the blood back to the heart. The blood cycles to the lungs for more oxygen, then repeats the journey again.

HEALTHY HEART

The heart works hard day and night, always pumping to keep you alive. If you use up more oxygen than usual, such as when you exercise and are breathing harder, the heart needs to pump even harder to keep up. A healthy heart will eventually return to its normal rate of beating after the exercise stops.

STAGES OF FOOD

The food on our plate is delicious to eat. It looks and tastes good. But as it is, it can't actually DO anything for the body. It needs to be broken down into simper materials to be of use.

DIGESTIVE SYSTEM

Digestion means breaking down food into substances that the body can absorb and use. The **digestive system** is the group of organs that process food through all stages. The **digestive tract** travels all the way from your mouth to your bottom!

TAKE A BITE

The first step in a food's journey is when it enters the **mouth**. The teeth chew it into pieces small enough to be swallowed. It is then pushed into a **muscular tube**, the food pipe, which squeezes it down to the **stomach**.

BREAKING DOWN

Food sits in the **stomach** for several hours, while powerful muscles and juices break it down into smaller pieces yet again. This slushy substance then travels into the **small intestine**, where many of the nutrients are absorbed into the bloodstream.

MOUTH

FOOD PIPE

SMALL INTESTINE

🔵 HELPERS

An **acid** in the stomach helps break down food and get rid of anything harmful. In the small intestine, **bile** (a liquid produced by the liver) helps break down fat. To break down food really well, the organs also have help from **enzymes**. These are proteins made by the body that speed up chemical reactions. In a chemical reaction, two or more materials react with each other, forming new materials. In the mouth, enzyme-carrying **saliva** starts the digestive process as it mixes with food.

?

OUT OF CURIOSITY

In your lifetime, your body produces enough saliva to fill two whole swimming pools!

STOMACH

LARGE INTESTINE

🟡 IRRITATION

If the body is unable to break down a certain type of food, the person suffers a **food intolerance**. For example, people who are lactose intolerant are usually missing an enzyme that can digest the sugar called lactose in milk products. Some chemicals added to food can also irritate a person's digestive system.

🟡 MOVING OUT

RECTUM

ANUS

Finally, the mush moves on to the **large intestine**. Water and remaining nutrients are absorbed, leaving anything else to dry out. This waste then moves to the **rectum** where it is stored as poop. Eventually, it is pushed out of the body through the **anus**.

SENSING YOUR WORLD

Making sense of our surroundings begins with the sense organs. Special receptors around your body take in information from the world and pass it to your brain. Your brain carries out the process of making sense of your surroundings so that you can live safely and happily.

SENSES

Your body has many special **receptors** that can sense the world. They take in information about what is sweet, soft, hot, and more, and send it to the brain to process. There are five main **senses**—sight, smell, taste, touch, and hearing.

SIGHT

Your **eyes** sense shades, shapes, brightness, and distance. Light reflects off objects, then enters through the central black **pupil** and passes through a **lens** to the back of the eye. Millions of receptors gather information about brightness and color, then send it on to the brain through the **optic nerve**. The brain can then put together an image and understand the object that you see before you.

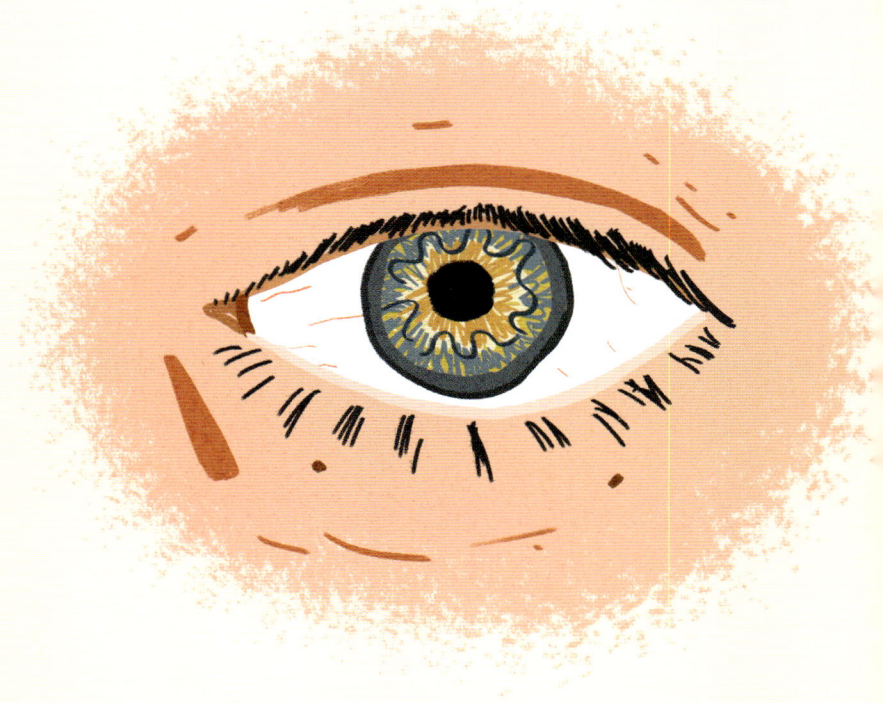

SMELL

When we breathe in through the **nose**, smells (which are chemicals) enter the body. Slimy **mucus** traps the chemicals at the back of the nose, where receptors send signals to the brain. The brain can then figure out what the smell is. Humans are able to make out about 10,000 different smells.

TOUCH

Covering the whole body, our **skin** plays a huge part in sensing the world. Just under the surface, receptors sense pressure, heat, cold, and pain. They send signals through the nervous system to help the body react to the touch. If the body feels cold, for example, its little hairs will react by standing on end to trap warm air. The feet contain more sense receptors than most parts of the body. This is why they are so ticklish! They might react by kicking, without you even thinking about it.

TASTE

Your **tongue** is covered in thousands of tiny **taste buds** to help you taste the food you eat. Each taste bud is a sense receptor that sends a signal to the brain about the food—whether it's sweet, salty, bitter, sour, or umami (tasting rich, like meat or mushrooms). The brain puts all the signals together to understand the taste of the meal. The sense of smell works very closely with taste to give a full understanding of food. These senses help you enjoy a delicious dish, but they can also warn the brain if a food is unsafe to eat!

HEARING

Sounds enter the body through the **ears**. Sound waves (vibrations that travel through air or water) travel through the ear canal to the ear drum. This vibrates when it feels sound waves—the louder the sound, the bigger the vibration! The vibrations move on to hearing receptors that turn them into signals for the brain. The brain makes sense of them.

AND MORE

Proprioception is often described as the sixth sense. It makes use of receptors in muscles and joints to help you understand your body's position in space. Without it, you would fall over all the time!

THE CHANGING HUMAN BODY

Just like any other life form, the human body changes over time.
It is born, grows bigger, and gets older—with lots of excitement along the way!

BABY

When cells from a mother and a father join inside the mother, a baby's journey begins. It stays inside the mother's **womb** for nine months, growing and developing until it is ready to enter the world. Once born, it is small and depends on its parents for food, getting around, and safety. The baby very quickly grows and learns, soon recognizing faces and exploring its surroundings with its hands, mouth—and all its senses.

CHILD

Learning continues at a speedy rate as children learn to walk and to talk. Language grows as children hear words repeated, then begin to connect them to their meanings—and finally to use them! Twenty baby teeth start forming before a child is born, but they move down from the gums between the ages of 6 months and 12 years. Between age 6 and adulthood, baby teeth fall out as the 32 larger, permanent teeth move into place.

ADOLESCENT

Between the ages of 8 and 14, girls start going through **puberty**. Boys start a little later, between 9 and 16. During puberty, the body changes so that—when its owner is old enough—it would be able to make a baby, if they wanted! **Adolescents** have a growth spurt, when they grow taller quite fast. They grow hair in new places, start to sweat more, and may develop acne. Girls develop breasts, and boys' voices become deeper.

ADULT

Around age 21, a human has usually reached their full height and may have their complete set of **adult** teeth. Adults may choose to start a family. When a woman has a baby in her womb, she is said to be **pregnant**.

OLD AGE

After many years of adulthood, a person begins to approach **old age**. Their skin becomes less firm, causing wrinkles, and their hair may turn white or start to fall out. Their cells are less able to repair themselves or make good-quality copies of themselves. Some organs and systems of the body start to work less well.

? OUT OF CURIOSITY

There are around 8 billion people living across the world. The average age of all those human beings is 29.

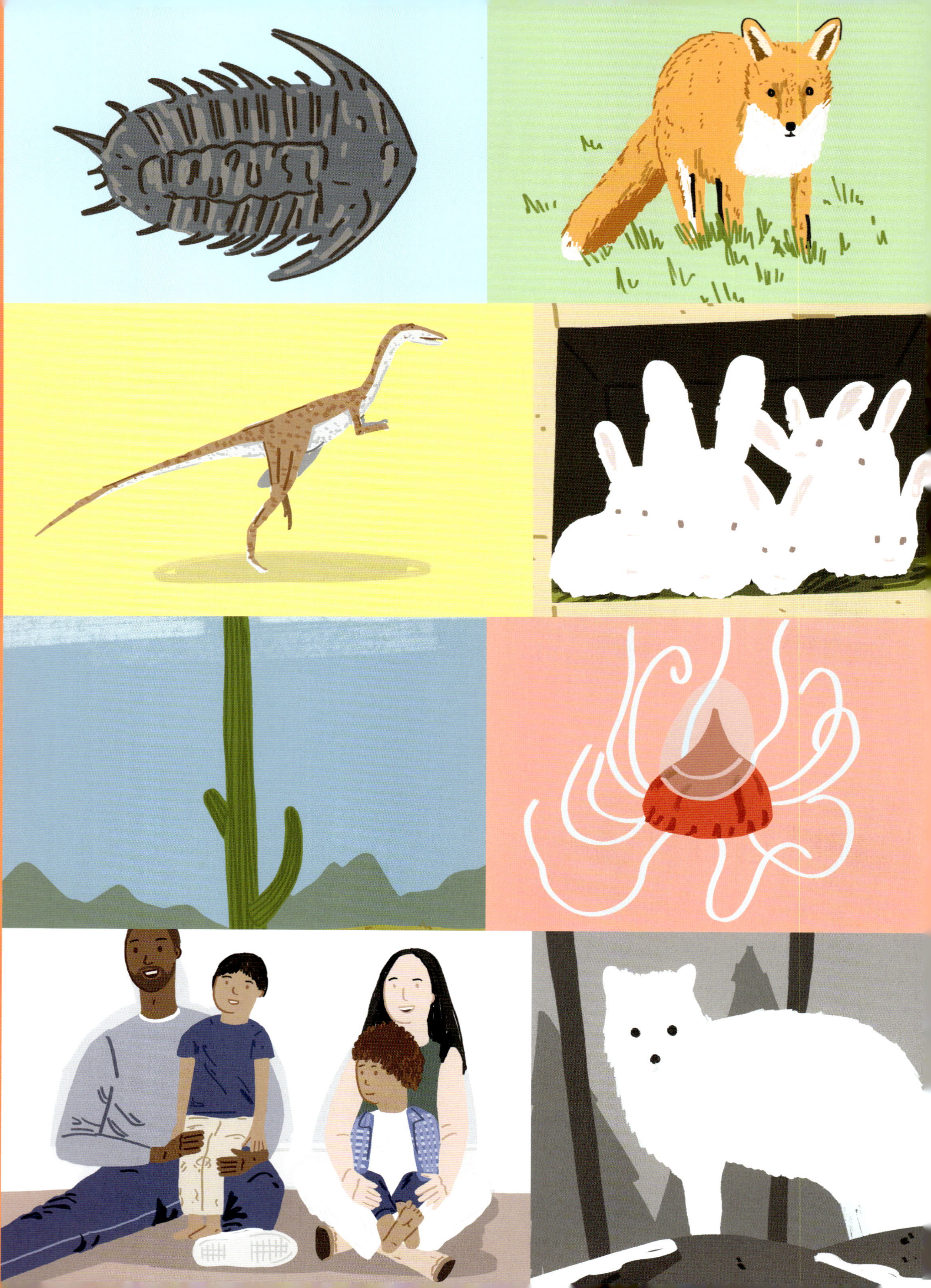

CHAPTER 6

EVOLUTION: FROM PAST TO PRESENT TO FUTURE

In the grand scheme of Earth, humans have been around for only a very short period of time. There is a rich history to be discovered long before our lives here. How did life begin on this planet? How has it changed, or evolved, over time? Where is it going next?

Evolutionary biology is the study of the processes of evolution that have led to the many living organisms found in our world today. Travel through time in this chapter as we explore where it all began, how characteristics are passed on from one generation to the next, and how different creatures adapt to the world in order to survive.

THROUGH TIME

From tiny organisms to enormous creatures, Planet Earth has seen many things come and go during its time in the Solar System.

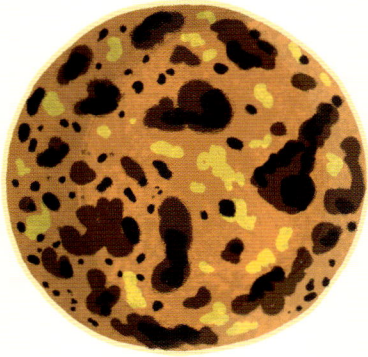

4.5 billion years ago:
Earth forms, but it is nothing like we know today. Its surface is hot, molten rock. It is millions of years before Earth cools and rain begins to create oceans.

3.8 billion years ago:
The first life appears! These are simple single-celled organisms that live in the oceans. Over millions of years, they start to provide oxygen to the water and atmosphere.

1.5 billion years ago:
More complex cells, with internal structures capable of doing different jobs, start to form in the oceans.

395 million years ago:
The first four-legged animals appear. They are amphibians, able to move between water and land.

312 million years ago:
Reptiles evolve from amphibians. Around 80 million years later, a group of reptiles called dinosaurs has evolved.

150 million years ago:
Birds have evolved from a group of small, feathered dinosaurs. Birds are the only "dinosaurs" alive today.

665 billion years ago:
The first animals, which are simple invertebrates (without a backbone), evolve in the ocean.

520 million years ago: Vertebrates (with backbones) emerge. They are simple, jawless fish.

1 billion years ago:
Living things made of more than one cell appear.

540 million years ago:
Some invertebrates start to grow shells.

OUT OF CURIOSITY

If you shrunk the history of Earth down to a 24-hour period, humans would only appear in approximately the last minute! So much has gone on before us.

65 million years ago:
The dinosaurs are wiped out after the impact of a giant space rock. Over millions of year, mammals grow larger.

350,000 years ago:
Modern humans have evolved. We are descendants of great apes that lived 4–7 million years ago.

PASSING IT ON

Evolution is possible because characteristics are passed from parent organisms to their babies. In organisms that reproduce asexually (make copies of a single parent), change only happens when there are mistakes in the copying, called mutations. But in organisms with two parents, features can be mixed and matched quickly and easily.

INHERITANCE

When a baby is born, it inherits its features from its parents. This includes characteristics such as eye shade, hair type, and height. Because babies form from cells from both parents, they have a mix of features—some from the mother, and some from the father.

CHILDREN WITH FEATURES FROM BOTH PARENTS

VARIATION

All living things pass on characteristics to their offspring. But not all offspring are alike. **Variation** makes differences between them. You and your siblings each have different combinations of your parents' features. And within the species, you are similar to every other human around the world (two legs, intelligent brain, etc.), but there are differences. Some people have blue eyes, and some have brown. Some people are tall, some are short, and some are somewhere in between.

VARYING TO SURVIVE

Variation means that there is variety in the organisms in a species—they are not all **identical**. It comes about by mixing genes from two parents and by mutation, which sometimes changes a feature of an organism slightly. Sometimes one variant of a feature is more helpful to an organism than another. In a snowy environment, an animal born with lighter fur might survive better as it can hide from predators. It will succeed and reproduce, passing on its genes. Over time, more animals will have lighter fur. Variation helps species adapt, over time, to changes in their environment. This process is called **natural selection**.

VARYING TO EVOLVE

Over time, the variations in each new generation lead to evolution. When a species evolves so much that it has wings rather than arms, feathers rather than scales, and a beak rather than teeth, we can say that it is a different type of animal—a bird rather than a dinosaur! Variation has led to the existence of millions of different species on Earth!

ADAPTING TO THE WORLD

In the competitive world of nature, species must fight to survive.
This isn't always a physical battle—sometimes it's all about
finding a particular habitat where there is less competition for food.

ADAPTATION

Over time, a species becomes more and more suited to its environment. This is called **adaptation**. Living things also adapt to the arrival of other species in their environment, perhaps growing larger or sharper-toothed to fight off bigger predators. Over many generations, animals may move into a less crowded habitat, such as the treetops or underground burrows, to avoid competition. Slowly, species adapt to this environment, evolving wings for flight or large paws for burrowing.

PERFECT FIT

We can see adaptations in every animal if we look closely enough! Over time, polar bears have grown thick fur to adapt to their cold land. Elephants, on the other hand, have finer hair as well as large ears that they can fan to keep cool in the heat of their sunny home. Plants also adapt to their surroundings. A cactus has become well suited to its desert habitat. Its long roots can stretch far to collect water, and its thick stem can hold on to the water for far longer than many other plants.

FENNEC FOX

A TALE OF THREE FOXES

A fox is a mammal. But there are dozens of different species of foxes, each adapted to their own habitat. A **fennec fox** has a unique look, for example. Its huge ears help it release heat and cool down in its hot desert home. Living in the chilly north, the **Arctic fox** doesn't need this feature. Instead, it has adapted to have fur on its paws to keep them warm and stop them from sliding on the ice. Yet another fox species, the **red fox**, has adapted to be resourceful to find food in human settings, such as farms and cities.

RED FOX

ARCTIC FOX

ADAPTING TO CHANGE

A species is adapted to survive in its part of the world. But what if that habitat changes? If the polar bear's land heats up, its characteristics are no longer suited to its home and it will struggle to survive. Species need to adapt quickly enough to live in changing homes, or move on to new ones.

SECTION 2: COOL CHEMISTRY

Chemistry is the study of the "stuff" that the world is made from—**matter**. All matter is made from tiny building blocks called **atoms**. Chemistry is the study of how atoms join together to create every material we know.

HEALTH

Chemistry is important in many areas of life. For example, it keeps us healthy. Lots of medicines are developed each year using chemistry, and many tests are carried out in hospitals using chemicals.

CHEMISTRY AT WORK

Chemistry is a vital part of industry. New materials are developed all the time as a result of work carried out by chemists. Chemists are constantly working to find new, environmentally friendly fabrics, plastics, and more. Even some of our food is developed by chemists, such as new types of healthy food created from fungus.

There are lots of different types of chemistry, which can be broken down into five main branches or "disciplines."

ORGANIC CHEMISTRY

Organic chemistry is the study of chemicals that contain atoms of carbon. Most of the chemicals necessary for living things to flourish are carbon-based. Organic means "living."

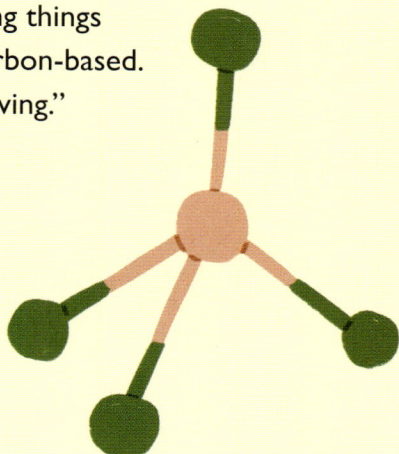

INORGANIC CHEMISTRY

Inorganic chemistry is the study of chemicals that are not usually found in living things. These chemicals are often found in rocks or **minerals** dug from the ground. Currently, a lot of inorganic chemists are concentrating on the materials used for computers and for energy production.

PHYSICAL CHEMISTRY

Physical chemistry studies how atoms bond together to create groups of atoms called **molecules**. A physical chemist might study **chemical reactions**, which is when the atoms in molecules are rearranged, creating new substances.

BIOCHEMISTRY

Biochemistry is the study of the chemical reactions that take place in living things—even you! Biochemists study the processes that take place in cells, and develop new treatments for diseases.

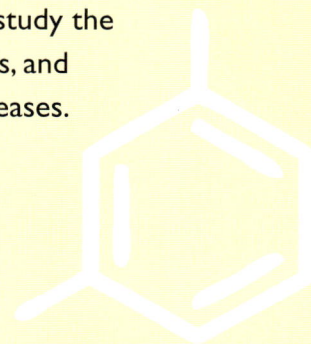

ANALYTICAL CHEMISTRY

Analytical chemistry is the study of the way matter is composed. It looks at how materials in samples of matter can be identified, separated, and quantified (finding out how much of a thing there is). Analytical chemists use a wide variety of complex instruments and experiments to find out about matter.

CHEMISTRY IS EVERYWHERE!

So—chemistry is going on all around us, every day—and lies behind lots of the things we take for granted in our lives, from computers to clothes and food!

SOLID STATE

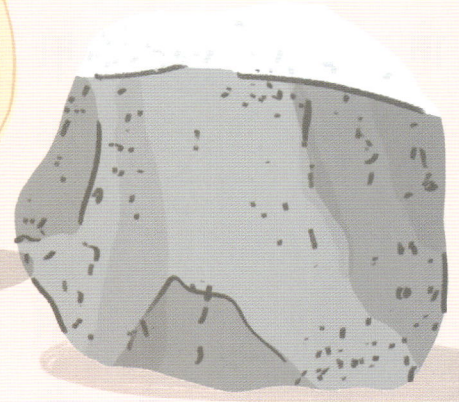

LIQUID STATE

GAS STATE

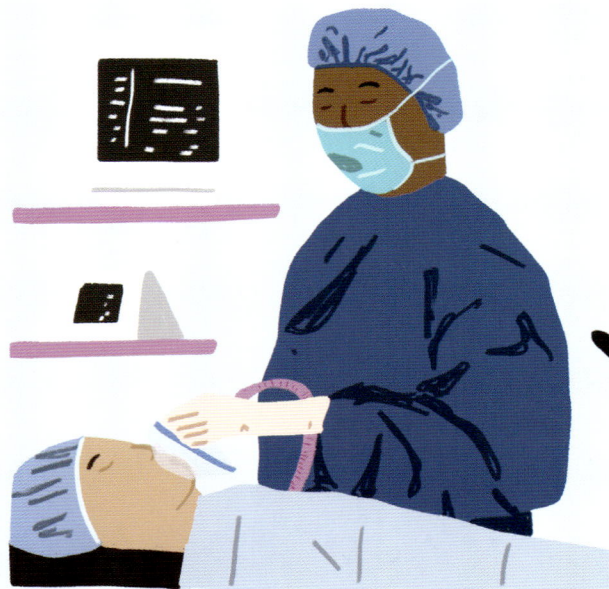

CHAPTER 7

STATES OF MATTER

There are four main common states (or "phases") of matter in the Universe:

SOLID	LIQUID	GAS	PLASMA

Matter is everything that has mass (or weight), and takes up space. Matter is made up of atoms and bonded groups of atoms, called molecules. Millions of them fit together to make all of the things we see and use every day—your home, trees, plants, and animals—even you are made of atoms!

SOLIDS

The ground you walk on is a solid, as are the chair you sit in, the plate you eat from, and a book you read—all solid things. Solids are "hard" things that you can hold.

LIQUIDS

Liquids can be poured. They take on the shape of the containers they are put into. The juice you drink is liquid. Seawater, blood, milk, and water are all liquids.

GASES

The air you breathe is a gas. Molecules of gas are much farther apart than molecules in liquids. Gases are often invisible and we sometimes smell them rather than see them. Gases take on the shape and volume of the container they are held inside.

PLASMA

We don't see plasma as often as solids, liquids, and gases. It is like a gas, but in this case some of the molecules have changed—they lose some of their electrons, and become ions. Plasma was only identified relatively recently in scientific terms—in 1879, by William Crookes.

CHANGING STATES

Sometimes, things change state. The molecules themselves don't change, but the way they move does. A water molecule is H_2O: two hydrogen atoms and one oxygen atom. That stays the same whether it is a liquid, solid (ice), or gas (steam). However, its physical state changes. Matter changes state when energy is applied, such as pressure or heat.

At room temperature, water is a liquid. The molecules can move about easily, so water drips and flows. It can change to a solid, as ice, when it freezes. In this form, the molecules are held together tightly and do not move easily. If we add heat energy, water can change into vapor called steam as it boils, like water in a kettle. The molecules move faster and are spread far apart.

◆ SOLIDS ◆

How do we recognize when something is solid?
Ask yourself these questions:

- DOES IT STAY IN ONE PLACE?

- DOES IT FLOW? IF IT DOES, IT IS NOT A SOLID.

- DOES IT HOLD ITS SHAPE? IF IT SPREADS OUT INTO THE AIR, IT IS NOT A SOLID.

- CAN IT BE SQUASHED OR COMPRESSED INTO A SMALL VOLUME? SOLIDS CAN'T CHANGE THE VOLUME THEY OCCUPY AS THE MOLECULES CAN'T MOVE CLOSER TOGETHER WITHOUT A CHANGE IN TEMPERATURE.

Don't be fooled by powders such as salt or sand—they are still solids even though they can be "poured." Each tiny grain keeps the same shape and volume, so these are solids.

◆ SOLID STATE

Molecules vibrate as they have **kinetic energy**—they vibrate as they bump into each other. In a solid, forces keep the molecules tightly together and they vibrate (jiggle) in place. They don't move around past each other. The **electrons** move, but the atoms are locked into position.

Molecules in a solid are stuck in a rigid arrangement of atoms. They can't be compressed as there is nowhere for them to go. Strong forces bond the molecules, keeping them attracted to each other, keeping the solid together.

SOLID STATE

EXAMPLES OF SOLIDS

Solids can have lots of different textures—soft like fur and fabric or tough like stone and wood. Solid objects can be huge like cliffs at the coast or tiny like grains of sand.

SKIN

FUR

SAND GRAINS

FABRIC

STONE

WOOD

INTERMOLECULAR FORCES

All substances have forces that act to bring molecules together or apart— we call them intermolecular forces.

The molecules in solids are locked together. Liquids have cohesive (sticky) forces that pull molecules together, while molecules in gases spread out.

LIQUIDS

We use liquids every day. We drink water and juice; we wash clothes and dishes; and we shower or bathe. We use gasoline in our cars. We fry foods in oil. Think about the properties of all of these liquids for a moment:

- THEY CAN BE POURED FROM ONE CONTAINER TO ANOTHER.

- THEY TAKE ON THE SHAPE OF THE CONTAINER THEY ARE IN.

- THEY CANNOT EASILY BE HELD IN YOUR HAND WITHOUT RUNNING THROUGH YOUR FINGERS.

MOVEMENT

These properties that we can see are created by properties we cannot see. The molecules and atoms of liquids are free to move about, even though they are fairly close together. The particles are arranged in a random way and move around each other, so liquids flow. This is why liquids take on the shape of the container they are poured into.

Liquids have an almost fixed **volume** but no fixed shape. **Gravity** causes liquids to take on the shape of containers. Liquids cannot easily be compressed because the particles are close enough together that they have nowhere to move to.

LIQUID STATE

VISCOSITY

Scientists talk about the viscosity of fluids. Water has low viscosity as it flows freely. Tar is a thick, sticky liquid that flows so slowly, it almost seems like a solid. It has high viscosity.

COHESIVE FORCES

Most liquids have strong cohesive (sticky) forces, which pull the molecules to keep them together. You can see that in action in your bathroom! When water drops onto a smooth surface such as a ceramic tile or glass, it makes a drop. It's the cohesive forces that stop the water molecules from spreading out.

The same force acts on a droplet of water dripping from a tap. The water sticks together until it is too heavy and it falls—that's what makes that classic "drop of water" shape.

SURFACE TENSION

The same cohesive forces cause surface tension. It acts like a "skin" on the water, but there is no real skin—just forces at work. It happens because the forces at the surface work on the water molecules in a different way. In the main body of the liquid, the molecules are all pulled in every direction by the other molecules.

The molecules at the surface are pulled down and this squeezes them. The surface of the water seems to be elastic, like there was a skin. That's surface tension—and why pond skaters and water spiders can walk on water!

USES OF LIQUIDS

Liquids have lots of uses. They are used as solvents (to **dissolve** things). When things are dissolved in a liquid it is called a solution. Paints and most glues contain solvents. The solvents are very volatile, which means they disperse into the air easily—that's why we need to use them in well-ventilated spaces.

Liquids are also used as lubricants. They are used in engines, gear boxes, and machinery.

Hydraulic systems use liquids to transmit power. Oil is forced through hydraulic pumps, which transmit this power to move hydraulic cylinders to drive machinery.

Liquids are used as coolants. The fact that they flow means that they can be used to run through machines to remove excess heat. Water and glycol are used in engines for this purpose.

OUT OF CURIOSITY

There is even a liquid rock, called magma! It is found deep under the Earth. When it comes to the surface in a volcanic eruption, the flow is called lava.

Fridges, air conditioners, and heating systems use liquids to move heat from one place to another. Our bodies even use a liquid—sweat—to keep us cool as it evaporates.

GASES

Gas is all around us—the air we breathe is a gas!
The atmosphere is a layer of gases that surrounds Earth.

That hissing noise you hear when you open a can of soda? It's gas that has been held under pressure escaping. That's the same reason champagne corks make a popping sound when they come out of the bottle neck.

GAS STATE

USES OF GAS

Doctors use gas in hospitals—for example, to put people to sleep when they have operations (nitrous oxide). Divers also use gas tanks to breathe underwater (oxygen, nitrogen, helium).

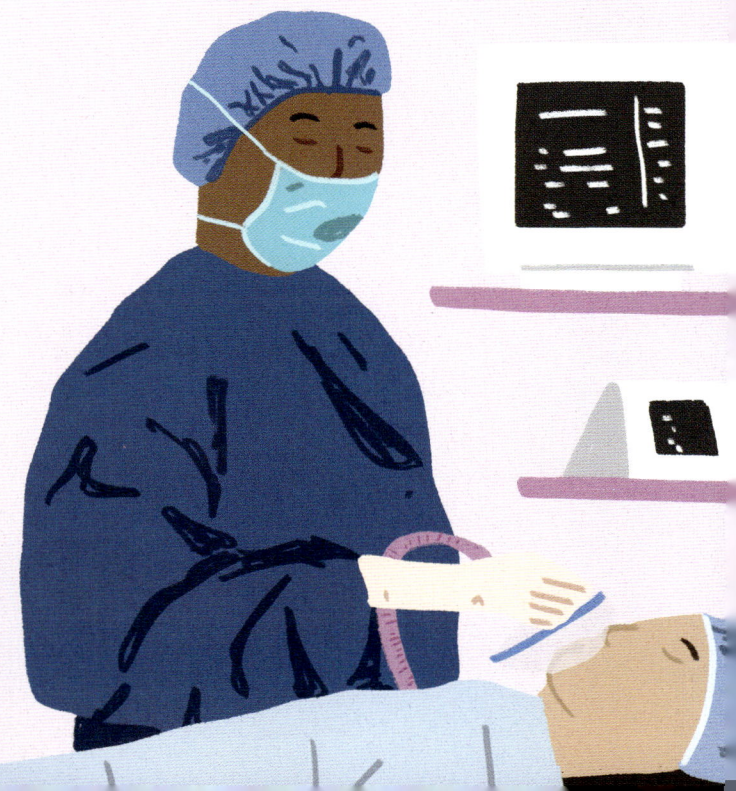

PLASMA

Plasma is found in stars and lightning. It is like a gas, but some of the molecules have changed—they lose some of their electrons, and become **ions**. Plasma is the most abundant state of matter in the Universe!

FLOW

Gas particles are far apart, and randomly spaced. The attractive forces between the particles are weak, and they move quickly in all directions, independently of one another.

As a result, gas particles flow and completely fill a container, no matter how large it is. The particles spread out to fill the whole space equally.

HOW GAS MOVES

Have you ever seen smoke drifting above a fire? Or steam rising above a pan? They show us how gas moves. It flows like a liquid, and spreads or diffuses. That's why smoke and steam both seem to "disappear" into the air.

Gases have low density and low viscosity.

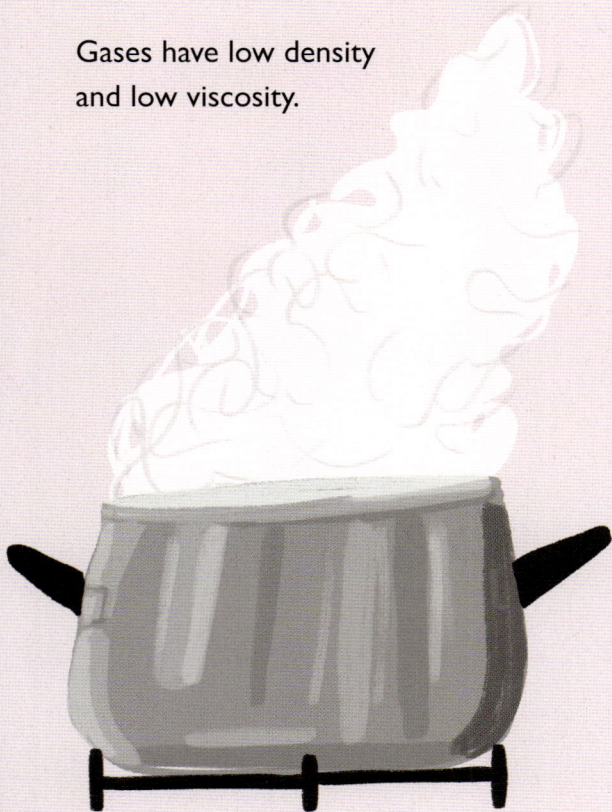

COMPRESSION

Gases can be compressed as the particles are far apart and have space to move into.

PRESSURE

When gas particles hit the side of a container, it creates pressure. If the temperature is increased, the particles move faster and hit the side more frequently, increasing pressure.

If the size of the container a gas is put into is decreased, the particles hit the side more often and this also increases the pressure. The weight of gas can create pressure on anything under it—on a planet, for example, this is called atmospheric pressure.

CHANGING STATE

Gases can change state, like other states of matter. If a temperature is low enough, gases can condense and turn into a liquid. If the temperature is low enough it can even change straight to a solid through a process called deposition. This process makes grass frosty in winter, when water in gas form is chilled and turns into solid ice.

OUT OF CURIOSITY
So what about vapor?
The word vapor describes gases that are usually liquid at room temperature—like water (H_2O). Water vapor, for example, is just water in its gaseous state.

MELTING POINT

The melting point of a substance is the temperature at which it changes from a solid state to a liquid one. Heat changes the state of the matter by affecting the bonds between particles.

FLOW

When temperature rises, the molecules have more energy. They start to move faster, and soon have enough energy to break free from the solid structure, and flow as they move more easily. The substance has changed state, melting from a solid to a liquid.

MELTING ICE

For pure water, the melting point of the solid state—ice—is 0° Celsius (or 32° Fahrenheit). If you add other substances to water, such as salt or sugar, the melting point lowers—that's why salt works on icy roads in winter.

DIFFERENT MELTING POINTS

Every element has a melting point—but some are much higher than others. Some substances are liquid at room temperature—this is around 18° Celsius (64.4°F). Olive oil, for example, is liquid at room temperature.

The element gallium (Ga) is a soft, silvery metal used in the manufacture of electronics. It melts at a low temperature—around 29° Celsius (84°F)—so it could melt from the heat of your hand!

MELTING AND FREEZING POINTS

An interesting point to note is that the melting point of a solid is the same as the freezing point of the substance in its liquid form. It makes sense, if you think about it!

MELTING POINTS:

WATER (H_2O): 0° CELSIUS (32°F)

CHOCOLATE: 35° CELSIUS (95°F)

PHOSPHORUS (P): 44° CELSIUS (111°F)

BEESWAX: 64° CELSIUS (147°F)

LEAD (PB): 327° CELSIUS (620°F)

IRON (FE): 1,538° CELSIUS (2,800°F)

BOILING POINT

The boiling point is the temperature at which a substance boils—which means it reaches a state of rapid evaporation, changing state from a liquid to a gas. When a liquid becomes a gas we call the process vaporization. The molecules have been heated to such a point that they vibrate quickly and bonds between them are weakened until they break free to become a gas.

WATER

For pure water, boiling point (bp) is 100° Celsius (212°F). Have you ever watched a kettle boil and seen steam come out of the spout? The kettle turns off when the water reaches boiling point—and we have to be very careful or we can get scalded.

AIR PRESSURE

Amazingly, the boiling point of a liquid depends on the pressure of the surrounding air. High air pressure increases the boiling point, whereas low air pressure makes the boiling point drop. At the top of a high mountain, such as K2 or Mount Everest, there is lower air pressure. The top of Mount Everest is 8,848 m (29,029 ft) above sea level. The air is so "thin" and the air pressure so much lower than at sea level, that water boils at a lower temperature, at about 70° Celsius (156°F). Celebrating the climb with a "quick" cup of tea or coffee takes on a new meaning!

ADDING SUBSTANCES

Boiling points can be changed by the addition of other substances to the liquid. For example, adding salt or sugar to water changes its boiling point.

OUT OF CURIOSITY

Evaporation is what happens when a liquid becomes a gas—but only at the surface of the liquid. It does not need a high temperature or boiling point for that to occur. Think about a puddle on the ground. The molecules at the surface are in contact with the air and on a sunny day the puddle dries quickly. As it does so, the liquid water has become water vapor.

⊙ ELEMENTS ⊙

A chemical element is a substance that contains one type of atom (if a substance has more than one type of atom, it is a compound). An element is any substance that cannot be broken down by ordinary chemical processes into simpler substances.

Elements are the building blocks of all substances, and can be in any state of matter—solid, liquid, or gas—but most are solids at room temperature. There are only 11 elements that are gases at room temperature (the noble gases plus hydrogen (H), oxygen (O), nitrogen (N), fluorine (F), chlorine (CL)) and two liquids (bromine (Br) and mercury (Hg)).

⊙ NUMBER OF ELEMENTS

There are 118 chemical elements known to chemistry today. Only 92 of these are found in nature, the last of which to be discovered was uranium (U), discovered in 1789. The rest are made in laboratories. The first element made in this way was technetium (Tc) in 1937.

⊙ THE PERIODIC TABLE

Scientists have arranged the chemical elements on the **periodic table**. Their position tells us about their properties. They have chemical symbols which are used across the world. That means that scientists use the same symbol, wherever they are located, and whichever language they speak! The symbols come largely from their Latin names.

GOLD – symbol Au from Latin for gold: *aurum*

SILVER – symbol Ag from Latin for silver: *argentum*

LEAD – symbol Pb from Latin: *plumbum*

SODIUM – symbol Na from Latin: *natrium*

1 H																	2 He
3 Li	4 Be											5 B	6 C	7 N	8 O	9 F	10 Ne
11 Na	12 Mg											13 Al	14 Si	15 P	16 S	17 Cl	18 Ar
19 K	20 Ca	21 Sc	22 Ti	23 V	24 Cr	25 Mn	26 Fe	27 Co	28 Ni	29 Cu	30 Zn	31 Ga	32 Ge	33 As	34 Se	35 Br	36 Kr
37 Rb	38 Sr	39 Y	40 Zr	41 Nb	42 Mo	43 Tc	44 Ru	45 Rh	46 Pd	47 Ag	48 Cd	49 In	50 Sn	51 Sb	52 Te	53 I	54 Xe
55 Cs	56 Ba	57-71	72 Hf	73 Ta	74 W	75 Re	76 Os	77 Ir	78 Pt	79 Au	80 Hg	81 Tl	82 Pb	83 Bi	84 Po	85 At	86 Rn
87 Fr	88 Ra	89-103	104 Rf	105 Db	106 Sg	107 Bh	108 Hs	109 Mt	110 Ds	111 Rg	112 Cn	113 Nh	114 Fl	115 Mc	116 Lv	117 Ts	118 Og

57 La	58 Ce	59 Pr	60 Nd	61 Pm	62 Sm	63 Eu	64 Gd	65 Tb	66 Dy	67 Ho	68 Er	69 Tm	70 Yb	71 Lu
89 Ac	90 Th	91 Pa	92 U	93 Np	94 Pu	95 Am	96 Cm	97 Bk	98 Cf	99 Es	100 Fm	101 Md	102 No	103 Lr

ATOMIC NUMBERS

The **atomic number** of an element is the number of **protons** in each atom. The atomic number of an element affects its position on the periodic table. Hydrogen (H) is the first element and has the atomic number 1 because it has one proton. Gold (Au) has the atomic number 79 because it has 79 protons in each atom.

PROPERTIES

On the periodic table, elements are grouped together in families according to their specific properties. Noble gases are one family. Helium (He), xenon (Xe), neon (Ne), radon (Rn), and argon (Ar) are all classed as noble gases.

EARLY IDEAS

For 2,000 years, starting from about 450 BCE, people in Europe believed the elements were Earth, Air, Fire, and Water. In the Middle Ages, **alchemists** added two new elements of a different kind, sulfur (which meant combustibility to them), and mercury (which meant volatility). A third, salt (solidity), was added in the 1500s.

?

OUT OF CURIOSITY

Hydrogen (H) is the lightest element—and it is the most abundant element in the Universe.

In 1661, the English chemist Robert Boyle proposed a new model of the elements, based on tiny particles (that we now call atoms) that can combine to make other substances.

In 1789, the French chemist Antoine Lavoisier published the first list of elemental substances based on Robert Boyle's definition, looking at the way substances could be combined and decomposed. Lavoisier's first list contained 33 elements, of which 23 are still considered elements.

COMPOUNDS

A chemical compound is a chemical formed from the atoms of different chemical elements.

The atoms are bonded together and the chemical compound behaves like a single substance with properties of its own—which may be different from the properties of the elements it is made from! Salt, or sodium chloride, is a perfect example.

SALT

Sodium chloride (NaCl) is made up of one atom of sodium and one atom of chlorine. Now, sodium (Na) is a metal that burns in the presence of water, and chlorine (Cl) is a poisonous gas— but put together in equal proportions, they make the salt we use to safely season our food!

WATER

Water (H_2O) is also a compound. It is made up of hydrogen and oxygen atoms. There are two hydrogen (H) atoms and one oxygen (O) atom.

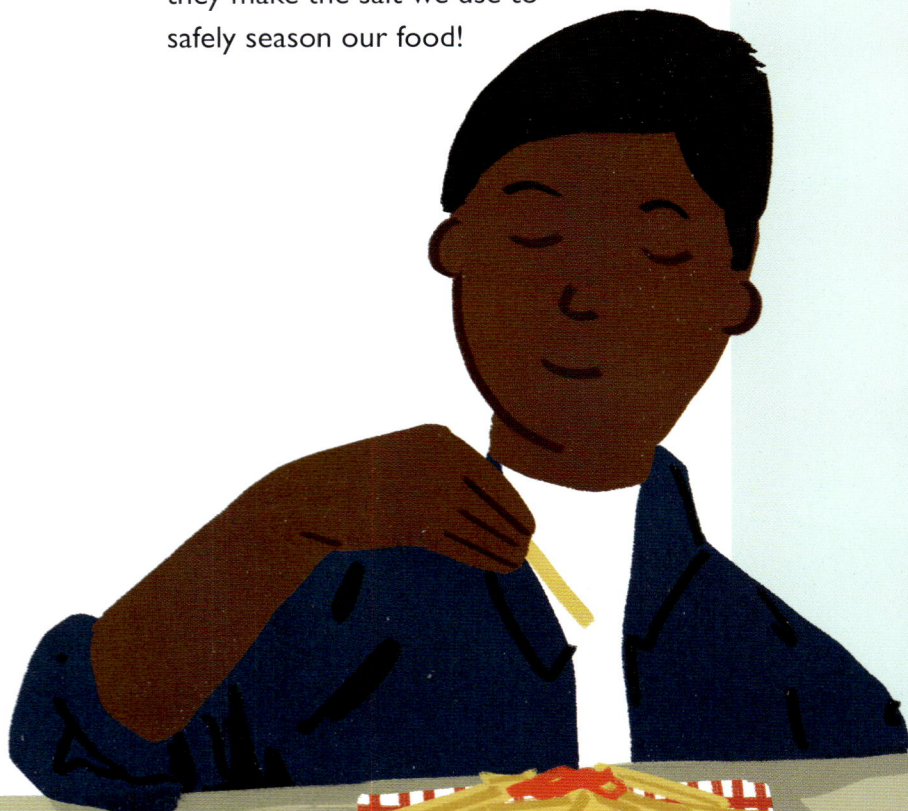

COMPOUNDS ALL AROUND

There are a huge number of compounds—maybe as many as 61 million! More compounds are discovered by scientists working in laboratories every day. Compounds can even be made by combining other compounds to create new chemicals.

The chemical reaction that takes place when a substance is heated, for example, may join atoms together to create a new compound or even several new compounds. The possibilities are exciting and seemingly endless.

RESEARCH

Chemists work to find new medicines, cleaning materials, glue, and more—and businesses employ scientists to research and develop these new compounds to make their products work better.

BONDS

Once compounds have been made, they can be hard to break down. They are not like mixtures, which are just physically combined and can be easily separated again. **Chemical bonds** are created when compounds are made. They have combined to make a completely new substance.

MIXTURES

In chemistry, a mixture is a substance containing two or more elements or chemical compounds. Mixtures can be solids, liquids, or gases. Mixtures are different from compounds because the combined substances do not chemically react to form new molecular bonds. Each component or part of the mixture keeps its original properties.

Mixtures can be separated into their component parts by physical processes such as **filtration**, **evaporation**, and **distillation**. Seawater, for example, can be separated by evaporation into its two main components, which are water (H_2O) and salt or sodium chloride (NaCl). There are also other compounds in seawater.

SEAWATER

Seawater is an example of a solution. This is created when one substance dissolves into another.

Another example would be sugar being stirred into hot water until it dissolves.

SOLUTIONS

Solutions combine a solute (the substance that dissolves) and a solvent (the thing the solute is dissolved by).

Solutions are known as homogenous mixtures. This means all of the substances are evenly distributed (spread) through the mixture. In seawater, the salt is the solute and the water is the solvent.

SUSPENSIONS

Other mixtures are suspensions. Muddy water is a suspension of soil in water. The soil does not dissolve; it merely floats in the water.

Sand in water is a heterogenous mixture, which means that there is not an even distribution of substances throughout.

If you stir a heterogenous mixture and leave it to settle, some of the solids will sink to the bottom of the container. These particles could be removed by filtration.

MIXTURES

Solids can also be mixtures. Most soils and rocks are mixtures of different materials.

Liquids can be mixtures too, such as salad dressing that combines oil and other liquids to create an emulsion. Over time, these settle and separate, and we shake them before we use them to mix them up again.

MIXED GASES

Gases can be mixtures too, such as the air we breathe, which is a mixture of nitrogen, oxygen, and other gases.

It is much more difficult to separate gases mixed together as the particles are too small to separate by physical means. One method is to find a solvent that will dissolve one of the gases, and remove the gas from the solution by itself.

COLLOIDS

Do you like to drink milk or put it on your cereal? Believe it or not, milk is a mixture. It is an example of a colloid. That is a heterogenous type of mixture. Tiny particles of liquid butterfat are suspended in water. Particles in colloids do not sink to the bottom over time, but stay suspended.

ALLOYS

Alloys are mixtures of different metals. The combined metals have different properties from separate metals. For example, nickel (Ni) or chromium (Cr) might be added to steel to help it to resist rust.

CHAPTER 8

CHEMICAL BUILDING BLOCKS

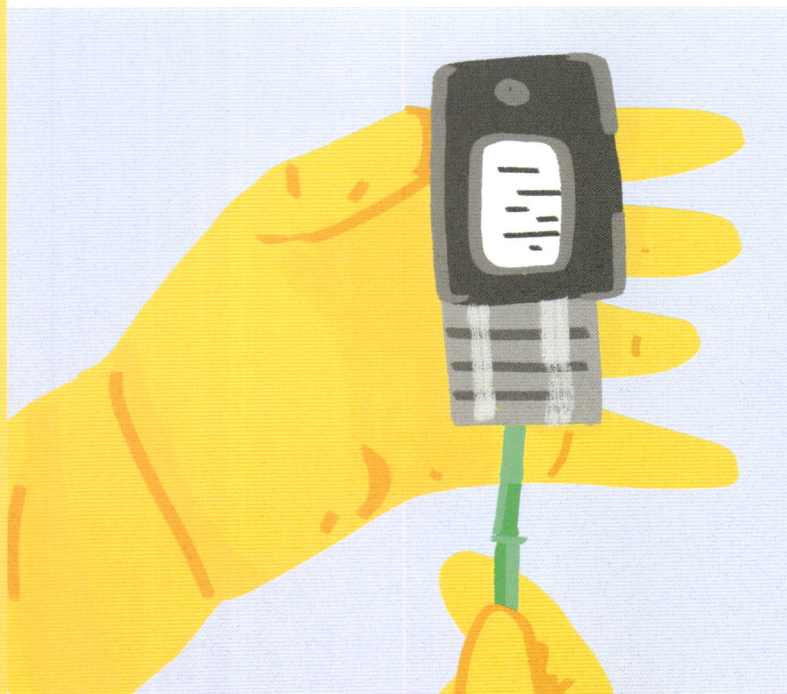

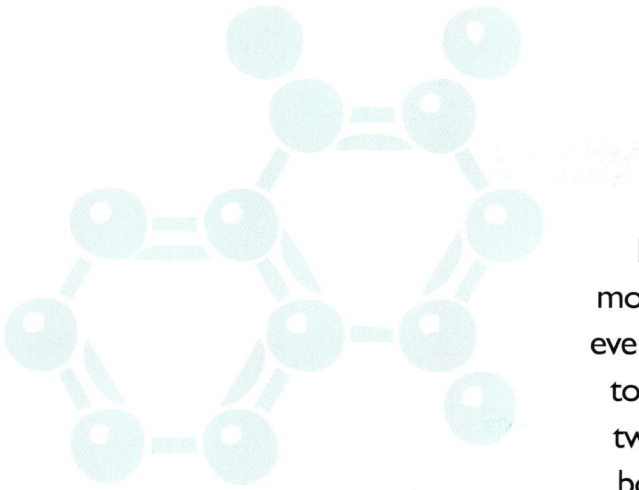

We live in a Universe made up of "matter." That means any substance that has mass (measured in kilograms or pounds) and takes up space by having volume (size).

Matter is made up of tiny particles called atoms and molecules. These microscopic things combine to make up everything. Atoms are like building blocks that fit together to make different substances. Molecules are made up of two or more atoms that are held together by chemical bonds. Polymers are big molecules, made up of smaller molecules joined together.

MORE THAN ATOMS

When scientists first began to understand atoms in the early 20th century, they thought they were about to understand the basis of all matter—but they were wrong.

Swiss astronomer Fritz Zwicky began to argue that parts of the Universe had to be made of other things entirely in the 1930s.

DARK MATTER

Scientists think that the Universe also contains a different form of matter, called dark matter. Dark matter cannot be seen directly; it does not absorb, reflect, or give off light. No wonder it is called "dark" matter! Scientists are still finding out about dark matter and how it works.

Normal matter is not boring just because it is "normal"!

Tiny atoms are part of everything you can see and touch. Isn't that amazing?

ATOMS

Atoms are the building blocks that join together to make all of the ordinary matter in the Universe. They are incredibly small—smaller than a pinprick. You can only see them with an incredibly powerful microscope. There are about 7 billion billion billion atoms in a human, which is octillions!

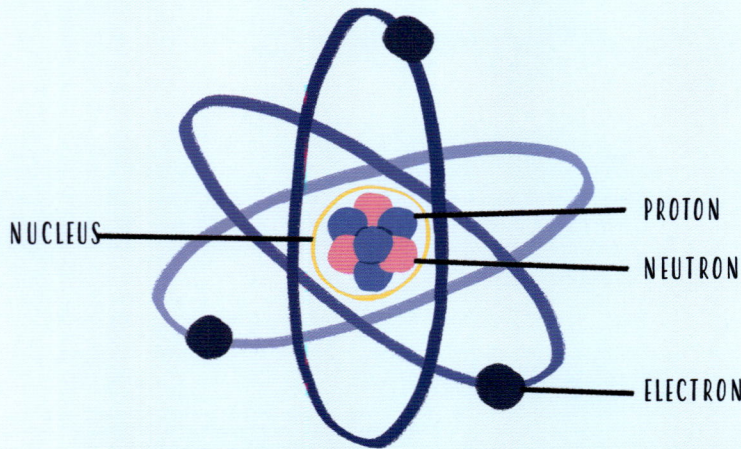

NUCLEUS

PROTON

NEUTRON

ELECTRON

Atoms are made up of even smaller particles: **electrons**, **protons**, and **neutrons**.

In the middle of an atom is the nucleus, made up of positively charged protons and neutral neutrons. The negatively charged electrons are attracted or pulled toward the protons because they have the opposite charge. They spin around the nucleus in tiny orbits, like a satellite orbiting Earth.

THE PERIODIC

1 H								
3 Li	4 Be							
11 Na	12 Mg							
19 K	20 Ca	21 Sc	22 Ti	23 V	24 Cr	25 Mn	26 Fe	27 Co
37 Rb	38 Sr	39 Y	40 Zr	41 Nb	42 Mo	43 Tc	44 Ru	45 Rh
55 Cs	56 Ba	57-71	72 Hf	73 Ta	74 W	75 Re	76 Os	77 Ir
87 Fr	88 Ra	89-103	104 Rf	105 Db	106 Sg	107 Bh	108 Hs	109 Mt

57 La	58 Ce	59 Pr	60 Nd	61 Pm	62 Sm	63 Eu
89 Ac	90 Th	91 Pa	92 U	93 Np	94 Pu	95 Am

Each element is a different type of atom. The number of protons an atom contains decides what kind of element it is. That gives the element its "atomic number."

The **periodic table** is arranged in atomic number order—take a look! An atom with one proton in the nucleus is hydrogen (H). An atom with two protons is helium (He). Can you find them on the periodic table?

In chemistry, we look at the way the electrons in an element pair up or share with other atoms. Sometimes, they even shift to other atoms completely, and create **ions**—atoms or molecules with an electric charge.

TABLE

							2 He
			5 B	6 C	7 N	8 O	9 F	10 Ne
			13 Al	14 Si	15 P	16 S	17 Cl	18 Ar
28 Ni	29 Cu	30 Zn	31 Ga	32 Ge	33 As	34 Se	35 Br	36 Kr
46 Pd	47 Ag	48 Cd	49 In	50 Sn	51 Sb	52 Te	53 I	54 Xe
78 Pt	79 Au	80 Hg	81 Tl	82 Pb	83 Bi	84 Po	85 At	86 Rn
110 Ds	111 Rg	112 Cn	113 Nh	114 Fl	115 Mc	116 Lv	117 Ts	118 Og

64 Gd	65 Tb	66 Dy	67 Ho	68 Er	69 Tm	70 Yb	71 Lu
96 Cm	97 Bk	98 Cf	99 Es	100 Fm	101 Md	102 No	103 Lr

MOLECULES

Molecules are two or more atoms held together by a **chemical bond**. A molecule is the smallest "unit" of a substance that has the properties of the substance.

The chemical name for water is H_2O. That means there are two hydrogen atoms and one oxygen atom in each molecule of water. The atoms do not make water until they are chemically bonded—just mixing the two gases together doesn't make water vapor.

BONDS

Atoms are bonded when they share electrons. Electrons are found in the outer shell of an atom. When atoms combine, as in water, they each share shareable electrons. This holds the bond together.

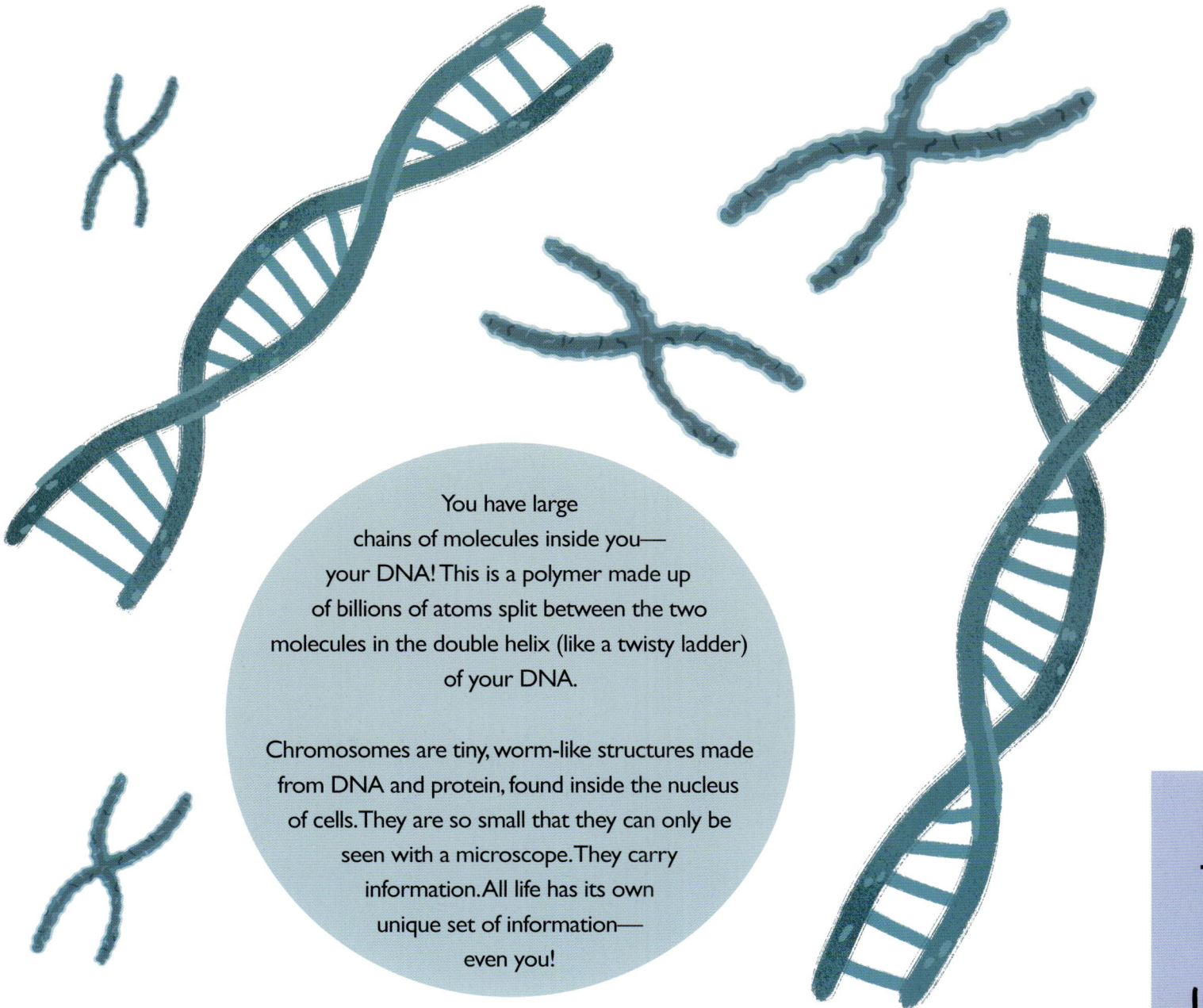

h O h

You have large chains of molecules inside you— your DNA! This is a polymer made up of billions of atoms split between the two molecules in the double helix (like a twisty ladder) of your DNA.

Chromosomes are tiny, worm-like structures made from DNA and protein, found inside the nucleus of cells. They are so small that they can only be seen with a microscope. They carry information. All life has its own unique set of information— even you!

POLYMERS

Have you drunk from a plastic bottle today? Or used a plastic bag for shopping? Have you worn nylon fleece or a raincoat? Or maybe written on a piece of paper? If so, you have used a **polymer**!

Some polymers are found in nature. Cellulose is a strong polymer found in the cell walls of plants that helps them to stand up. Wood, paper, and cotton all contain cellulose. Cellulose is what makes fibers in plants, like hemp and cotton. It is the strength of these natural polymers that allows us to twist fibers into strong thread that can be used to make fabric.

Cellulose is the fiber in our foods, such as vegetables. We cannot digest fiber, but it helps us to keep our digestive systems healthy.

ARTIFICIAL POLYMERS

Artificial polymers are big molecules made up of smaller molecules (called **monomers**) laid out in a repeating pattern.

Some plastics are made from crude oil that has been extracted from the ground. It is refined and broken down into monomers which are then used to create the polymers for plastic.

The polymers can be created to form hard, rigid, flexible, or soft plastic, depending on how they are made.

AMAZING AMBER

Amber is fossilized tree resin and a natural polymer. It started as sticky sap and hardened over time. That means amber can be found with ancient insects trapped inside—just like the mosquito in the film, *Jurassic Park*.

In the movie, fictional scientists extracted dinosaur blood and the all-important DNA that started everything—not that that would be possible in real life!

☢ ISOTOPES ☢

Isotopes are atoms of an element with the same number of protons, but a different number of neutrons—sometimes more and sometimes less. This makes them less stable than normal atoms. An atom of a radioisotope gives off energy or particles. It may change the number of protons it has and so "decay" into a different element. Being exposed to this energy, called radiation, is usually thought of as being harmful to the human body, but radioactive decay can make isotopes useful in medicine.

For example, doctors use barium isotopes to trace food as it passes through the gut, as the barium appears white in x-rays. This can help them to diagnose and treat health problems.

Technetium-99m is used as a tracer. It can be injected or inhaled by the patient. It then travels through the body and the radiation it gives off can be tracked. Doctors can look at images and see organ function and bone growth.

Radioisotopes used in this way decay quickly, before they can cause any harm to the patient's body.

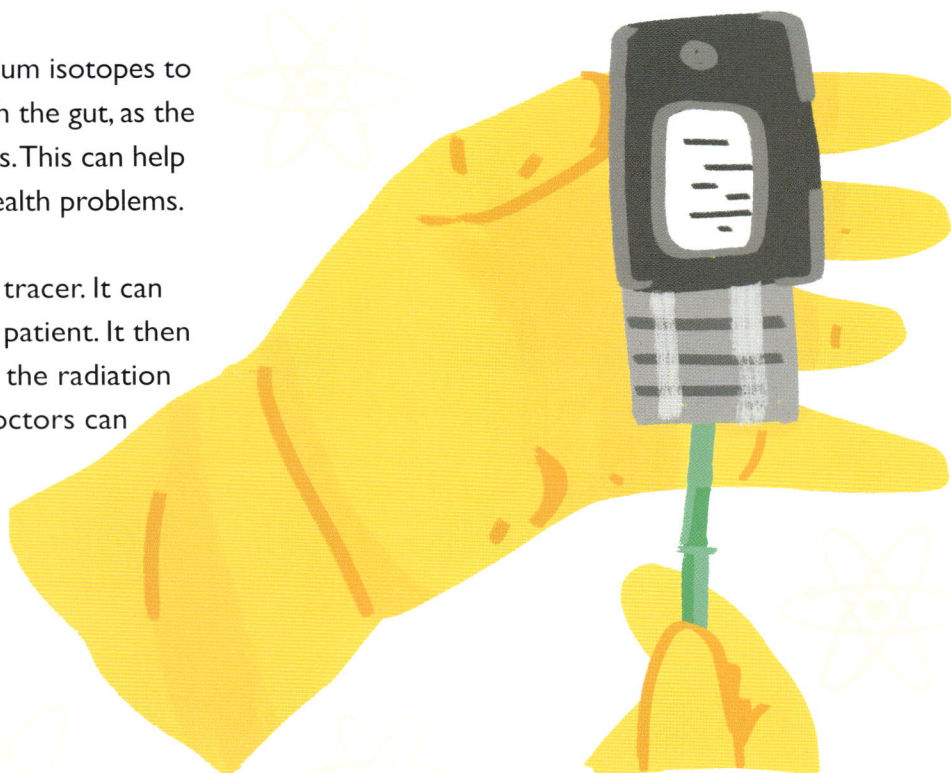

☢ RADIOTHERAPY

Radiotherapy uses radioisotopes to treat cancer. This disrupts the molecules of the tissue treated, and causes breaks in the DNA molecule. This kills cancer cells. It can cause unpleasant side effects that make patients feel ill, but it is an important tool in the fight against cancer.

☢ DANGER!

Isotopes can also be dangerous. Plutonium-239 and Uranium-235 are used to make nuclear weapons—perhaps the most destructive and deadliest weapons in the world.

Nuclear fission happens when a single free neutron strikes the nucleus of an atom of radioactive materials such as plutonium or uranium. When this happens, it bumps into two to three more neutrons, which split off from the nucleus, releasing energy. The freed neutrons strike other nuclei and set off a chain reaction. More and more energy is released with terrible effects.

☢ ATOMIC BOMBS

At the end of World War II in 1945, atomic bombs were exploded at Hiroshima and Nagasaki by US air forces.

They caused catastrophic damage. In Hiroshima, 18,000 people were killed. In Nagasaki, between 50,000 and 100,000 died.

In the decades that followed, many more people died as a result of the radiation from these atomic bombs. By 1950 over 340,000 had died.

Many people around the world believe that nuclear weapons are too dangerous and should never be used again.

NANOPARTICLES

Nanotechnology is a part of science that deals with things on an atomic or molecular scale. That means things that are 100 nanometers or less in size. One nanometer (nm) is 0.000000001 meters. "Nano" means "billionth," so a nanometer is a billionth of a meter. To give an idea of just how small that is, it is about 1/25,000th of the diameter of a human hair. Your fingernails grow a nanometer per second—amazing!

TINY MOVEMENTS

Nanoparticles are tiny. We can only see them with a special electron microscope. They may be small—but they can be incredibly useful! Nanoparticles of an element often behave differently from larger particles of the same material.

Gold, for example, is usually not very **reactive**. On the nanoscale, it becomes very chemically active. On this scale, it is easier for atoms and molecules to move around. They have much more surface area exposed to other nanoparticles, and this makes it easier for chemical reactions to take place.

EVERYDAY NANOPARTICLES

Nanoparticles are used in many areas of everyday life. Sunscreen often contains nanoparticles of zinc or titanium oxide to block the sun's ultraviolet (UV) rays—so they save you from sunburn! Cosmetics also can contain nanoparticles.

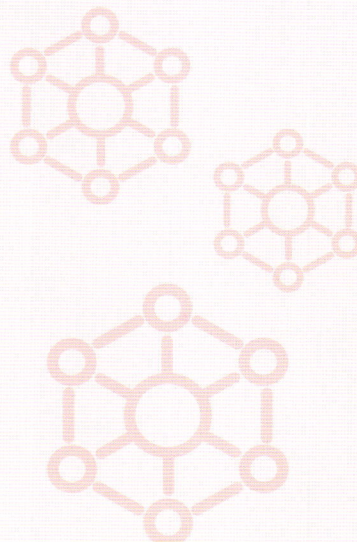

NANOWHISKERS

Some materials contain "nanowhiskers"—tiny fibers that coat the fabric and keep it clean.

Nanowhiskers can be used to help to make things like car bumpers scratch-resistant, and paint that is corrosion-resistant.

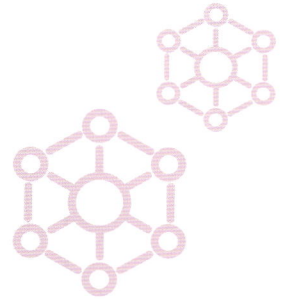

DRESSING IN SILVER

Nanoparticles such as colloidal silver are also used in some dressings to care for wounds, to keep them clean and free from infection.

pH

Scientists use a **pH** (power of hydrogen) scale to measure how acidic or basic a solution is. A pH scale is numbered from 0 to 14. Low numbers from 0–7 are acids. The lower the number, the more acidic the liquid is. Battery acid from a car would have a pH of 0, and lemon juice would be about 2.

TESTING ... TESTING ...

pH can only be tested when a solution is aqueous—that means, it is in water. Some liquids such as vegetable oil or pure alcohol have no pH value at all.

BASE

Liquids numbered from 7–14 are **bases**. The higher the number, the stronger the base. Liquid drain cleaner would have a pH of 14, and bleach would be 13.

LITMUS TEST

There are lots of ways to measure the pH of a liquid. Litmus paper is cheap and easy to use. When you touch a piece of the paper to a liquid, it changes its shade to show if the liquid is an acid or base. If the paper goes red, then the liquid is acidic, but if the paper turns blue, it is basic.

NEUTRAL

If the pH is 7, the liquid is neutral. That would be a liquid such as distilled water.

DISTILLED WATER

?

OUT OF CURIOSITY

A healthy person's blood has a pH of around 7.4—quite neutral!

EXAMPLES

pH

BASE

pH	
14	→
13	→
12	→
11	→
10	→
9	→
8	→
7	→ NEUTRAL
6	→
5	→
4	→
3	→
2	→
1	→
0	→

ACID

Liquid drain cleaner
(pH = 14)

Bleaches, oven cleaner
(pH = 13.5)

Ammonia solution
(pH = 10.5–11.5)

Baking soda
(pH = 9.5)

Seawater
(pH = 8)

Blood
(pH = 7.4)

Milk, urine, saliva
(pH = 6.3–6.6)

Black coffee
(pH = 5)

Grapefruit juice, soda, tomato juice
(pH = 2.5–3.5)

Lemon juice, vinegar
(pH = 2)

Battery acid, hydrochloric acid
(pH = 0)

ACIDS

Acids are chemicals with a low pH. Acids have a pH lower than 7. Always be careful around acids as they can be very dangerous! Strong acid can burn skin badly.

POWER OF HYDROGEN

All acids contain hydrogen. That's why pH contains hydrogen's symbol— the letter "H." When they are dissolved in water, acids lose some of their hydrogen in the form of electrically charged atoms, or ions. Strong acids (with a pH of 1–3) lose all of their positive hydrogen ions instantly, and those ions may bond with other chemicals in powerful reactions. Weaker acids (pH 4–6) hold on to some of their ions. The amount of ions that an acid releases tell us its *power*—which gives us the "p" in pH!

DANGER!

Always remember that acids can be very dangerous, so check with an adult first and never touch anything marked with a warning sign.

ACIDS:

- Can sting the skin or damage it
- Turn litmus paper red
- Conduct electricity (acid is used in batteries)
- Can corrode metal
- Contain hydrogen

OUT OF CURIOSITY

You even have some acids in your body! Your DNA is a type of acid, called a nucleic acid. You also have hydrochloric acid in your digestive system, to help you to digest food.

KEEP AWAY!

Some creatures produce acid as a defense! Ants produce formic acid, and some octopi produce magneta, a black inky acid.

BATTERIES CONTAIN
SULFURIC ACID

VINEGAR CONTAINS
ACETIC ACID

CITRUS FRUITS
CONTAIN
CITRIC ACID

YOGURT CONTAINS
LACTIC ACID

BASES AND ALKALIS

A base is the "chemical opposite" to an acid. It is a substance that can accept a hydrogen ion from another substance. Some bases are weak and others are strong. An **alkali** is any solution with a pH of more than 7. It is created when a base is dissolved in water. It can be neutralized, or brought down to a pH of 7, by adding an acid to the mix.

DANGER!

Alkalis can be very dangerous and burn your skin. Never touch any chemicals without an adult present and using proper skin and eye protection.

ALKALIS:

- Feel "soapy"
- The higher the number on the pH scale, the stronger the alkali is
- Edible alkalis can have a bitter taste
- Are easily dissolved in water
- Turn litmus paper blue
- Can conduct electricity

EXAMPLES OF ALKALIS IN EVERYDAY LIFE

Soap and toothpaste contain weak alkalis. Sodium hydroxide is used in making detergent, soap, and even paper.

HELPFUL ALKALIS

Potassium hydroxide is used to make soil less acidic so plants will grow. Magnesium hydroxide is used as an indigestion remedy to make stomach contents less acidic.

BLEACH

Some heavy-duty cleaning products like bleach and drain cleaner contain strong alkalis and they can damage your skin.

OUT OF CURIOSITY

The word "alkali" comes from the Arabic word "*quali*" which means "from the ashes." Ashes were used in traditional soap making—and most cleaning products are alkali!

BUILDING BLOCKS

Calcium carbonate is used in building. It is chalk lime, used in some mortar and cement, and also makes up stones called marble and limestone.

UNIVERSAL INDICATOR

Universal indicator (UI) can be used to find out the pH of a liquid. UI is used either as a strip of paper, or as a liquid. It shows pH values precisely, from 0–14. UI is made from a clever mixture of different substances that change their shade at different pH values.

SMART SHADES

Indicates strong acid

Indicates neutral

Indicates strong base

KEYS

When you buy commercial universal indicator paper or solution, it comes with a special key to tell you what each shade means. This chart is used by comparing the shade of the paper or solution used against the key. Then you can "read" the result.

OUT OF CURIOSITY

The pigment found in red cabbage juice is a naturally occurring universal indicator! You can easily make some yourself and use it to test drinks in the kitchen and hand soap in the bathroom to find their pH value.

Chop up red cabbage and boil it for a few minutes. Wait until it is completely cool and strain off the liquid. You can put the liquid in containers and add drops of different but safe-to-use liquids, to test their pH.

RED CABBAGE UNIVERSAL INDICATOR

0 1 2 3 4 5 6 7 8 9 10 11 12 13 14

ACIDIC ← pH → ALKALINE

CHAPTER 9

THE CHEMISTRY OF LIFE

All living things use chemicals and chemical reactions to live. Plants, humans, and other animals—we all need chemicals and chemical processes to function. All life is carbon-based, which means it contains carbon atoms. There's a lot of carbon stored out there in trees, plants, your cat—and even you! Carbon is the fourth most common type of element in the whole Universe.

Other chemicals are also widely used by living things, including hydrogen, oxygen, and nitrogen. In addition, sulfur and phosphorus are key building blocks for all life on Earth. Living **organisms** have processes that use these chemicals to form molecules such as carbohydrates and proteins that we need to live, grow, and be healthy.

WATER

Most of the Earth is covered with water—that's why it looks so blue from space. An amazing 71% of the surface of the Earth is covered by oceans, lakes, and rivers.

Water is transparent, tasteless, and smell-free. This might make it sound less than exciting—but if you have ever seen a roaring river, a pounding waterfall, or stormy seas, you know it is anything but! Water is everywhere, in the form of a liquid, gas, and solid. Drops of liquid water fall as rain. Water vapor is an invisible gas that floats in the air. Water freezes into solid ice at the North and South Poles.

WATER FOR HEALTH

Without water, there would be no life on Earth, as all living things need water to survive. You are made up of around 60% water. If you don't drink enough, you soon feel tired and grumpy, and even become ill.

Water carries essential materials around the body. Many of the chemical processes that happen in your body require water, and if you get **dehydrated** they don't work properly. That's bad news for you and your health!

Have you ever seen a plant wilting? It cannot function correctly without water, so the plant droops and will eventually dry out and die.

COOL, COOL WATER

Water is useful for regulating temperatures on Earth, too. The oceans store heat from the sun, which affects global temperatures and weather systems. Water also cools humans down. When we get too hot, we sweat. Sweat is 90% water. As the sweat evaporates, or turns to invisible gas, we cool down. This is because it takes heat to evaporate the sweat, and that heat comes from our body.

WHAT MAKES WATER?

Water is made of tiny molecules, each of them made of one atom of oxygen and two atoms of hydrogen that are bonded together. Hydrogen is the lightest and most common type of atom in the Universe. Oxygen is the third most common type of atom. It easily joins with other atoms to form molecules.

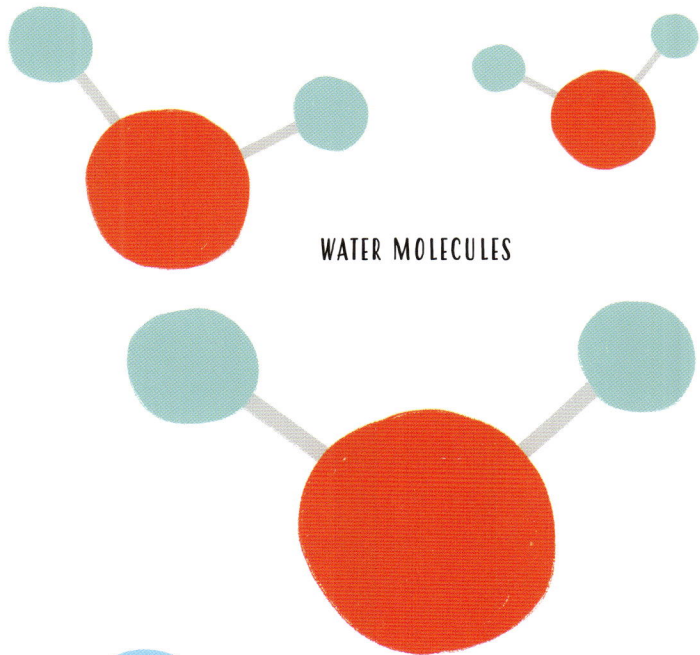

WATER MOLECULES

OUT OF CURIOSITY

When water gets very cold, it changes state from a liquid to a solid—ice. You will be familiar with that if you have seen frozen puddles on a wintry day or you have enjoyed ice pops and ice cream. But did you know that ice is less dense than water? That's why it floats! Density is a measure of how tightly packed the molecules in a substance are. Materials that are less dense than water—like ice and foam swimming floats—will float on water.

OXYGEN

O_2

Without oxygen we could not live on Earth! From the tiniest beetle to the biggest whale, almost all living things—including us—need oxygen to live. Without it, we could not breathe.

THE OXYGEN CYCLE

Most of the oxygen in the air is produced by plants. Animals, including us, breathe that oxygen in. We use the oxygen to make the systems in our bodies work.

We breathe out carbon dioxide. Plants take in this carbon dioxide and use the carbon to create sugars—food. Plants then give off oxygen and the cycle begins again.

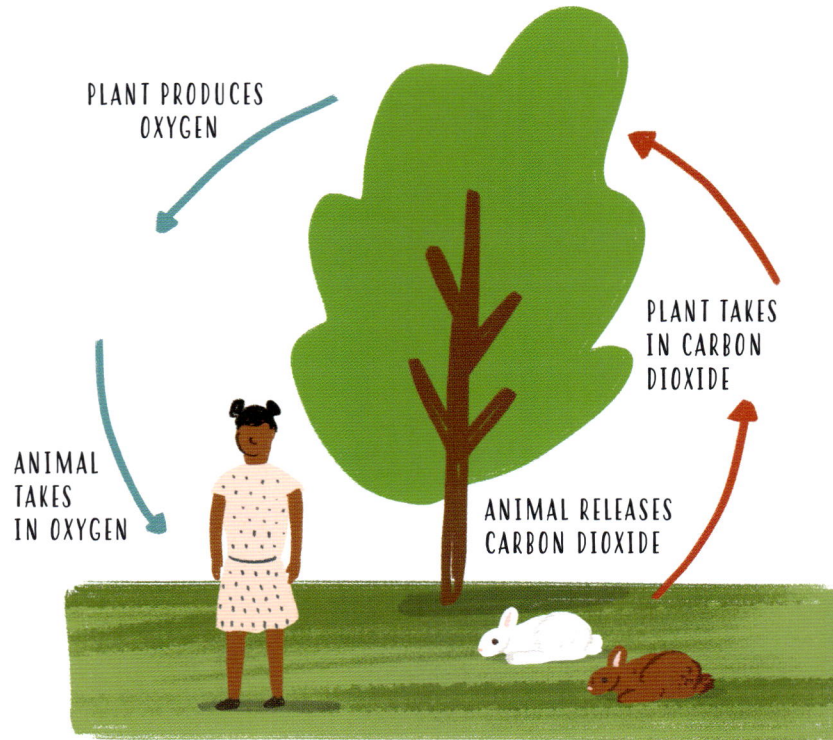

PLANT PRODUCES OXYGEN

PLANT TAKES IN CARBON DIOXIDE

ANIMAL TAKES IN OXYGEN

ANIMAL RELEASES CARBON DIOXIDE

O_2 TAKE A DEEP BREATH

All animal cells need oxygen for **respiration**. Every animal cell needs oxygen to function. Animals take in oxygen and it reacts with the glucose (sugar) from food to create energy.

Respiration is the process that takes in oxygen and exchanges it for carbon dioxide and water, which are waste products. Humans breathe and the oxygen needed for respiration is transported throughout our body in red blood cells.

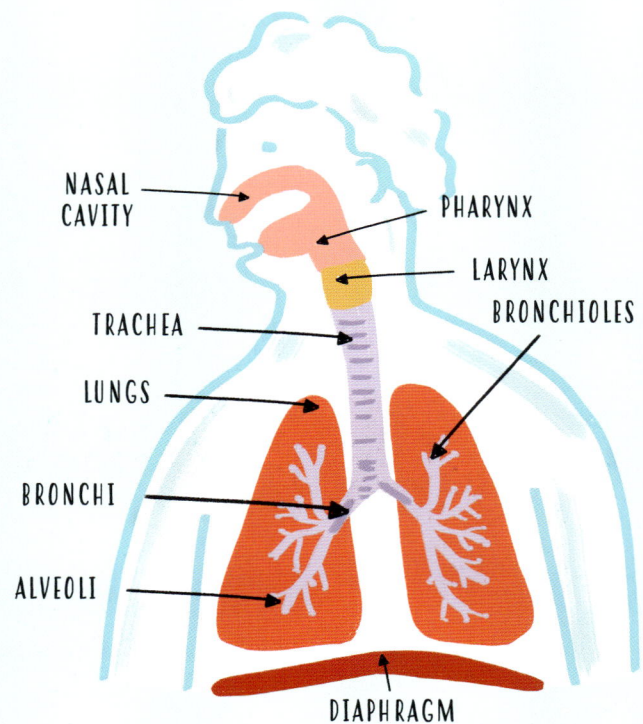

NASAL CAVITY

PHARYNX

LARYNX
BRONCHIOLES

TRACHEA

LUNGS

BRONCHI

ALVEOLI

DIAPHRAGM

Carl Wilhelm Scheele discovered oxygen in 1772. He called it "fire air" because it was needed for things to burn. Scientists call burning **combustion**. It is a chemical reaction. The **exothermic** reaction gives off heat, light, and other chemicals.

Fires start when combustible material (something that burns), together with oxygen, is heated. If it is above the "flash point" for the material, a fire starts. Flames are the part of fire that we can see.

Flames are made up of oxygen, water in gas form, and carbon dioxide. The shade of the flame depends on the material being burned and any impurities. We just see the flames as pretty reds, oranges, and yellows!

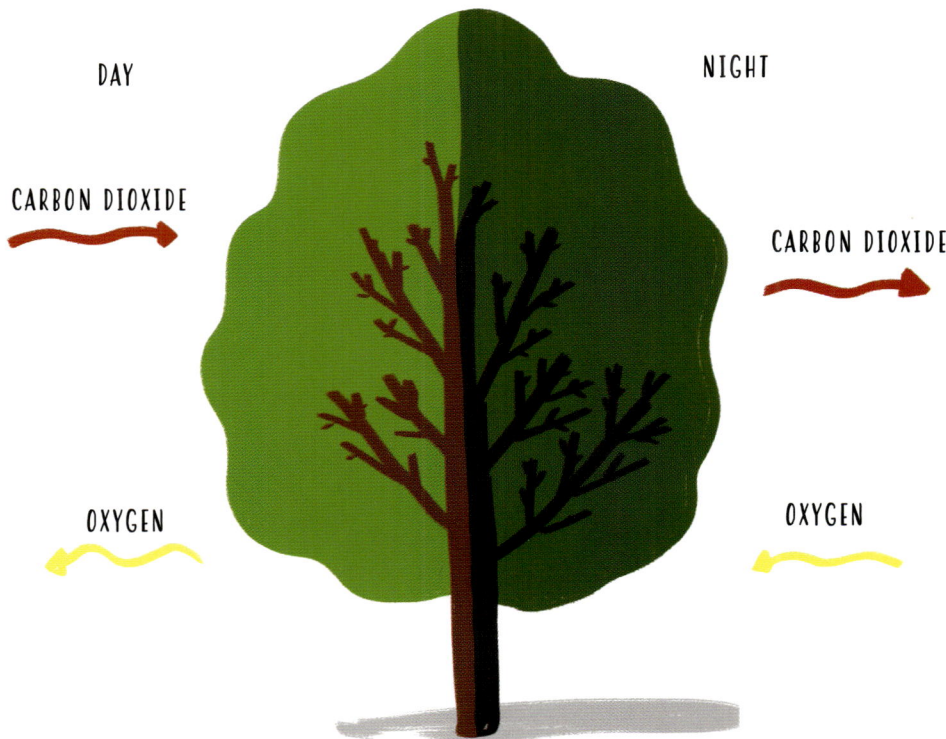

DAY

NIGHT

CARBON DIOXIDE

CARBON DIOXIDE

OXYGEN

OXYGEN

Plants also use respiration to create energy (for growth and reproduction) from the sugars they make during photosynthesis.

When it is dark, plants respire, but do not photosynthesize as this requires light. That means they take in oxygen and release carbon dioxide at night. During the day, in bright light, plants photosynthesize faster than they respire, so oxygen is released and carbon dioxide is taken in.

OUT OF CURIOSITY

Many animals that live in water can absorb oxygen that is dissolved in water using body parts called gills. Some water-living animals, such as seals and crocodiles, have lungs that take in oxygen from the air. They need to swim to the water surface to breathe.

CARBON DIOXIDE

Do you like fizzy drinks? Those sparkling bubbles that stream to the top of your glass, and make that yummy fizzy taste, are carbon dioxide!

CO_2

Carbon dioxide is about much more than soda, though. Its chemical **formula** is CO_2, which means that each molecule is made of one carbon and two oxygen atoms. This common chemical makes up around 0.041% of Earth's atmosphere.

PHOTOSYNTHESIS

When trees and plants **photosynthesize** (use the energy from the sun to create food; see pages 27 and 140) they remove CO_2 from the air. That is a good thing, because too much CO_2 building up in the atmosphere is bad for the planet.

CO_2 is a **greenhouse gas** (see pages 138–139), which means that too much can cause climate change. Plants and trees extract CO_2 from the air during the day, but animals and humans breathe it out.

FRESH AIR

If you are in a room that feels stuffy and you are drowsy, it may be because there are lots of people in there breathing out CO_2. Carbon dioxide is a waste product of our body processes, so you need to open a window to get some "fresh" air!

OUT OF CURIOSITY

CO_2 has quite a high freezing point, so it can be frozen and stored as "dry ice" to use in stage shows! Dry ice can make fog when it is dropped into warm water. Carbon dioxide gas is released from the ice as a very cold gas. This makes the water in the air condense and form droplets which we see as "fog."

CARBON

Carbon is absolutely fundamental to life, because it is found in all organic compounds. Organic compounds make up cells and carry out life processes—such as when animals eat and digest food, or breathe.

CARBON CYCLE

When animals (including humans) eat, they take in carbon in the form of proteins and carbohydrates. Oxygen in the cells of animals combines with the food and produces energy. That allows animals to move and grow, for example. A waste product of this process is carbon. The carbon is combined with oxygen to form carbon dioxide, which animals release into the atmosphere as they exhale, or breathe out. See also page 57.

Carbon atoms are constantly moving through living things, in the atmosphere, in the oceans, in the soil, and in the Earth's crust. This is called the carbon cycle.

DIAMOND

The abundant **element** of carbon can take many different forms. It can be a super-hard substance used in cutting machinery and engagement rings. Diamond crystals can develop into several different shapes. The most common is the diamond shape. Diamond crystals can also form cubes. These are very strong structures—that's why diamonds are so strong!

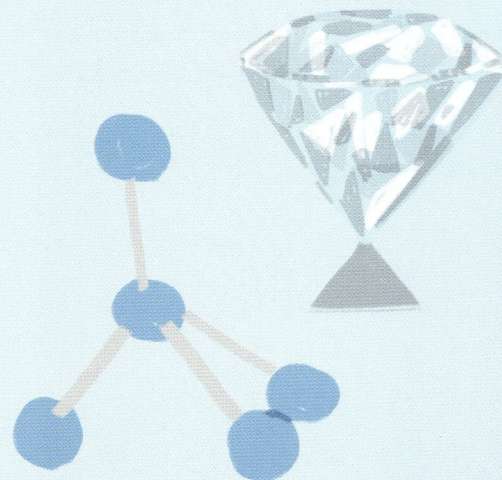

DIAMOND MOLECULE

GRAPHITE

Carbon can also be a slippery, electrical **conductor**—graphite. Graphite is used as a **lubricant** to make things move more easily (such as machine parts) and can also be used for drawing as, when it is rubbed on paper, some of the graphite is left on the page. Graphite has carbon atoms arranged in hexagons.

PENCIL LEAD IS MADE OF GRAPHITE

GRAPHITE MOLECULES

BUCKMINSTERFULLERENE

Another form of carbon is buckminsterfullerene, or C_{60}. These were the first **nanoparticles** ever discovered, back in 1985. They are made up of 60 carbon atoms and shaped like a hollow soccer ball.

Buckminsterfullerene is unique—the only molecule of a single element to create a hollow spherical "cage." Its atoms are arranged in a collection of 12 pentagons and 20 hexagons. Nicknamed 'buckyballs,' these molecules are named after American inventor Buckminster Fuller, who designed many buildings based on geodesic domes, which are round structures that can withstand heavy loads.

C_{60} is very stable and this means scientists see a world of possibilities for this tiny "cage." Research is ongoing into using buckyballs for super-powerful batteries, cancer treatments, rocket fuel, and new types of plastics.

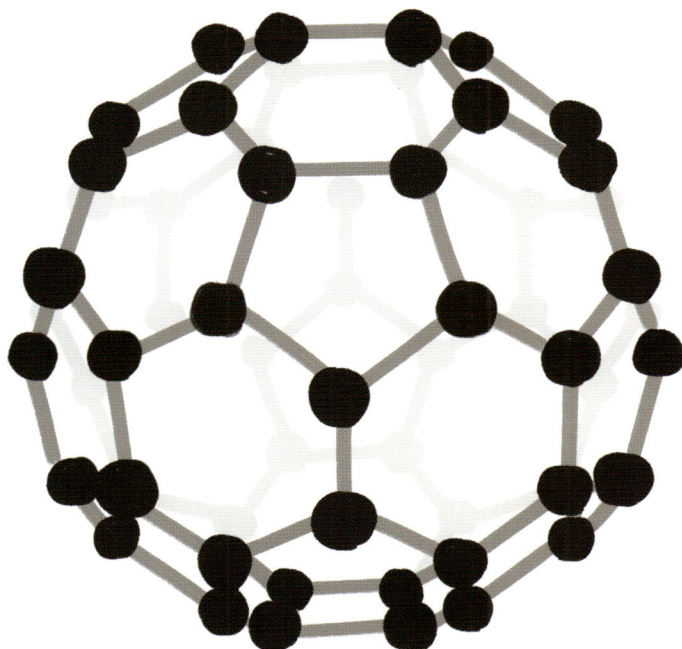

BUCKYBALL MOLECULE

NITROGEN

Do you think oxygen is the main element found in air?
If so—think again! Nitrogen (N) makes up an amazing 78%
of the air we breathe. It is a clear, smell-free, taste-free gas.

CHLOROPHYLL

Nitrogen was discovered in 1772 by Daniel Rutherford. It is vital to many processes in living things. It is found in **chlorophyll** in plants (see pages 27 and 140–141), in protein, and in **DNA** in animals—including you.

Plants are hungry for nitrogen, and that is why it is sometimes applied to soil to make it more fertile—to feed and nourish those hungry plants.

There is a downside though. Man-made nitrogen compounds can pollute when they run off in rain into streams and rivers. Nitrogen can poison aquatic life, like fish.

FIZZY DRINKS

Although many fizzy drinks have bubbles of carbon dioxide, the bubbles in beer are often nitrogen—though there is frequently some carbon dioxide as well. Nitrogen makes smaller bubbles than carbon dioxide, and the nitrogen bubbles make the smooth, creamy head that some beers have.

COOL...

Nitrogen is used in some food packaging to push out oxygen and prevent the food from spoiling. Some microbes (tiny forms of life) that can spoil food need oxygen for respiration, and cannot use nitrogen, so food stays fresher. It is also used as a coolant, in computers, to stop them from overheating. Nitrogen treatment is even used to treat warts and verrucae by freezing them!

NITRO-POWER!

The nitrogen-containing compound nitrous oxide is a gas sometimes used in hospitals and dental clinics. It can reduce pain and relax people who are having procedures that might make them anxious. Nitrous oxide is sometimes known as "laughing gas" because it makes people giggly. This gas can also be used to increase the power of engines in racing cars—and then it gets called "nitrous."

BOOM!

Another nitrogen-based compound, nitroglycerin, is a liquid that can be used to create dynamite for the construction industry. It is a dangerous explosive that uses chemistry to create a big bang to demolish things, and prepare ground and rock for work.

OUT OF CURIOSITY

Titan is the largest moon of Saturn. 95% of its atmosphere, which is 4 times denser than Earth's atmosphere, is made up of nitrogen.

OZONE

Have you ever smelled a tangy, electrical smell when there has been a lightning storm? That's ozone (O_3)—three bonded atoms of oxygen! Ozone is sometimes produced when a charge of electricity (in this case, lightning) passes through the air.

Ozone can be both a blessing and a curse. It is not found in living things, but plays a key role in protecting them. As a gas in Earth's upper atmosphere, it shields the planet from **ultraviolet** (UV) rays from the sun. Without it, life on land would be damaged.

THE OZONE LAYER

A thin layer of ozone circles the Earth 10 to 50 km (6 to 31 miles) up. Humans cause problems by releasing chemicals that damage this precious ozone layer. The first of these to be identified was chlorofluorocarbons (or CFCs), which are used in aerosol sprays such as hair spray and deodorant. The production of CFCs is now banned around the world, but other chemicals, including nitrous oxide (see page 135) from car exhausts, still cause damage.

Chemicals that damage the ozone layer have made thin patches in it, usually called holes, which grow larger and smaller each year. The holes allow dangerous ultraviolet rays to travel through. They can cause cancer, eye diseases, and other health problems. The ozone layer seems to be healing itself and by 2170 might be fully repaired.

SMOG MAKER

When found lower down in the atmosphere, far below the natural ozone layer, ozone can be very polluting. Ozone is created in the lower atmosphere when gases from car exhausts mix with sunlight. Ozone can create smog (smoky fog) in cities and cause breathing difficulties. So we need ozone—but only in the right place!

GREENHOUSE GASES

Like ozone, greenhouse gases can both help and harm living things. These gases in our planet's atmosphere trap heat. They allow sunlight to pass through, but do not let all the heat back out of the atmosphere again, so the Earth stays warm. By absorbing **infrared radiation** and reflecting it back to Earth, they enable living things to survive.

If a planet has too many greenhouse gases in its atmosphere, it gets too hot. This means that water cannot remain in a liquid form. It evaporates. This happened to the planet Venus! Water is a vital ingredient in the process of photosynthesis, which is the basis for all life on Earth.

The main greenhouse gases are:

CARBON DIOXIDE   **METHANE**   **WATER VAPOR**

OZONE   **NITROUS OXIDE**

FOSSIL FUELS

The actions of human beings can increase the amount of greenhouse gases in the atmosphere. Burning fossil fuels such as coal, oil, and natural gas releases greenhouse gases. Chopping down forests (called deforestation) means there are fewer trees to absorb carbon dioxide—and it releases the carbon stored by the trees.

This leads to **climate change** as the Earth gets hotter. Global warming causes habitats to change, and animals and plants cannot adapt quickly enough to keep up. They may go hungry and even become extinct as a result.

Climate change also causes extreme weather patterns, such as typhoons and hurricanes. Sea levels rise as the polar ice caps melt, and flooding occurs.

Sunlight passes through the greenhouse
gases and warms the Earth

OUTER SPACE

ATMOSPHERE

GREENHOUSE GASES

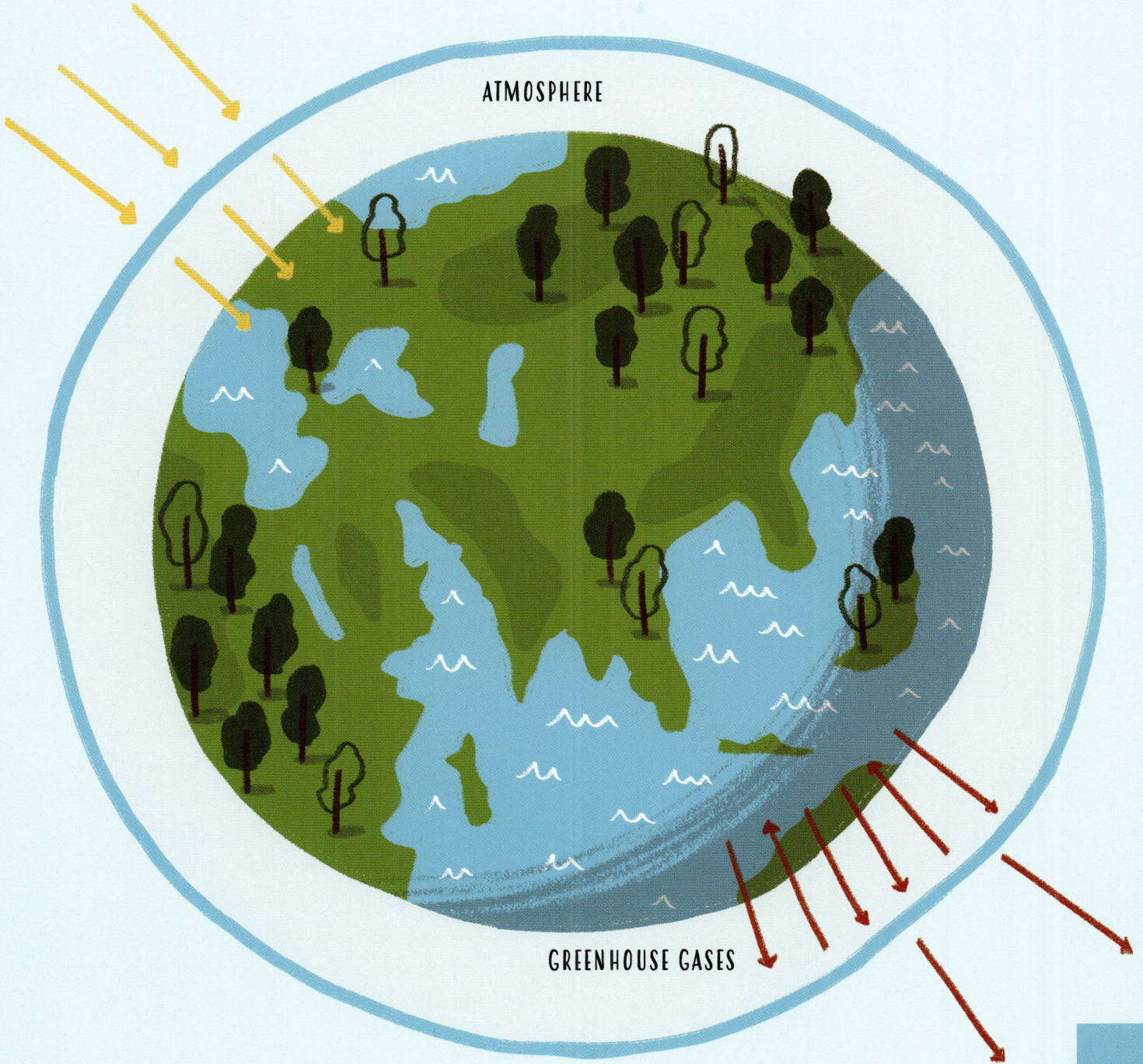

The Earth warms up and gives out heat.
Some heat passes back out through the
greenhouse gases, but some is trapped
inside, keeping the Earth warm.

CHLOROPHYLL

Chlorophyll is like green magic! This organic compound is found in **chloroplasts**—the tiny "factories" inside leaves. Chloroplasts use water, carbon dioxide, and energy from sunlight to produce food for the plant in the form of glucose, a type of sugar. Chlorophyll is the key to this process, which we call **photosynthesis**. It also make leaves green!

CHLOROPLAST

CHLOROPHYLL

Chlorophylls are special **pigments** found inside chloroplasts. Chlorophyll is the material that absorbs light and turns it into chemical energy, via photosynthesis. Chemical energy is stored in the bonds of chemical compounds, such as between atoms and molecules. The energy is released when chemical reactions happen. Without this process, plants could not live. Plants are at the bottom of most food chains, so without chlorophyll it would be hard for many living things to find food.

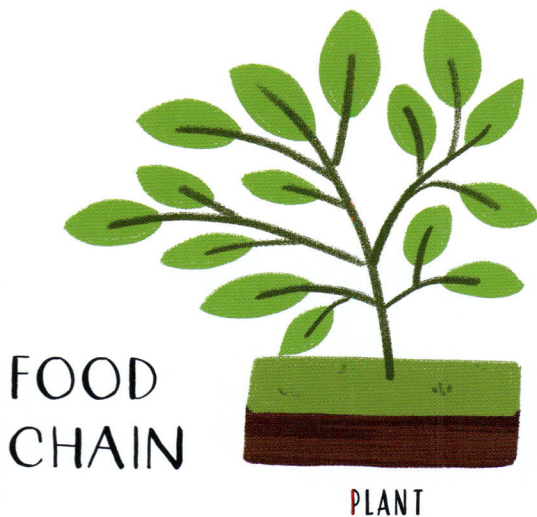

FOOD CHAIN

PLANT

INSECT

AUTUMN SHADES

We see chlorophyll as green, because it doesn't absorb the green wavelengths of light. Those are reflected from plants, so they appear green. The three pigments that shade leaves are chlorophyll, anthocyanins (which cause red leaves), and carotenes (which cause yellow leaves). As the temperature falls before winter, chlorophyll breaks down in deciduous trees (the ones that lose their leaves later in the year), so the leaves change their shade as the green fades. That's why we see trees in blazing oranges, reds, and yellows!

MOUSE

OWL

The chemical energy stored in photosynthesis travels up the food chain, as animals eat plants and other animals.

PROTEIN

Proteins make up all of the major structural tissue (such as muscle tissue) in animals—and that includes you! Proteins are long **polymers**—molecules shaped like a chain. Our bodies can produce 13 types of amino acid (the building blocks that make up protein), but there are nine we need and cannot make.

We obtain these essential amino acids by eating food that is rich in protein. Complete protein contains all of the amino acids we need. It is found in dairy products, eggs, soy, meat, and fish.

Incomplete protein sources include nuts, grains, some vegetables, and fruit. Vegetarians combine foods carefully to make sure their bodies take in all of the amino acids they need for their bodies to grow and repair. Eggs are considered to contain the highest-quality, most usable protein of all foods. The proteins in some foods, such as gluten in wheat, can cause allergic reactions in some people.

PROTEIN IN OUR BODIES

Fibrous protein molecules are long chains that group together into bundles and are differently arranged to make muscle, fingernails—and even hair. The protein that makes up hair, nails, and outer layers of skin is called keratin. After water, protein is the most common type of substance found in the human body.

SKIN CELLS

SUPER USEFUL

Proteins help to regulate and maintain life processes, speeding up **chemical reactions** in your cells. The instructions for making proteins are coded into your **genes**. An example of a protein found in your body is hemoglobin. This protein is found in red blood cells and it contains iron. It transports oxygen around your body.

OUT OF CURIOSITY

Insects contain high levels of protein, and are a nutritious food source. Some insects contain more protein than meat or fish!

CHAPTER 10

THE PERIODIC TABLE

The **periodic table** is a table that arranges the known elements in a list in order of their atomic number. It was invented by the Russian chemist Dmitri Ivanovich Mendeleev in 1869.

The first periodic table did not look the same as the version we use now: it was revised several times as scientists discovered more about different elements and their properties. The version scientists use today has been the same since the mid-1900s.

Legend:
- ALKALI METALS
- ALKALINE EARTH METALS
- LANTHANIDES
- ACTINIDES
- TRANSITION METALS
- UNKNOWN PROPERTIES
- METALLOIDS
- POST-TRANSITION METALS
- OTHER NON-METALS
- HALOGENS
- NOBLE GASES

1 H								
3 Li	4 Be							
11 Na	12 Mg							
19 K	20 Ca	21 Sc	22 Ti	23 V	24 Cr	25 Mn	26 Fe	27 Co
37 Rb	38 Sr	39 Y	40 Zr	41 Nb	42 Mo	43 Tc	44 Ru	45 Rh
55 Cs	56 Ba	57-71	72 Hf	73 Ta	74 W	75 Re	76 Os	77 Ir
87 Fr	88 Ra	89-103	104 Rf	105 Db	106 Sg	107 Bh	108 Hs	109 Mt

57 La	58 Ce	59 Pr	60 Nd	61 Pm	62 Sm	63 Eu
89 Ac	90 Th	91 Pa	92 U	93 Np	94 Pu	95 Am

ATOMIC NUMBER

The atomic number of an element is the same as the number of protons in the atom of the element. The periodic table starts with the lowest atomic number and moves through the elements to the highest number. The table is used by chemists to observe patterns and relationships between elements.

The table is arranged into periods, which are the rows across the table. Each period has a number from 1 to 7. Every element in the first period (the top row) has one **orbital** for its electrons. All of the elements in the second period have 2 orbitals and so on.

GROUPS

Columns of elements are called groups. These groups are numbered 1 to 18.

Elements arranged in groups have electrons arranged in similar ways. This means they behave in similar ways, and have similar chemical properties. That helps chemists to predict how elements might react in a given situation.

For example, magnesium (Mg) and calcium (Ca) are both in column 2 and share similarities.

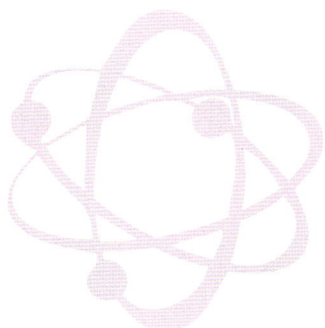

OUT OF CURIOSITY

Francium is the world's rarest naturally occurring element—only a few grams are on Earth at any one time!

					2 He
5 B	6 C	7 N	8 O	9 F	10 Ne
13 Al	14 Si	15 P	16 S	17 Cl	18 Ar

28 Ni	29 Cu	30 Zn	31 Ga	32 Ge	33 As	34 Se	35 Br	36 Kr
46 Pd	47 Ag	48 Cd	49 In	50 Sn	51 Sb	52 Te	53 I	54 Xe
78 Pt	79 Au	80 Hg	81 Tl	82 Pb	83 Bi	84 Po	85 At	86 Rn
110 Ds	111 Rg	112 Cn	113 Nh	114 Fl	115 Mc	116 Lv	117 Ts	118 Og

64 Gd	65 Tb	66 Dy	67 Ho	68 Er	69 Tm	70 Yb	71 Lu
96 Cm	97 Bk	98 Cf	99 Es	100 Fm	101 Md	102 No	103 Lr

NON-METALS

Non-metals are elements that are usually solid or gas under standard conditions. They are found in the top right-hand corner of the periodic table, except hydrogen. They have similar chemical properties that are different to elements that are metals:

NON-METALS

1 H																	
3 Li	4 Be												5 B	6 C	7 N	8 O	9 F
11 Na	12 Mg												13 Al	14 Si	15 P	16 S	17 Cl
19 K	20 Ca	21 Sc	22 Ti	23 V	24 Cr	25 Mn	26 Fe	27 Co	28 Ni	29 Cu	30 Zn	31 Ga	32 Ge	33 As	34 Se	35 Br
37 Rb	38 Sr	39 Y	40 Zr	41 Nb	42 Mo	43 Tc	44 Ru	45 Rh	46 Pd	47 Ag	48 Cd	49 In	50 Sn	51 Sb	52 Te	53 I
55 Cs	56 Ba	57-71	72 Hf	73 Ta	74 W	75 Re	76 Os	77 Ir	78 Pt	79 Au	80 Hg	81 Tl	82 Pb	83 Bi	84 Po	85 At
87 Fr	88 Ra	89-103	104 Rf	105 Db	106 Sg	107 Bh	108 Hs	109 Mt	110 Ds	111 Rg	112 Cn	113 Nh	114 Fl	115 Mc	116 Lv	117 Ts

57 La	58 Ce	59 Pr	60 Nd	61 Pm	62 Sm	63 Eu	64 Gd	65 Tb	66 Dy	67 Ho	68 Er	69 Tm	70 Yb	71 Lu
89 Ac	90 Th	91 Pa	92 U	93 Np	94 Pu	95 Am	96 Cm	97 Bk	98 Cf	99 Es	100 Fm	101 Md	102 No	103 Lr

- DULL, NOT SHINY
- POOR CONDUCTOR OF ELECTRICITY
- NOT DUCTILE (STRETCHABLE)
- BRITTLE, NOT EASILY BENT IN A SOLID STATE
- GOOD INSULATORS AGAINST COLD AND HEAT
- GAIN ELECTRONS DURING REACTIONS

PROPERTIES

Non-metals usually have lower densities than metals, and have lower melting and boiling points (except carbon). Non-metals also form many more compounds than metals.

LIVING THINGS

Living things are made up almost entirely of non-metals. The human body is around 65% oxygen, 18% carbon, 10% hydrogen, and 3% nitrogen.

TABLE OF NON-METALS

NUMBER	SYMBOL	ELEMENT
1	H	Hydrogen
2	He	Helium
6	C	Carbon
7	N	Nitrogen
8	O	Oxygen
9	F	Fluorine
10	Ne	Neon
15	P	Phosphorus
16	S	Sulfur
17	Cl	Chlorine
18	Ar	Argon
34	Se	Selenium
35	Br	Bromine
36	Kr	Krypton
53	I	Iodine
54	Xe	Xenon
85	At	Astatine
86	Rn	Radon
117	Ts	Tennessine
118	Og	Oganesson

OUT OF CURIOSITY

Two of the non-metal gases, hydrogen and helium, make up 99% of normal matter in the Universe. Nitrogen at 78% and oxygen at 21% make up most of Earth's atmosphere. Our water is made from the non-metals hydrogen and oxygen.

HALOGENS

Halogens are the elements in group 17 of the periodic table. Halogen means "salt-becomer," because the Greek word "*hals*" means "salt," and "gen" means "to make."

Halogens are very reactive, with fluorine being one of the most reactive elements in existence. The reactivity of the halogens decreases as you move down the column in the periodic table.

HALOGENS

1 H													5 B	6 C	7 N	8 O	9 F	2 He
3 Li	4 Be												13 Al	14 Si	15 P	16 S	17 Cl	10 Ne
11 Na	12 Mg												31 Ga	32 Ge	33 As	34 Se	35 Br	18 Ar
19 K	20 Ca	21 Sc	22 Ti	23 V	24 Cr	25 Mn	26 Fe	27 Co	28 Ni	29 Cu	30 Zn		49 In	50 Sn	51 Sb	52 Te	53 I	36 Kr
37 Rb	38 Sr	39 Y	40 Zr	41 Nb	42 Mo	43 Tc	44 Ru	45 Rh	46 Pd	47 Ag	48 Cd		81 Tl	82 Pb	83 Bi	84 Po	85 At	54 Xe
55 Cs	56 Ba	57-71	72 Hf	73 Ta	74 W	75 Re	76 Os	77 Ir	78 Pt	79 Au	80 Hg		113 Nh	114 Fl	115 Mc	116 Lv	117 Ts	86 Rn
87 Fr	88 Ra	89-103	104 Rf	105 Db	106 Sg	107 Bh	108 Hs	109 Mt	110 Ds	111 Rg	112 Cn							118 Og

57 La	58 Ce	59 Pr	60 Nd	61 Pm	62 Sm	63 Eu	64 Gd	65 Tb	66 Dy	67 Ho	68 Er	69 Tm	70 Yb	71 Lu
89 Ac	90 Th	91 Pa	92 U	93 Np	94 Pu	95 Am	96 Cm	97 Bk	98 Cf	99 Es	100 Fm	101 Md	102 No	103 Lr

DANGER!

The elements in this group are fluorine (F), chlorine (Cl), bromine (Br), iodine (I), and astatine (At). Halogens are all quite toxic. Fluorine gas is lethal. Breathing air that contains a tiny 0.1% concentration of fluorine can kill you!

COMPOUNDS

Halogens form acids when combined with hydrogen (H). Compounds containing halogens are called halides. Halogens have low melting points and low boiling points.

WHERE IN THE WORLD?

All halogens are found in compounds in the Earth's crust. Fluorine and chlorine are abundant, but iodine and bromine are quite rare. Astatine, on the other hand, is one of the rarest naturally occurring elements on Earth.

USES FOR HALOGENS

Halogen light bulbs and lamps have a tungsten filament in a quartz container. The gas around the filament is a halogen.

Halogen lamps glow with a whiter light than other bulbs, and get up to a higher temperature. The bulbs need to be made from fused quartz to reduce breakage.

Chlorine and bromine are both used as disinfectants, to sterilize things and to kill bacteria, even in wounds and drinking water. That smell in swimming pools is chlorine.

Fluoride is added to water and toothpaste in tiny quantities to fight tooth decay.

Sodium hypochlorite is produced from chlorine, and is the main ingredient of bleach. It is used for cleaning, laundry, and for bleaching paper and fabric. It burns the skin and eyes, so never touch it.

OUT OF CURIOSITY

Bromine smells bad. It gets its name from the Greek word "bromos," which means stench!

NOBLE GASES

Noble gases are in group 18 of the periodic table. They do not react with other elements. They have no smell and they are clear. As you move down the periodic table, the elements become rarer.

There are six noble gases:

HELIUM (He)	NEON (Ne)	ARGON (Ar)
KRYPTON (Kr)	XENON (Xe)	RADON (Rn)

 WILLIAM RAMSAY

Many of the noble gases were discovered (or isolated) by Sir William Ramsay. He received the Nobel Prize for Chemistry in 1904 for the discovery of "inert gaseous elements in air."

?

OUT OF CURIOSITY

Helium has the lowest melting point (-272°C, or -458 °F), and boiling point (-268.9°C, or -452.1 °F) of any substance.

USES FOR NOBLE GASES

Noble gases have very low boiling points. That makes them useful as refrigerants, to keep things cool. Helium in a liquid form is used by hospitals in MRI (Magnetic Resonance Imaging) machines. MRI scanners use strong magnets (which the helium keeps cool) and a type of radio wave to examine organs and structures in the human body.

Helium is also added to the breathing mix used by divers on deep dives. Gases such as nitrogen and oxygen are absorbed by your blood and your body tissues, but helium is not highly soluble in liquids. Adding it to tanks used by divers avoids **oxygen toxicity**, which is lung damage caused by breathing too much oxygen.

Helium is also useful as a "lifting gas"— you may have seen helium balloons floating at parties. Helium is less dense than air, so things filled with helium rise. Helium is also used for huge balloons or blimps, as it is very light and does not burn, so it is safe.

Noble gases are often used in lighting because they are not very reactive. Noble gases glow brightly, in different shades—and they are found in "neon" lights.

Noble gases are used in medicine, for example in lasers used by surgeons. Helium is effective as an asthma treatment. Xenon puts people to sleep for operations. Radon is used in radiotherapy.

Noble gases are very helpful to chemists. They are used in laboratories to stabilize reactions that would normally happen too quickly.

Argon is used in welding. It is denser than air, so it stops air from getting to the metal being welded. It is inert (does not react), so the hot metal does not **oxidize**. That would spoil the welded piece.

ALKALI METALS

Alkali metals are in group 1 of the periodic table, although hydrogen isn't one of them. Pure forms of the alkali metals are silver in shade and soft—you could cut them easily with a knife.

They react really strongly with water—some explosively—and have to be stored carefully. They are mostly stored under a layer of oil to stop them from **reacting**. In the air, they react to the oxygen (oxidize) and turn black. They are **malleable** and **ductile**, and good conductors of both heat and electricity.

POTASSIUM

The alkali metals are:

LITHIUM (Li)	SODIUM (Na)
POTASSIUM (K)	CESIUM (Cs)
FRANCIUM (Fr)	RUBIDIUM (Rb)

UNSTABLE

Alkali metals are never found in nature in their pure forms, as they are so unstable that they react quickly and combine to make other substances.

Sodium is in sodium chloride (NaCl) or table salt—the type used in cooking! It is also in sodium hydroxide (NaOH), commonly called caustic soda. This is used in cleaning and is a very strong and corrosive base.

ATOMIC CLOCKS

Caesium and rubidium are used to make atomic clocks. Caesium clocks are said to be the most accurate clocks, keeping the best time.

Potassium is used in the manufacture of fertilizers.

FERTILIZER

FLAME FACTS:

Alkali metals burn with a variety of tinted flames.

SODIUM

LITHIUM

CESIUM

POTASSIUM

RUBIDIUM

ALKALINE EARTH METALS

Alkaline earth metals are the second group on the periodic table. They are related to, but not as reactive as, the alkali metals. They are mainly silver in shade and soft, and react with halogens to form salts—compounds called halides. They occur in nature, but only as compounds and **minerals**.

The alkaline earth metals are:

BERYLLIUM (Be)

MAGNESIUM (Mg)

CALCIUM (Ca)

STRONTIUM (Sr)

BARIUM (Ba)

RADIUM (Ra)

Many of the alkaline earth metals were discovered by Sir Humphry Davy (the man who invented the Davy safety lamp for miners), including calcium, barium, strontium, and magnesium.

OUT OF CURIOSITY

Radium is formed by the radioactive decay of uranium and is dangerous to handle. It is scary to think that it used to be an ingredient in glow-in-the-dark paints which were used for many items around the house. It was discovered by Marie and Pierre Curie. It has been used in medicine, creating radon gas from radium chloride to be used in cancer treatments such as radiotherapy.

pH

Alkaline earth metals form solutions with a pH greater than 7. This makes them bases, or "alkaline."

Calcium and magnesium are important to living things. For example, magnesium is found in chlorophyll in green plants.

HUMAN BODIES AND ALKALINE METALS

Humans and many animals use calcium to build strong bones and teeth. Magnesium helps to regulate your body temperature.

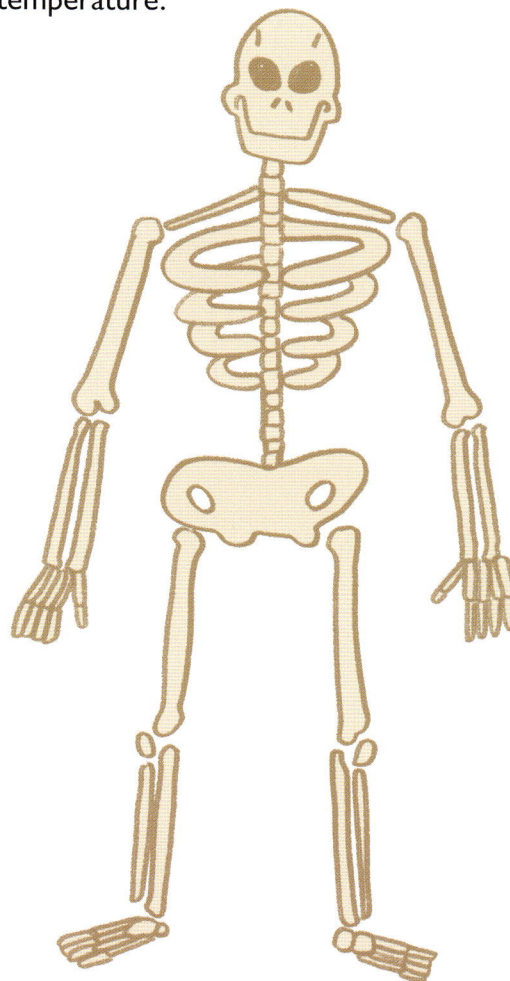

FLAME FACTS:

Alkaline earth metals burn with tinted flames.

BERYLLIUM

MAGNESIUM

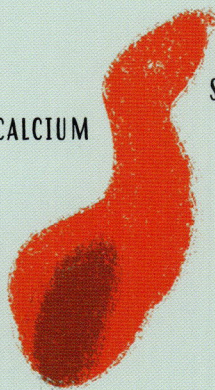

CALCIUM

STRONTIUM

RADIUM

TRANSITION METALS

Transition metals are found in the middle of the periodic table, called the "d block." There are 35 elements in this section. They all have similar properties.

They are harder than alkaline earth metals and less reactive. They make up the largest section of the periodic table, from columns 3 to 12, although sometimes the elements in column 12 are not included as part of the transition metal group (zinc (Zn), cadmium (Cd), mercury (Hg), and copernicium (Cn)). Most metals are transition metals.

COMMON PROPERTIES

Transition metals can form many compounds. They conduct electricity and have high melting and boiling points. They have higher densities than the alkaline earth metals.

When they are freshly cut, transition metals are shiny. They are strong and hard.

PRECIOUS METALS

"Precious" metals, such as the types we wear as necklaces and rings, are transition metals: silver, gold, copper, platinum, and titanium.

REACTIONS

Transition metals react slowly with oxygen at room temperature, but some (like copper) react with oxygen when they are heated. Copper (Cu) + oxygen (O) = copper oxide (CuO).

Transition metals react slowly with cold water, or not at all. Iron (Fe) reacts with water (H_2O) and oxygen (O) to make rust, or iron oxide (Fe_2O_3).

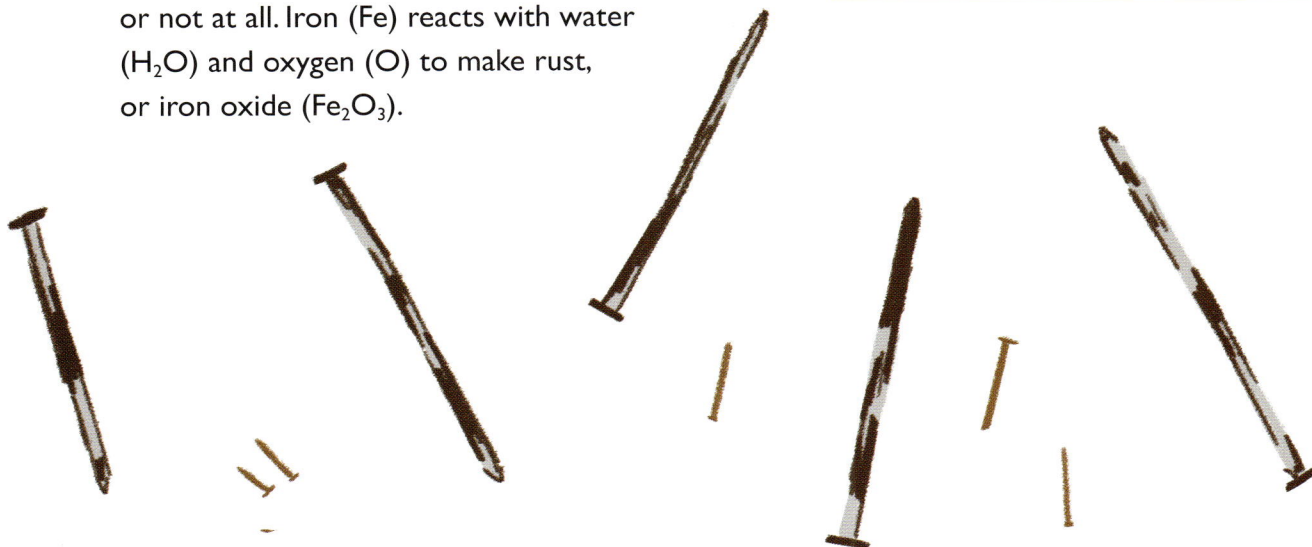

HEALTHY BODIES

Some transition metals are needed by the human body to keep it healthy. We need iron to make blood, and zinc and chromium for other key processes in our bodies.

METALLOIDS

A metalloid is a strange element that has the properties of both metal and non-metal elements. For example, it might be brittle like a non-metal, but shiny like a metal. It could be a conductor of electricity like a metal, but dull like a non-metal.

Metalloids can form alloys with metals. Some are semi-conductors, like silicon and germanium. That means they only conduct electricity under special conditions.

WHERE IN THE WORLD?

The most abundant (found most often) metalloid on Earth is silicon (Si), and the rarest is tellurium (Te).

Other metalloids are boron (B), germanium (Ge), arsenic (As), and antimony (Sb). Selenium (Se) and polonium (Po) are sometimes included in this group as well.

Unlike other families of elements, metalloids are arranged in a diagonal line on the periodic table.

METALLOIDS

1 H																	2 He
3 Li	4 Be											5 B	6 C	7 N	8 O	9 F	10 Ne
11 Na	12 Mg											13 Al	14 Si	15 P	16 S	17 Cl	18 Ar
19 K	20 Ca	21 Sc	22 Ti	23 V	24 Cr	25 Mn	26 Fe	27 Co	28 Ni	29 Cu	30 Zn	31 Ga	32 Ge	33 As	34 Se	35 Br	36 Kr
37 Rb	38 Sr	39 Y	40 Zr	41 Nb	42 Mo	43 Tc	44 Ru	45 Rh	46 Pd	47 Ag	48 Cd	49 In	50 Sn	51 Sb	52 Te	53 I	54 Xe
55 Cs	56 Ba	57-71	72 Hf	73 Ta	74 W	75 Re	76 Os	77 Ir	78 Pt	79 Au	80 Hg	81 Tl	82 Pb	83 Bi	84 Po	85 At	86 Rn
87 Fr	88 Ra	89-103	104 Rf	105 Db	106 Sg	107 Bh	108 Hs	109 Mt	110 Ds	111 Rg	112 Cn	113 Nh	114 Fl	115 Mc	116 Lv	117 Ts	118 Og

57 La	58 Ce	59 Pr	60 Nd	61 Pm	62 Sm	63 Eu	64 Gd	65 Tb	66 Dy	67 Ho	68 Er	69 Tm	70 Yb	71 Lu
89 Ac	90 Th	91 Pa	92 U	93 Np	94 Pu	95 Am	96 Cm	97 Bk	98 Cf	99 Es	100 Fm	101 Md	102 No	103 Lr

SILICON

Silicon is a common metalloid. It is a **semiconductor**, which makes it incredibly useful for technology.

Silicon is one of the most important materials in the manufacture of electronics such as mobile phones and computers. You will have technology containing silicon in your house right now!

SILICON VALLEY

This is an area near San Francisco where many computer-related companies are based. The silicon wafers used in computers are made by melting sand (silica). These are polished and then made to hold thousands of tiny transistors, which can amplify or switch electronic signals. Tiny triangles of these wafers are then cut and fitted into central processing units (CPUs), just like the one in your computer.

DANGER!

Arsenic is a highly poisonous metalloid. In fact, it is one of the most poisonous elements that exists! Arsenic is used to harden alloys, especially copper and lead alloys. It is also used as an ingredient in some wood preservatives, pesticides, and types of glass.

Antimony is used today in making metal alloys, but was used in cosmetics 5,000 years ago by the ancient Egyptians.

ACTINIDES AND LANTHANIDES

When you look at the periodic table, you see two rows at the bottom. These are sometimes called the "f block" of the periodic table.

One of the rows is called the actinides and the other is called the lanthanides. Some people call them rare-earth metals, and others call them inner-transition elements. There are 15 actinides—which are shown in purple at the bottom of page 161—and 15 lanthanides—shown in blue.

WHERE IN THE WORLD?

Actinides and lanthanides are highly reactive with halogens. Lanthanides are naturally occurring on Earth. Some of the actinides are not naturally occurring and are only made in laboratories.

Lanthanides are metals that slowly turn into their hydroxides (react and combine with hydrogen molecules) when they are placed in water. They form a coating of oxide when exposed to air, like most metals.

USES FOR ACTINIDES AND LANTHANIDES

Hybrid cars use lanthanides such as lanthanum, terbium, neodymium, and dysprosium in their batteries.

Americium (Am) is a synthetic radioactive element. It is an actinide, and is used in making smoke detectors.

URANIUM

Uranium (U), used in nuclear reactors to provide power, was once used to make glass—until it was found to be radioactive!

PLUTONIUM

Plutonium (Pu) was used to create the bomb that destroyed Nagasaki at the end of World War II. The bomb harnessed the awful power of a nuclear chain.

? OUT OF CURIOSITY

The name actinium comes from the Greek word "aktis," which means beam or ray.

IT'S ALL IN THE NAME...

All of the elements in the actinide series are radioactive. Take a look at the list of names below—can you read them out loud? Some sound like names from science fiction, rather than science "fact"!

ACTINIUM (Ac)	THORIUM (Th)	PROTACTINIUM (Pa)	URANIUM (U)	NEPTUNIUM (Np)
PLUTONIUM (Pu)	AMERICIUM (Am)	CURIUM (Cm)	BERKELIUM (Bk)	CALIFORNIUM (Cf)
EINSTEINIUM (Es)	FERMIUM (Fm)	MENDELEVIUM (Md)	NOBELIUM (No)	LAWRENCIUM (Lr)
LANTHANUM (La)	CERIUM (Ce)	PRASEODYMIUM (Pr)	NEODYMIUM (Nd)	PROMETHIUM (Pm)
SAMARIUM (Sm)	EUROPIUM (Eu)	GADOLINIUM (Gd)	TERBIUM (Tb)	DYSPROSIUM (Dy)
HOLMIUM (Ho)	ERBIUM (Er)	THULIUM (Tm)	YTTERBIUM (Yb)	LUTETIUM (Lu)

POST-TRANSITION METALS

Post-transition metals, or "poor metals," are to the right of transition metals and to the left of metalloids on the periodic table.

There are discussions about which elements to include, but typically they include metals from groups 13, 14, and 15. They tend to be softer than other metals and have lower melting points. Post-transition metals are ductile and malleable, and conduct heat and electricity.

Included in this group are:

ALUMINUM (Al)   GALLIUM (Ga)   INDIUM (In)   TIN (Sn)

THALLIUM (Tl)   LEAD (Pb)   BISMUTH (Bi)

DECISIONS, DECISIONS...

Nihonium (Nh), flerovium (Fl), moscovium (Mo), and livermorium (Lv) are sometimes classified as post-transition metals—but not always. It's quite confusing!

ALUMINUM

The most common naturally occurring post-transition metal on Earth is aluminum. It is the third most abundant element in the Earth's crust.

Aluminum is light and relatively strong, so it is used to make containers, such as cans for carbonated (fizzy) drinks.

Aluminum was first identified as an element in 1825 and it was at first so expensive to produce that it was more highly valued than gold! Napoleon III was fascinated by it and funded experiments for using the element in the military.

HEALTH

Bismuth is used to make remedies for indigestion and heartburn. One dose contains around 262 milligrams of bismuth subsalicylate.

INDIUM

Indium is used to make electronics such as flat screens and touchscreens.

LEAD

In the past, lead was used to make toys because it could be melted and poured into molds easily and cheaply. Lead was also added to paint, but then it was found to cause poisoning.

Today, lead is still used in some products such as car batteries, but people understand that it can cause health problems if it is in regular contact with skin.

CHAPTER 11

CHEMICALS ALL AROUND US

As you have seen, everything in the world is made up of chemicals. Most of those chemicals are compounds, which are combinations of different elements. Some of those compounds are very complicated and are made of lots of different atoms, such as the chemicals in living things, including you.

You are now in a good position to spot chemicals in the world around you. Most animals take the chemical world as they find it, eating food and breathing in the air. Humans have gone far beyond that to use Planet Earth as a source of raw materials. We mine metals from the ground and mix them into alloys. We use chemical reactions to make entirely new chemicals, such as plastics, that don't occur naturally. We have made chemicals that help our plants to grow (fertilizers) and to change the taste of foods or keep them for longer (preservatives).

Humans use the resources of Earth like a vast chemistry set—often with good results, but sometimes with bad effects, too.

AIR

Air is made up of several different gases, including nitrogen (around 78%), oxygen (around 21%), and a small percentage of carbon dioxide (0.04%), along with a tiny amount of hydrogen and neon. Without air, we could not live on Earth—we need it to breathe.

THE ATMOSPHERE

Air surrounds the Earth, in a layer that is held in place by Earth's gravity. This blanket of gases is called the atmosphere. Near the surface of the Earth, the atmosphere is around 75% nitrogen and around 20% oxygen.

Greenhouse gases and ozone help to keep the planet warm and protect living things from dangerous radiation that comes from the sun's rays.

THANKS!

The fact that we now have oxygen in the air is due to simple living things called cyanobacteria that developed in the oceans billions of years ago. They make their food by photosynthesizing. Since photosynthesis makes oxygen, cyanobacteria were responsible for putting large amounts of oxygen into Earth's atmosphere.

Over 2.5 billion years ago, the atmosphere was made up of an unbreathable mixture of carbon dioxide (CO_2) and gases that belched from volcanoes, such as methane and ammonia.

POLLUTION

Air also contains aerosol particles—tiny airborne specks of things like dust, pollen, soot, car exhaust, and smoke. This causes air pollution. There are megatons of it in the atmosphere!

The air also contains tiny bioaerosols, microbes that are carried along on the air via wind or a sneeze or cough.

OUT OF CURIOSITY

Air is 'light," but there is a lot of it pushing down on the surface of the Earth. We call that air pressure. Air pressure is highest at sea level, and lowest on high mountains.

HUMIDITY

Air contains lots of water in gas form. Have you ever heard the word "humid"? It describes hot, damp air that contains lots of water.

High humidity can make it harder to breathe easily. Humidity is measured in percentages—you can see it on many weather forecasts. When humidity is 100%, it rains!

≋ SEAWATER ≋

Have you ever tasted salty seawater on your lips after swimming?
Or seen sparkly white salt on your skin as you dried in the sun?
Seawater is salty because of the minerals that are worn away from
rocks by rivers and raindrops, collecting in the sea.

The salt that is dissolved in the water can be extracted by
evaporation. When the water evaporates, sea salt (made up
of sodium chloride—NaCl—and small amounts of minerals)
is left behind—delicious sprinkled on your chips and fries.

There is an amazing 35 g (1.2 oz) of dissolved salt
in every kilogram of seawater—so it's no
wonder that it tastes so salty!

≋ GETTING SALTY

When the oceans first formed 3.8 billion years
ago, they were freshwater. Some of the ocean's
salts, including sodium, chlorine, and potassium,
came from underwater eruptions. Rain mixed
with carbon dioxide in the air to make a weak
acid that wore away rocks that also contained
salts. Rain and rivers carried salt into
the oceans.

≋ THE DEAD SEA

Things float more easily in seawater than freshwater, which makes swimming easier! Any material can float if it is less dense than the liquid it is in. One of the saltiest natural bodies of water is the Dead Sea, bordered by Jordan, Israel, and the West Bank. In Arabic, the sea is called Al-Bahr Al-Mayyit , or "The Sea of Death." Sounds spooky!

In reality, the name comes from the fact that most things cannot live in such salty water. Any fish carried down rivers into the Dead Sea die off quickly; only some forms of bacteria can live there. It's a great place for swimmers though, as the dense water helps people to float easily.

≋ FREEZING

Seawater freezes at a lower temperature than freshwater because salt lowers its freezing point. It freezes at around -2°C (28.4° Fahrenheit), instead of freshwater's 0° Celsius (32° Fahrenheit). The sea does freeze near the poles, where the temperature is very low. The polar ice cap at the North Pole is made of frozen seawater.

ROCK

Rock is a solid that makes up all of Earth's outer layer, which is called the crust—and without rock, there would be no land to live on! Have you ever looked closely at different types of rock? A good place to look is on the beach. That's because rocks from lots of different places are carried along by the action of waves to be deposited on pebbly beaches.

MINERALS

Minerals are solids that form naturally in the ground or in water. They sometimes contain a single element but are usually compounds. Rocks are mixtures of minerals.

Many rocks are made up of little grains. They can be broken back down into grains too, when sand is made. Rocks at the surface of the Earth are eroded by water, weather, and even wind. Next time you are at the beach, look very closely at a pinch of sand.

You could look with a magnifier for a closer view. You'll see many tiny specks of different rocks in each pinch of sand.

Rocks are formed in different ways. They are classified into three main groups, depending on the way they were made: sedimentary, metamorphic, and igneous.

SEDIMENTARY

Sedimentary rock is made when sand, mud, or the remains of living things become stuck together as they settle. Fragments drift down through water and create a tightly pressed mixture that hardens to become rock.

Sandstone is a sedimentary rock made from grains of broken rock. Mudstone and shale are made from hardened mud, while chalk is made from the shells of tiny ocean creatures. Fossils are found in sedimentary rock. They were made when dead creatures sank to the bottom of a body of water or mud and gradually their tissues were replaced by minerals.

IGNEOUS

Igneous rock is formed when molten rock, heated inside the Earth, cools. Magma is the name for molten rock inside the Earth. Molten rock is called lava when it comes out of volcanoes.

If it cools underground, magma will cool slowly. That gives **crystals** time to develop. A crystal is a mineral with an ordered structure. When magma cools underground, it forms intrusive igneous rock. These rocks often have large crystals that you can see with the naked eye. An example of this type of igneous rock is granite.

When lava erupts from a volcano, then cools and hardens into rock, it forms volcanic rock—or what scientists call extrusive igneous rocks. When lava cools quickly, crystals do not have time to grow. Basalt is a volcanic rock with small crystals. Obsidian, another volcanic rock, does not have crystals at all. There are more than 700 types of igneous rock!

METAMORPHIC

Metamorphic rock is created when the pressure and heat in the Earth's crust cause changes in the minerals that rock is made from. That's how they get the name "metamorphic"—think of the way that a tadpole changes into a frog when it undergoes metamorphosis to remind you.

Metamorphic rocks started out as sedimentary, igneous, or metamorphic rocks. An example of a well-known metamorphic rock is marble, which is the metamorphized version of limestone.

? OUT OF CURIOSITY

"Ore" is the name given to rocks that contain useful minerals, metals, and gems.

LAVA

MAGMA

MINERALS

Minerals are solids that occur naturally in the environment. They make up rocks. Minerals, unlike rocks, have a chemical structure that is the same throughout. They can be made of a single element, such as gold (Au) or copper (Cu). They can also be made up of a combination of elements. Scientists who study minerals are called mineralogists.

INORGANIC

Minerals are inorganic—that means they are not living organisms such as animals or plants. They usually have a crystal structure. There are many types of minerals but they are mainly divided by scientists into two groups, silicates and non-silicates. Silicates contain silicon and oxygen, and make up a huge 90% of Earth's crust.

Non-silicates include:

OXIDES

Chromite ($FeCr_2O_4$) is an oxide mineral made from oxygen (O), chromium (Cr), and iron (Fe).

CARBONATES

Calcium carbonate ($CaCO_3$) is a carbonate mineral that is found in coral skeletons and the shells of snails and oysters.

SULFIDES

One sulfide mineral is pyrite (FeS_2), which is made up of sulfur and iron (Fe). Pyrite is also called fool's gold because it looks a little like gold.

HALIDES

The salt we sprinkle on our dinner (NaCl) is a halide. It is made from the halogen chlorine (Cl) and sodium (Na).

I
N
C
R
E
A
S
I
N
G

H
A
R
D
N
E
S
S

 1) TALC

 2) GYPSUM

3) CALCITE

 4) FLUORITE

 5) APATITE

6) ORTHOCLASE FELDSPAR

 7) QUARTZ

 8) TOPAZ

 9) CORUNDUM

10) DIAMOND

Minerals are described by scientists according to their properties:

HARDNESS

Scientists use the Mohs scale to describe how hard a mineral is on a scale of 1–10, with 1 being the softest and 10 the hardest. If a mineral can be easily scratched, it is soft. If it cannot, like diamond, it is hard (in fact, the hardest mineral) and therefore a 10 on the Mohs scale.

LUSTER

Luster means how well minerals reflect light. A mineral might be described as dull, metallic, brilliant, or glassy.

SPECIFIC GRAVITY

Specific gravity (SG) is the density of the mineral. The mineral is always compared to water, which has an SG of 1. Quartz, for example, has an SG of 2.7.

STREAK

Streak is exactly that—the mark made when the mineral is rubbed across a rough surface such as a tile. The shade of the powder left behind is the streak. Weirdly, some minerals have a streak that is a different shade from their body!

CLEAVAGE

This means what happens when the mineral breaks into pieces. According to their structure, some may break into sheets and others into small cube-like shapes.

SHADE

Different minerals have different shades, depending on the elements they contain! The same mineral, such as corundum, can be shaded differently by the inclusion of tiny amounts of impurities—forming ruby or sapphire.

OUT OF CURIOSITY

A gem is a rare mineral such as emerald, ruby, sapphire, or diamond, that is cut and polished—and often worn as decoration.

METALS

The science of studying metals is called metallurgy. Metals are strong but flexible solids that are often found in rock ore, which is dug from the ground in great mines. To separate the metal from ore, the rock is crushed and heated to high temperatures in a process called smelting.

PROPERTIES

Metals are great conductors of heat and electricity—but some metals such as copper are especially conductive so they are used in electrical circuits. Conducting allows electricity to pass through a material. Metals are usually sonorous—they make a noise like a bell when they are struck.

Metals are malleable, which means they can be beaten into a thin sheet. They are also ductile, so they can be stretched out into thin wires. Metal is strong, so it is made into things like bridges and cars—and even coins, so they do not wear away with lots of use.

BONDS

It is their very strong, metallic bonds (the force that binds the atoms together) that give metals their properties of bendability and conductivity.

All metals are solids at room temperature, apart from mercury (Hg), which is a liquid. Their strong bonds also give most metals a high melting point. However, they can be melted to pour into molds to make components, tools, machinery, and electronics.

There are different types of metals:

BASE METALS

These reactive metals corrode (or break down) easily in the air. Oxidation happens when the metal combines with the oxygen in the air. Examples of base metals are zinc (Zn), copper (Cu), lead (Pb), and tin (Sn).

Did you know that "tin" cans are in fact made from several metals? Most drink cans—75% around the world—are made from aluminum. Most food cans are made from steel plated with tin or chromium.

OUT OF CURIOSITY

When copper corrodes it turns a blue-green shade. This is oxidation taking place. It's a chemical reaction where the copper reacts with the oxygen in air to create copper oxide.

In ancient times, Romans and Greeks corroded copper on purpose and used the green shade, called verdigris, as a pigment for paints and dyes.

NOBLE METALS

Noble metals are unreactive metals such as platinum (Pt), gold (Au), iridium (Ir), palladium (Pd), and silver (Ag).

They resist corrosion and oxidation, and because they are quite rare they are valuable. They are often made into necklaces, earrings, and rings or used in technology.

FERROUS METALS

Ferrous metals are iron and alloys of iron. Iron is attracted to magnets so ferrous metals are too. Examples of ferrous metals are steel, cast iron, and pig iron. Steel is mainly made from iron (Fe), carbon (C), and manganese (Mn).

⚙ ALLOYS ⚙

Alloys are metals that combine two or more elements. They are mixtures, made to combine the properties of different metals. They are produced to make stronger and corrosion-free metals for a variety of applications. Steel is one of the most useful and widely made alloys. Steel is made of iron, plus a variety of different ingredients. In industry and construction, steel is often made by combining iron and carbon.

Look around and you may find a type of steel in your cutlery drawer at home—this is stainless steel. It is made from steel and chromium, and is rust-free and easy to clean.

⚙ ALUMINUM ALLOYS

You may have held this alloy in your hand today, if you have drunk soda from a can. Aluminum is combined with elements such as silicon and copper to make an alloy.

It doesn't corrode and it is very light, so it is perfect for packaging. It's useful for other things that need to be strong but light, such as ladders and airplanes.

✳ BRASS

Brass is an alloy made from zinc and copper. You may have some in your house as it is often used to make ornaments and candlesticks.

✳ GOLD

Most wearable gold you see is an alloy, too. Pure gold is very soft and easily damaged, so it is often mixed with other metals to make it stronger. Look in a jewelry shop window. Find the labels on the gold. The higher the number, the more gold is used in the alloy: 24 karat gold is pure gold, 18 karat gold is made with 75% gold, and 9 karat gold contains just 37.5% of pure gold.

❓ OUT OF CURIOSITY

The first known alloy was made in ancient times—the Bronze Age! The Stone Age was before that, when people did not use metals. Bronze is a combination of tin and copper.

It was used to make tools, weapons, and utensils, as well as wearable art—and today, it is used for statues.

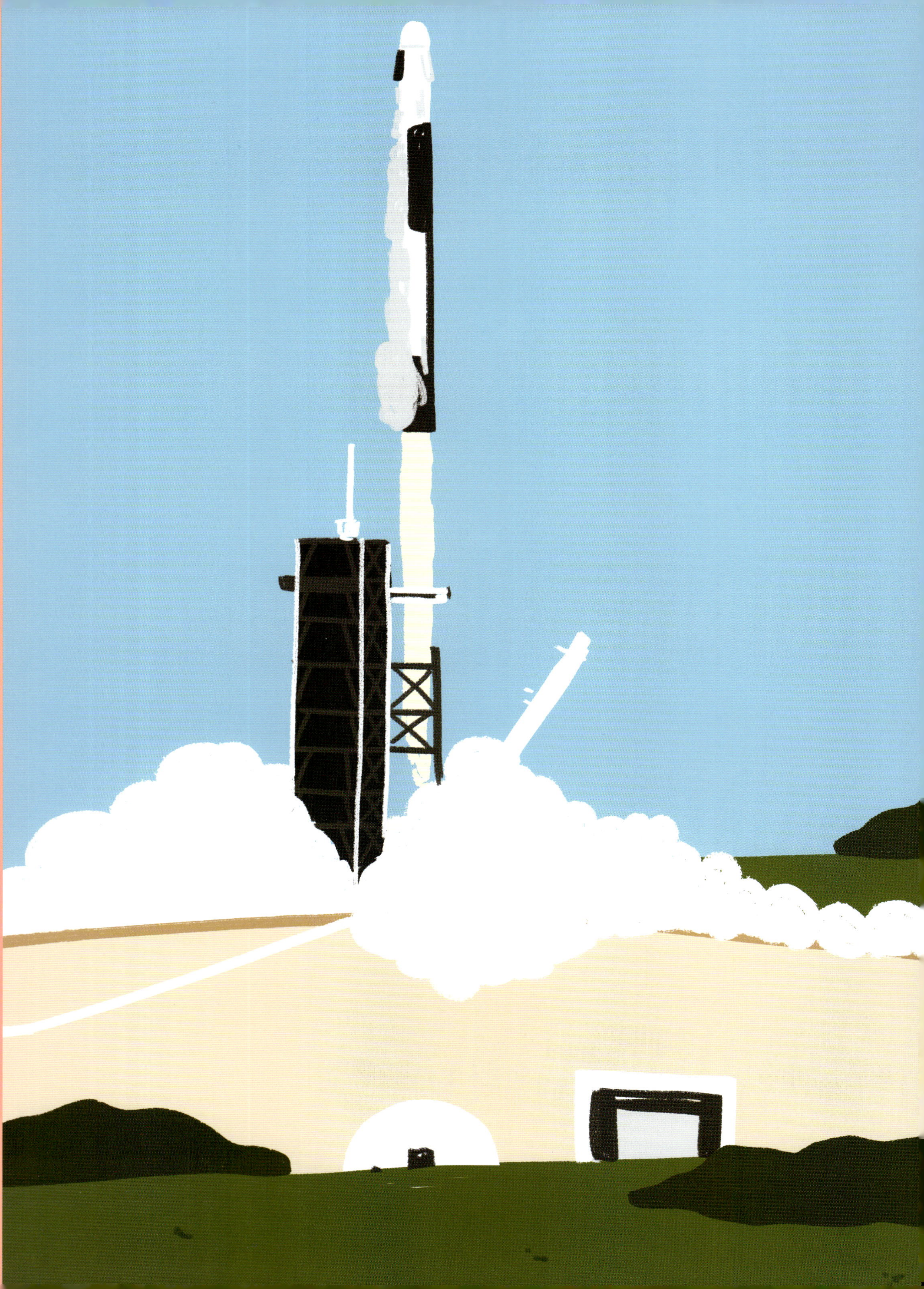

SECTION 3: PHENOMENAL PHYSICS

The earth-shaking blast of a rocket launching. The mysterious click of magnets coming together. The unbelievable heights of a bridge suspended over water. The light that helps us see. All of these have something in common. They can all be explained by **physics**.

Physics is the study of energy and matter and how they relate to each other in space and time. Physics can be as small as atoms or as big as the Universe! Some people look closely at the laws and forces of physics—for them it's all about the action! For others, it's about understanding how waves can make light and sound. Yet others look at energy, electricity, and even space.

The people who study physics are called **physicists**. They strive to understand how our great big Universe, and everything inside it, behaves.

Become a physicist yourself as you flip through these pages and discover mind-bending, fascinating facts about the world around you.

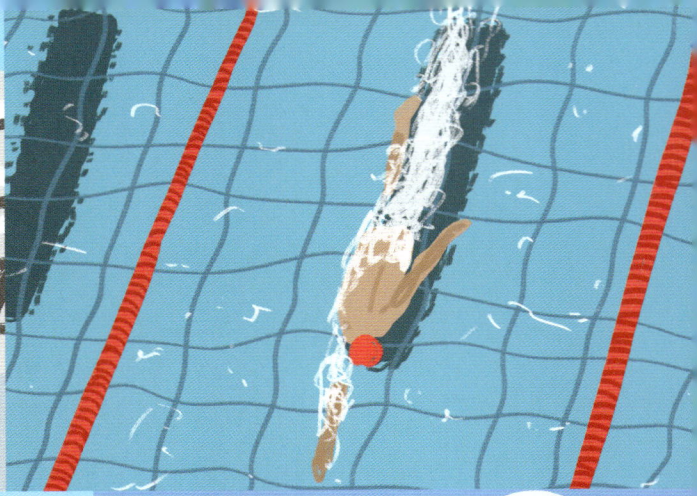

CHAPTER 12

DYNAMICS: FEELING FORCE AND MOTION

Forces are some of the fundamentals of physics. From the pull of gravity to the push of pressure, from floating to sinking, physics is there.

Dynamics is the study of the motion that occurs due to forces—the action that happens thanks to forces in our Universe. In this chapter, we'll look at forces including gravity, pressure, friction, resistance, buoyancy, and magnetism. Discover how a parachute works, why race cars are faster than heavy trucks, and what force holds our Universe together. Get ready for an action-packed ride!

FEEL THE FORCE

Forces allow us to go about life in the way we know it. They help us stay on the ground, walk along that same ground, and drive in cars, ice skate, or even fly, too. Without forces, life would be very different!

WHAT IS A FORCE?

Simply put, a force is a push or pull that can change the speed, direction, or shape of something. Some forces work when objects touch each other, such as bicycle wheels on the pavement. Other forces work when objects aren't touching at all. Have you ever seen a magnet pick up a paperclip from a table, pulling it through the air? That's a force at work!

FINDING BALANCE

Some forces are working all the time. Gravity, for example, is always pulling objects—and you!—toward Earth. Other forces happen with a little more effort. Things get especially exciting when forces become unbalanced. Take a look at the game of tug of war. Both teams try to pull the other over the middle line. If the pull forces are the same coming from each side, nobody moves. But if one team pulls harder than the other, we have a winner!

NEWTON'S LAWS OF MOTION

Sir Isaac Newton was a famous physicist born in 1642. He formulated three simple laws that explain how forces can make things move. These are called the **laws of motion**, and they can be used to explain everything from the actions of tiny atoms to super-sized spacecraft.

1. An object that isn't being pushed or pulled will stay in the same state of motion that it's in. This means that if an object isn't moving, it will continue to stay still. If it's in motion, it will continue to move at the same speed and in the same direction until a force changes that motion. For example, if you started gliding across a smooth ice rink, you would keep on going until you crashed into something to stop you!

2. The acceleration or deceleration of an object depends on the force acting on it, and the object's mass. Acceleration means speeding up, and **deceleration** means slowing down. Each of these happens quicker with lighter objects (objects with less **mass**). Race cars are much lighter than big heavy trucks, and so they can accelerate much quicker. This law also says that a bigger force will create faster acceleration or deceleration. The harder you push on something, the quicker it moves!

3. Every action has an equal and opposite reaction. Forces always work in pairs. If one object pushes on another, the second object pushes back with the same force. Rockets blast off using this principle. The **thrust** of the explosion within the rocket pushes down on the ground, which pushes back on the rocket with equal force—enough to launch it into space!

GROUNDED BY GRAVITY

Gravity keeps us grounded—literally. Without it, we would float away! Our homes, our pets, falling leaves . . . all would float out to space without this special invisible force pulling them down. Space itself would look very different without gravity keeping the Solar System intact.

MASSIVE DISCOVERY

Gravity was explained by Sir Isaac Newton in the late 1600s. It is a force you can find anywhere—the **force** that pulls objects with **mass** or energy toward each other. This force is stronger the closer objects are to each other. On top of that, the greater the mass of an object, the greater the **gravitational pull** it has. For example, Earth is so massive that it pulls all objects toward it, holding you down on the ground. The Earth is also pulled toward you, but only by the tiniest amount.

WORKING AGAINST GRAVITY

Objects speed up as they fall toward the Earth. But you may have noticed that not all objects fall in the same way. A rock seems to drop straight down, while a feather floats and flits back and forth before resting gently on the ground. **Air** works against gravity, pushing back on a moving object. The greater the surface area, the greater the force of air resistance. A parachute can slow down a skydiver due to air resistance. The parachute's curved design also traps air inside it, using air pressure to slow down the skydiver to a safe landing.

GRAVITY

AIR RESISTAN

SECURED IN SPACE

Gravity exists everywhere. Not limited to Earth, this powerful force can even be found in space. The Earth exerts gravity on the Moon, keeping it in **orbit** around our planet. The Moon exerts its own force back on Earth, pulling our oceans toward it and affecting the **tides**. Beyond that, the Sun pulls all the planets in the Solar System toward it using its gravity. Gravity holds our Universe together.

OUT OF THIS WORLD!

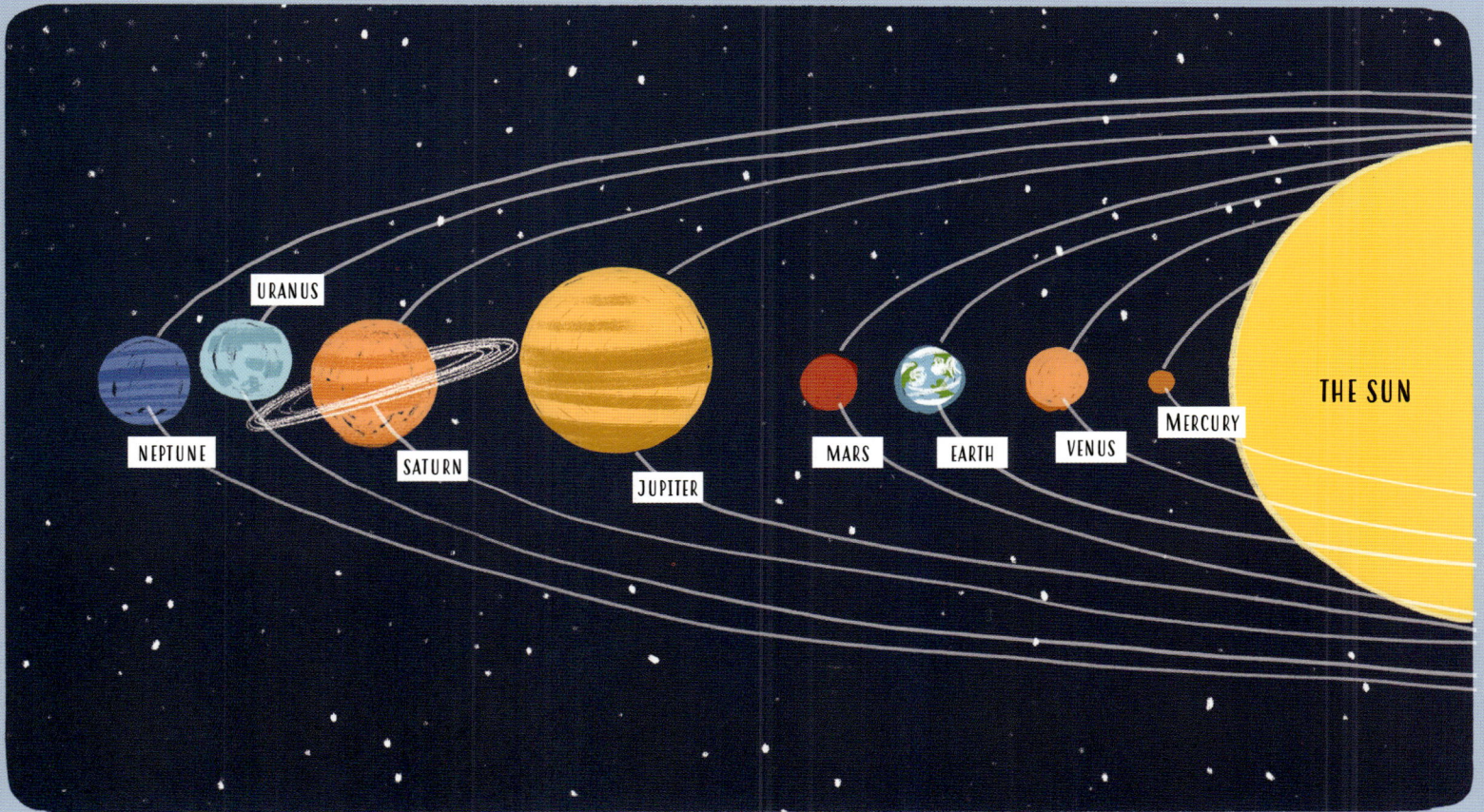

NEPTUNE   URANUS   SATURN   JUPITER   MARS   EARTH   VENUS   MERCURY   THE SUN

OUT OF CURIOSITY

Astronauts grow taller in space! This is because on Earth, the force of gravity pulls the bones in the spine downward and together. In space, low gravity allows these bones to spread out—making the astronaut up to 3% taller.

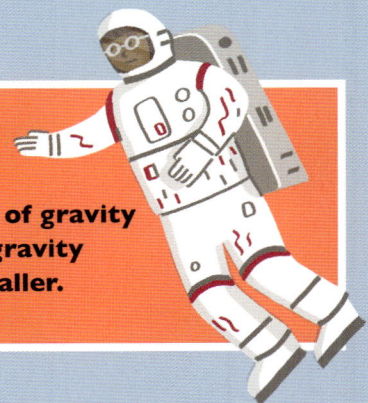

UNDER PRESSURE

We do not exist in empty space. Even while we stand still on Earth, various forces are at work on us. Gravity pulls us down to the ground, while the ground pushes back up on us. Air presses in from all directions, while our bodies push back on the air. Sometimes we don't notice, and sometimes we feel the pressure!

WHAT IS PRESSURE?

Pressure is the amount of pushing force acting over an area. A force can be strong or weak, spread out or working on a small space. Pressure helps us measure this. If you push strongly on a small area, you create high pressure. But if you push lightly with your hands spread out over a bigger area, the pressure will be weak. You can use this knowledge to your advantage—if you concentrate your force into a small space, you can suddenly feel much more powerful than if your pressure is spread out!

NO PRESSURE!

Take a balloon as an example. It is hard to burst a balloon by pushing on it with your finger. This is because the pressure is spread out across your fingertip, and it is not strong enough to pierce the balloon. However, what happens if you poke the balloon with a pin? Suddenly the pressure is much greater, because it is concentrated in one tiny area on the tip of the pin. The pin easily pierces the balloon's rubber, the gas bursts out, and … pop!

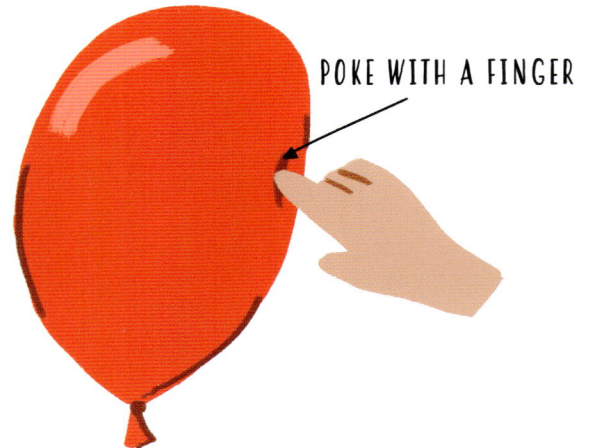

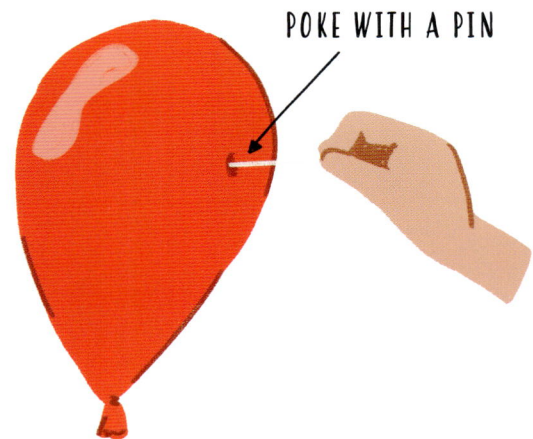

POKE WITH A FINGER

POKE WITH A PIN

POP!

WEIGHT ON YOUR SHOULDERS

We might not think of air as having any weight, but in fact gravity makes each air molecule weigh something. In big quantities, air can create pressure. The **atmosphere** is a big blanket of air wrapped around the Earth. It presses down on the surface and creates **air pressure**. Air pressure high up in the atmosphere is weak, since the atmosphere is thin. But closer to the ground, the air is thick, the weight of the air above presses down, and air pressure is high.

The same principle applies to water. **Water pressure** is the force of water's weight pressing down on you. Near the surface, water pressure is weak. But as you venture farther into the deep sea, the water pressure increases. This is because the weight of the water increases, with the water above pressing down. Deep-sea divers wear special suits and air tanks so that they can swim in these high-pressure conditions.

MEASURE THE PRESSURE

Air pressure changes with the weather. Scientists use a **barometer** to measure air pressure and predict the weather. If the air pressure is high, you can expect clear skies and cooler temperatures. But if the air pressure is low, there may be warmer weather and storms! Air molecules tend to move from high pressure to low pressure areas, so if there is a difference in pressure, forecasters would predict windy times ahead.

187

FIGHTING FRICTION

If you've ever tried running across an ice rink, you'll know how important the force of friction is. Without it, things—and people—would slip and slide all over the place!

WHAT IS FRICTION?

Friction is a force of **resistance** that slows things down. It works in the opposite direction to motion and happens when one object rubs against another.

The resistance depends on how smooth the surfaces are. Smooth surfaces create less friction, which means that things can slide over them easily. Ice skates glide across smooth ice, and skis slide easily over slippery snow. However, rough surfaces can create a lot of friction. It feels nearly impossible to push a sofa across a carpet, because the sofa is heavy and the carpet is rough!

SMOOTH RIDE

To get around the force of friction, objects can be designed to be as frictionless as possible. Skis slide on snow because they are smooth, light, and flat. This careful design means that there is very little resistance between the skis and the snow, and skiers can rush down hills with ease.

GET A GRIP

On the other hand, some objects are designed to work against friction and provide grip. Your shoes have bumpy treads that help you grip the surface you're walking on, so you don't slip everywhere. A bicycle is full of clever friction hacks for a smooth ride.

The bike chain is **lubricated** with oil. Lubricants are slippery materials that can reduce friction. Oil helps the bicycle chain move smoothly.

The handles, pedals, and seat have textured, bumpy surfaces to stop your hands, feet, and bottom from sliding off.

The bike's wheels are narrow so only a small surface area is in contact with the road. This reduces friction so the bike can keep moving.

WHEELS MOVE ACROSS THE GROUND

FRICTION WITH THE GROUND SLOWS THE WHEELS DOWN

Brake pads grip the wheel when you want to stop. Friction with the brake pads slows the wheels down.

HEATING UP

Friction can also create **heat**. If you rub your hands together, you'll notice them heating up. This is the same as car wheels spinning on the road. The smell of burning rubber comes from wheels spinning so quickly against the road that they overheat.

THE POWER OF RESISTANCE

Some forces, such as gravity, aren't very noticeable as you go about your daily activities. But others make some activities a real challenge! Air and water resistance create a force called **drag**, which can significantly slow you down.

✳ WHAT IS RESISTANCE?

Resistance comes from friction, the force that pushes back on objects in motion and slows them down. The faster the object, the greater the resistance.

✳ AIR RESISTANCE

Air resistance is a type of friction that occurs between an object and the air. You can experience air resistance working on you as you cycle fast and feel the air on your face. Cars, bicycles, and planes are designed to be **aerodynamic**—with a **streamlined** shape that reduces drag from the air moving past. The long, rounded shape of a plane means that air that comes into contact with the plane is quickly directed around and away. Thin, pointy objects experience less air resistance than those with wider, flatter surfaces.

?

OUT OF CURIOSITY

Even though cars are designed to be as streamlined as possible, over half of a car's fuel is used to overcome the force of drag.

✳ WATER RESISTANCE

Water resistance is a type of friction that occurs between an object and the water. In this case, it's water that slows down a moving object. Just like air resistance, the resistance of water is greater the faster an object is moving and the wider it is. And just like our aerodynamic cars and planes, many sea creatures have streamlined bodies that help them swim swiftly through the sea. The ocean's top predator, the great white shark, has a torpedo-shaped body to power through water and catch its prey!

When you go swimming, there is friction between your skin and the water particles. You need to work hard to overcome the water resistance and pull yourself through the water. You tuck your head in and stretch out your hands and arms, reducing the points where water can push back on you to slow you down. And you're off!

REDUCING RESISTANCE

BEING BUOYANT

When an object is in water, there are many different forces working on it.
We know that water resistance pushes back on the object when it tries to move.
But what about floating and sinking? How do objects sink or stay afloat?

SINK OR SWIM?

WHAT IS BUOYANCY?

Buoyancy is the ability of something to float in water or another liquid. An object that floats is said to be **buoyant**. When you try to swim down to the bottom of the deep end of a pool, you can feel a buoyant force trying to push you back up.

UPTHRUST

WEIGHT

STAYING AFLOAT

Every object in water has two forces acting on it. **Weight**—which is to say, the object's own weight—pulls it down. **Upthrust** is the force of the water pushing up on it. If these forces are equal, the object will be **suspended**. The object will **float**, and rise up to the surface, if the upthrust is greater than the weight. This is why a feather or a light stick can be seen floating above water on a lake.

?

OUT OF CURIOSITY

Our bodies become buoyant in the Dead Sea. This lake is so full of salt that the water is denser than normal. This makes your weight less than the upthrust, and you float!

BREAKING THE BALANCE

However, if the weight is greater than the upthrust, the object will **sink**. For example, a heavy anchor plunges straight down to the bottom of the lake and can hold a floating boat in place.

KETTLE OF FISH

Fish and other sea creatures have cleverly evolved to suit their underwater world. They need to be able to overcome the competing forces of weight and upthrust to stay in the water without floating or sinking. Normally these forces are about equal on most fish, so they naturally stay between the surface and the sea floor. However, fish have another trick up their sleeves (or fins!). They have a swim bladder that holds oxygen. If the fish begins to sink deeper, the swim bladder absorbs more oxygen. And if the fish begins to float too high, oxygen is released.

OPPOSITES ATTRACT

Magnets are a fascinating phenomenon, both in nature and when created by humans. They can cause objects to come together, push apart, or even dance in the sky. Magnets are a mystery of the world that scientists have come to understand through physics.

MAGNETIC FORCE

Magnetism is a force between two metallic objects. It is created by electric charge and can cause objects to **attract** (pull together) or **repel** (push apart). Each magnet has two **poles**: north and south. When two like poles are close together (such as north and north or south and south), the magnets repel. When two opposite poles are close together (north and south or south and north), the magnets attract.

ATTRACTION

REPULSION

MAGNETIC MATERIALS

Not all materials are magnetic. In fact, only a select few are! First, to be magnetic they must be made of **metal**. And second, the metal must be able to hold a magnetic charge. Iron, steel, nickel, and cobalt are magnetic metals. Metals such as silver and gold have no magnetic force.

Some metals are always magnetic—these are called **hard, permanent** magnets. The magnets on your fridge are a good example of this! Other metals become magnetic when a magnet is near them, but don't have magnetism on their own. These are **soft and temporary** magnetic materials.

OUR MAGNETIC WORLD

Magnets play an important part in our world. In fact, some can even help care for the planet, such as in a recycling plant. By using a huge magnetic crane, we can separate and pull out magnetic metals—ready for recycling. This saves them from going to a landfill. Magnets are also used for sophisticated, speedy trains—the futuristic maglev train uses magnetism to repel and levitate (hover) above its tracks.

Beyond that, Earth itself is a giant magnet! This is because of the movement of molten iron in the planet's core. This creates a **magnetic field** of invisible force between Earth's two poles. This field can attract magnetically charged particles from the Sun, which burn up as they enter the atmosphere. The resulting light show is called the aurora borealis, or the Northern Lights.

OUT OF CURIOSITY

If you stand at Earth's North Pole, the north end of a compass wants to point downward (instead of forward). And if you stand at the South Pole, the south end points down!

CHAPTER 13

ENERGETICS & ELECTRONICS: EVERYTHING ENERGY & ELECTRICITY

Energy lights up our world. Not only that—it makes things happen! Everything that moves uses energy, from plants growing to people dancing to cars racing. Energy can be used or changed, transferred or stored. Energy includes heat, light, electricity, and more. Energy really is everywhere!

Energetics is the study of energy—how it behaves, transfers, and changes. In this chapter, we'll look at where energy comes from, how it can be used, types of energy, and how we power our world. We'll also take a look at **electronics**, and how energy can travel through circuits. Be prepared to be **energized** as you make your way through these pages.

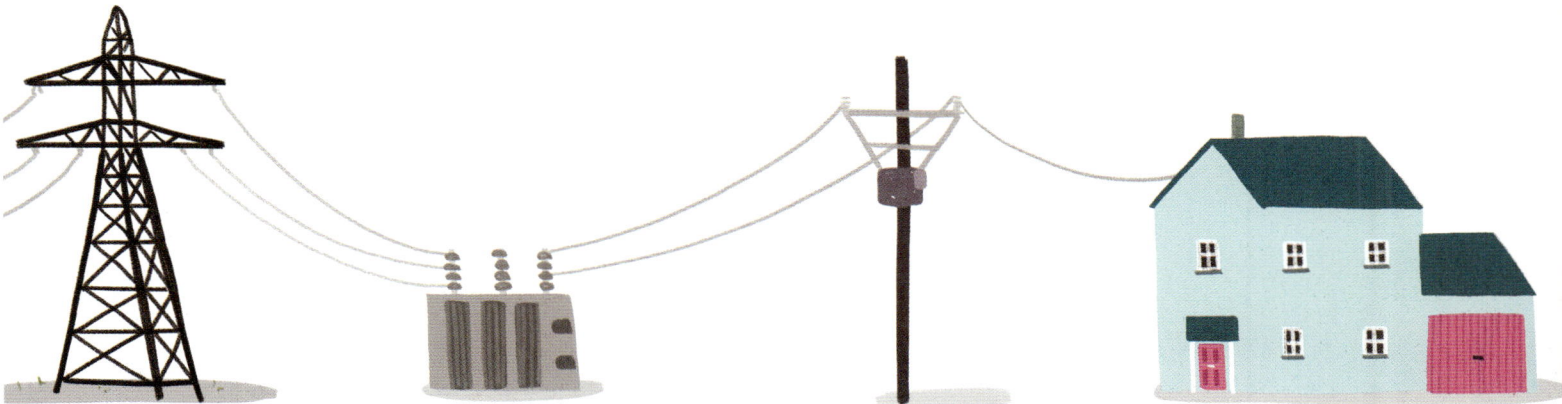

ENERGIZING OUR WORLD

Energy powers people, plants, cars, homes, and so much more.
Without it, our world would be cold, dark . . . and lifeless.

WHAT IS ENERGY?

Energy makes things happen. It helps anything in the Universe perform an action, from moving to glowing to heating up. It comes in many forms.

Heat energy makes things warm up. Energy from something hot moves to something cold. For example, as a fire burns, heat and light are released and transferred to people sitting nearby.

Light energy comes from glowing objects. It moves in a straight line and bounces off objects into our eyes.

Sound energy is produced by vibrations, which travel through the air to our ears.

Electrical energy comes from charged particles building up and moving together. The current of charge flows through wires to bring power to objects. It can also cause lightning!

POWERING THE PLANET

The **sun** provides a huge amount of energy to our planet. It transfers both light and heat, which help us see and stay warm.

The sun is made of mainly hydrogen atoms. It is so hot that these atoms lose their electrons, leaving only the nucleus of protons. These nuclei join together and make helium atoms. As the atoms fuse and create a heavier nucleus, energy is released. This process is called **nuclear fusion**, and it releases a whole lot of energy!

HOW DOES IT WORK?

Scientists believe that all energy in our Universe began with the **Big Bang** 13.8 billion years ago. Energy today is not created or destroyed. Instead, it can be transferred from one object to another. For example, energy from the sun is transferred to plants, which use it as food to help them grow. Animals might then eat the plants, and the energy is transferred to them. Energy can also be stored for later use, such as in a battery.

$E=mc^2$

Albert Einstein, born in 1879, is one of the most well-known scientists of the 20th century. His **equation**, $E=mc^2$, might be even more famous than he is! Einstein showed that matter and energy are the same thing. Matter is made up of particles that are essentially just energy, such as protons and electrons. His formula shows that the energy (E) emitted by matter can be determined by the amount of matter in kilograms (m) multiplied by the speed of light squared (c^2)—a very huge number! In simpler terms, this means that a small amount of matter can release a huge amount of energy, such as huge blasts created by an atomic bomb.

LYING IN STORE

You can think of energy a little bit like money. You can save your money, keeping it safe to spend later. Or you can spend it right away and make something happen. Energy works in a similar way. It can be saved with the potential to be used later, or it can be used straight away. Let's have a look at some more types of energy.

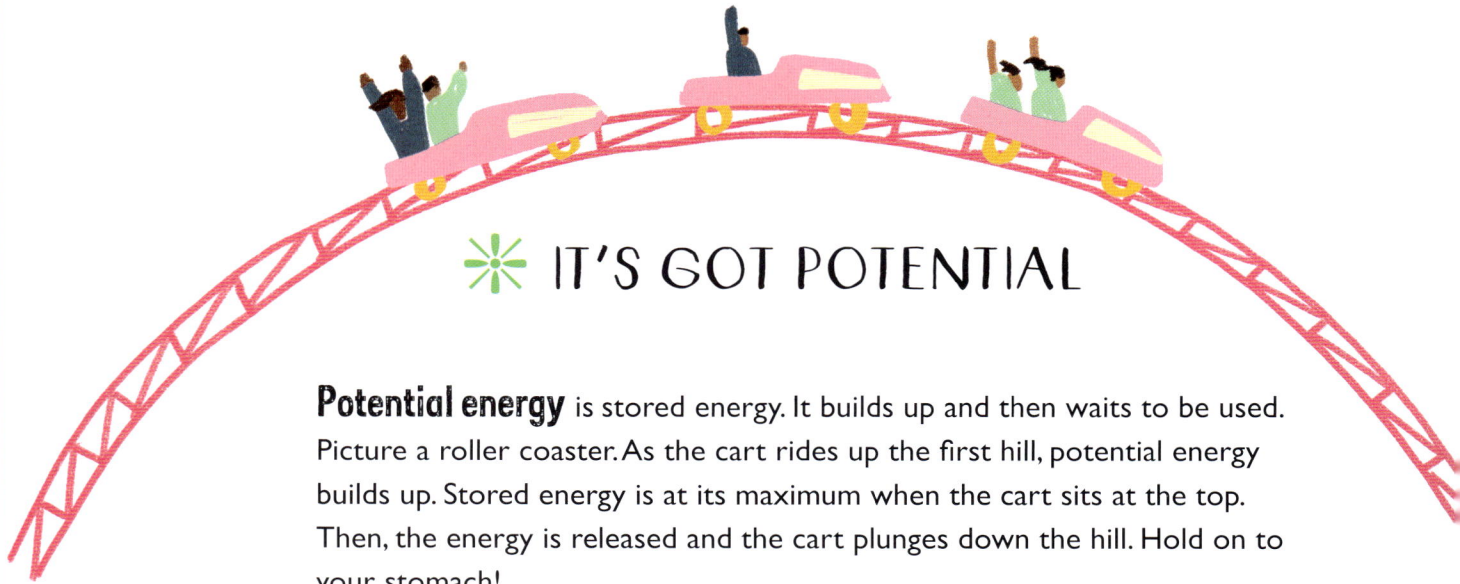

✳ IT'S GOT POTENTIAL

Potential energy is stored energy. It builds up and then waits to be used. Picture a roller coaster. As the cart rides up the first hill, potential energy builds up. Stored energy is at its maximum when the cart sits at the top. Then, the energy is released and the cart plunges down the hill. Hold on to your stomach!

✳ ELASTIC POTENTIAL ENERGY

When you push down on a spring, or pull on elastic, you have **elastic potential energy**. It is stored in a material that is squashed or stretched. The more the material is stretched or squashed, the more stored energy it has. Once the material has been pushed or pulled, energy is stored, ready to take the object back to its original position as soon as you let go.

✳ GRAVITATIONAL POTENTIAL ENERGY

All objects have **gravitational potential energy**, as the force of gravity pulls them toward Earth. The higher (and heavier) the object, the more gravitational potential energy it has. When you lift a ball above your head, you give it gravitational potential energy. As soon as you let go, this energy is released, and the ball falls to the ground (or on your head!).

✳ ON THE MOVE

Potential energy is often converted into **kinetic energy**. This is the energy of a moving object. The faster the object is moving, the more kinetic energy it has. When the car at the top of the roller coaster begins to roll down the hill, the potential energy turns into kinetic energy. Combined with gravity, this energy makes the car speed up. Anything in the Universe that moves has kinetic energy. A cheetah changes potential energy stored in its muscles into kinetic energy when it runs, speeding across the ground.

✳ BREAKING BONDS

Chemical energy is stored in all substances, in the bonds that hold atoms together in their molecules. When there is a chemical reaction and the bonds are broken, the energy is released. Fuel and food (or **biomass**) have plenty of chemical energy. When we eat, our bodies break down the bonds in chemicals in the food, and energy is released and transferred to us.

FEEL THE HEAT

Heat is a type of energy we come across—and feel—in our daily lives.
We might use a fire to heat up, or enjoy the warmth of the sunshine
on our skin. At other times, we might want to cool down!

WHAT IS HEAT?

Heat energy comes from the movement of atoms and molecules. The faster they move, the hotter the substance is. Cold objects contain molecules that are moving slowly and have very little heat energy. If the molecules could slow down completely, and come to a stop, they would reach a temperature called absolute zero.

HOT TO COLD

Heat energy always tries to move from something hot to something cold. It does this in three ways.

Conduction requires the movement of **electrons** between atoms. **Metals** are good conductors. Heat travels directly through them, spreading out from hot to cold. If your hand is colder than a hot pot, the heat travels from the pot to you when you touch it. Ouch!

Convection involves the movement of **atoms** or **molecules**. It happens in **liquids** and **gases**. As a liquid or gas heats up, the hot gas or liquid rises while cold gas or liquid sinks down to take its place. As water boils in the pot, steam and hot water rise to the top, and cold water takes their place below.

🔥 RISING UP

Soaring in the skies above, with only a basket, a burner, and an envelope full of air, a hot air balloon rises thanks to heat energy. Fire from a gas burner heats up the air inside the balloon. The hot air is trapped within the curved fabric. As the air heats up, the molecules move faster and spread out, filling the balloon. Due to **convection,** the hot air rises, pushing the balloon upward. The hot air inside the balloon is less dense than the cold air outside the balloon, so it continues to rise in the sky. As the balloon floats along, the air begins to cool, and the balloon dips down. A pilot gives a brief burst of flame from the burner to warm up the air again, and the balloon rises once more.

? OUT OF CURIOSITY

In 1783, the hot air balloon was the first technology that successfully allowed people to fly! The very first balloon flight, just months before, carried a chicken, a sheep, and a duck into the sky.

Radiation is the movement of energy as **waves**. It doesn't require any particles at all. Heat travels through air and space by invisible rays. Hot objects give off this **infrared radiation**, and this is how we feel heat. The rays from the sun or the heat from a fire **radiate** outward and warm us up.

IT'S ELECTRIC

Hundreds of years ago, instead of flicking a switch to turn on a light, people lit candles. Instead of turning on the heat, they built fire. The discovery of how to harness electricity changed our world.

WHAT IS ELECTRICITY?

Electricity is a type of energy. It can flow from place to place, or build up in one area. It is created by the tiny electrons that carry a negative electric charge. As these electrons whiz around atoms, they can jump from one atom to another. When trillions of electrons move in the same direction, they create an **electric current**.

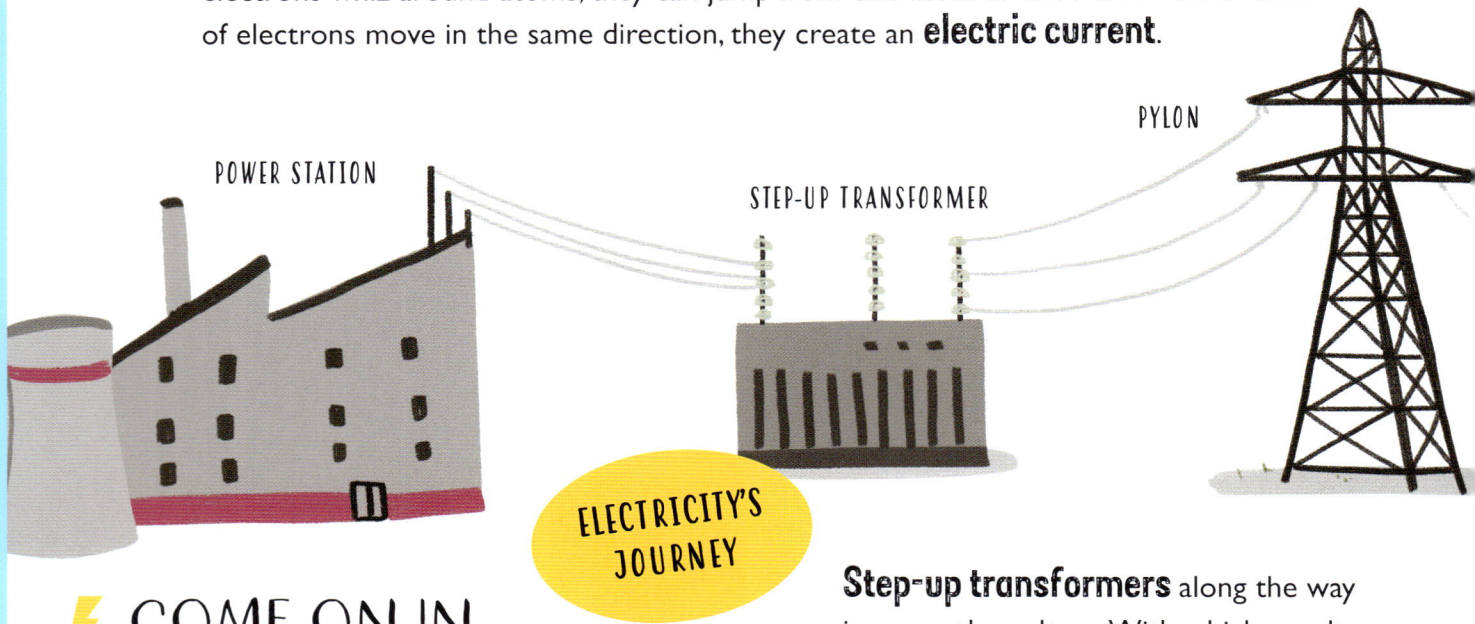

POWER STATION

STEP-UP TRANSFORMER

PYLON

ELECTRICITY'S JOURNEY

COME ON IN

Electricity exists in nature, but it's when it's **harnessed** and converted into power that it really becomes useful for us. **Generators** at power stations can capture energy from **fossil fuels**, sunlight, wind, and water and turn it into electrical energy.

Electricity travels from **power stations** to our homes through **cables**. Cables can run overground, held up by **pylons**, and underground, into buildings. These power lines take electricity all the way to the plug sockets where you plug in lamps, phone chargers, televisions, and more.

Step-up transformers along the way increase the voltage. With a higher voltage, there is lower current, and less energy is wasted as heat.

Step-down transformers reduce the voltage so it can enter your house safely.

ELECTRIC CURRENT

Electric current travels from place to place. It is the type of electricity that comes out of sockets. It can also come from **batteries**. Batteries use chemicals to produce electricity. The energy from the battery becomes the flow of electric curren

⚡ STATIC ELECTRICITY

Another kind of electricity is static electricity. This is when electricity builds up in one place. When two objects of certain materials rub together, the charged particles can move from one to the other. One object gains electrons and becomes negatively charged, leaving the other object positively charged.

When you rub a balloon on your head, the electrons from your hair move to the balloon. The balloon becomes negatively charged, and your hair becomes positively charged. When you lift the balloon higher above your head, your hair follows and sticks to it—its positive charge is attracted to the balloon's negative charge!

STANDING ON END

STEP-DOWN TRANSFORMER

POWER LINES

HOUSE

⚡ FLASH!

Lightning comes from static electricity. Ice particles in a cloud rub together and build up an electric charge. When this charge becomes too big, it jumps out to other clouds or to Earth as a flash of lightning.

?

OUT OF CURIOSITY

Lightning is so powerful that it produces heat, light, and sound. It comes with a crash of thunder, and it can be five times hotter than the surface of the Sun!

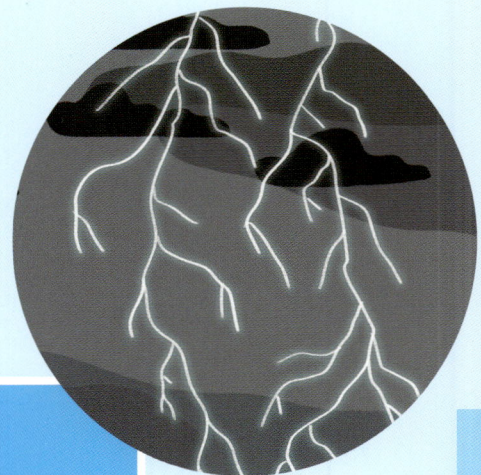

CIRCUITS OF POWER

Electricity is a lot like water. It flows along paths and likes to take the simplest route. And just as water flows through pipes, electricity flows through cables and wires.

WHAT IS A CIRCUIT?

A **circuit** is a loop that electricity flows through. If the loop is complete, the electricity can move. If the loop is broken, the electricity stops. The stream of electricity moves around as a **current**.

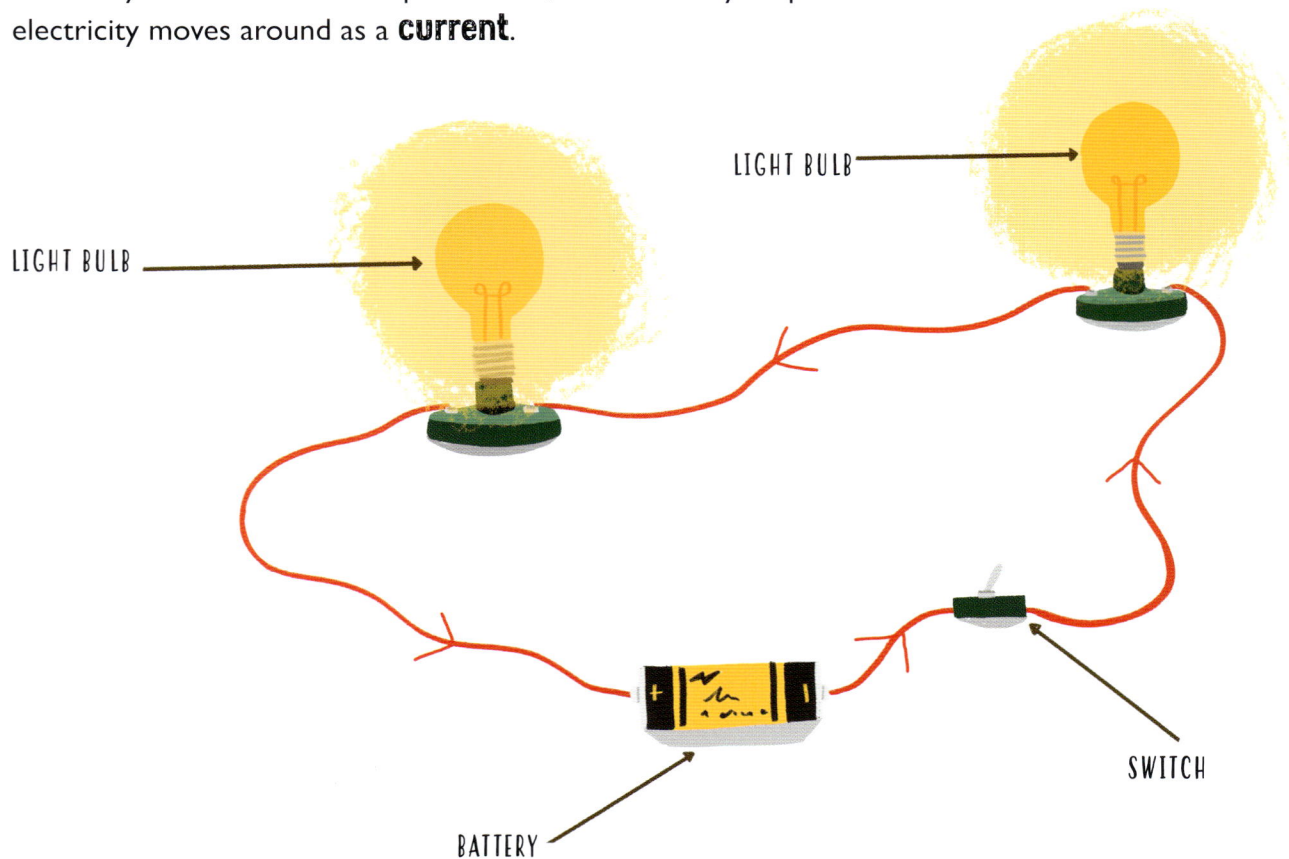

LIGHT BULB

LIGHT BULB

SWITCH

BATTERY

Every circuit needs a **power source**, such as a battery, with positive and negative ends. **Wires** connect the power source to the electrical components you'd like to power, such as a light bulb, and back again to complete the circuit. Electricity is carried along the wires by electrons and flows from negative to positive.

A **switch** turns the circuit on or off. When the switch is open, it creates a gap in the circuit, and the electricity stops. When the switch is closed, the circuit is complete and electricity can flow.

Light bulbs in the circuit above light up when the current of electricity reaches them. They change the electric energy into heat and light.

WILL IT FLOW?

Electricity passes through some materials much easier than others. **Conductors** are materials that allow electricity to pass through them easily, such as metal. Many wires are made of the metal copper. **Insulators** do not allow electricity to pass through them easily, such as plastic or fabric. Wires are coated in plastic **insulation** so that the electricity is trapped inside—and doesn't reach you directly!

SERIES CIRCUIT

A simple circuit with just one loop is called a **series circuit**. In this type of circuit, everything is connected to the same path. If you add an extra light bulb in a series circuit, the lights will dim, as the energy flowing through is shared between them. And if you add an extra power source, such as another battery, more power is produced to brighten the lights!

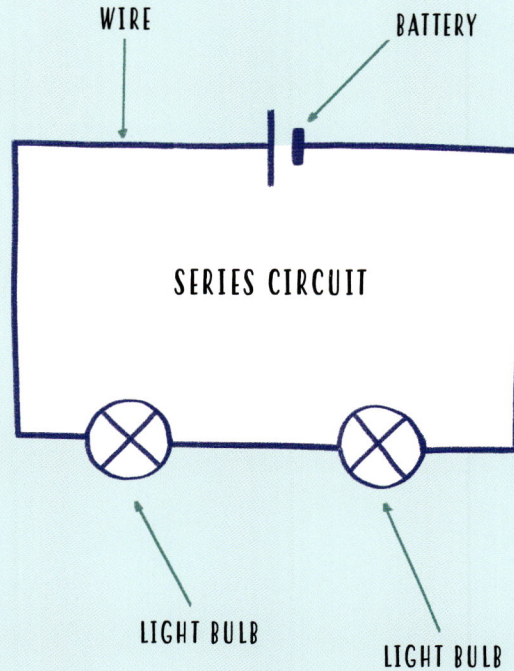

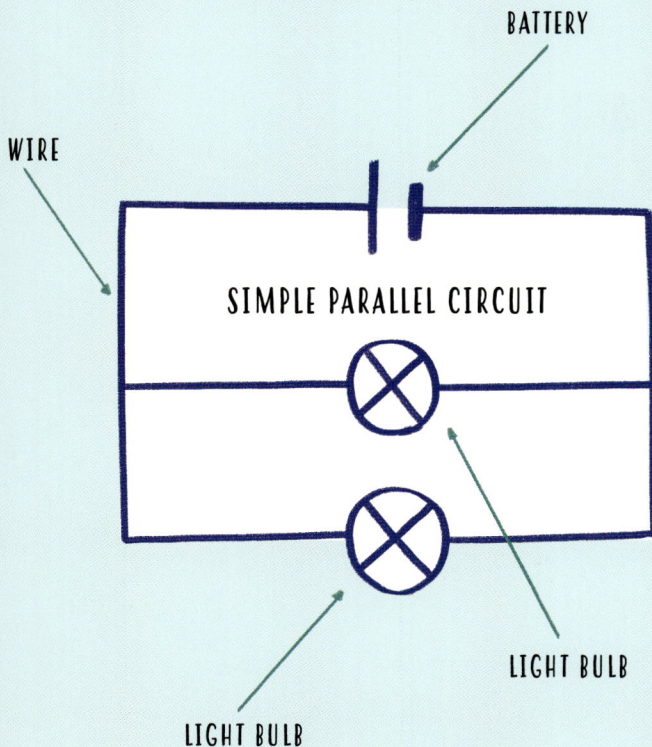

WIRE   BATTERY

SERIES CIRCUIT

LIGHT BULB

LIGHT BULB

BATTERY

WIRE

SIMPLE PARALLEL CIRCUIT

LIGHT BULB

LIGHT BULB

PARALLEL CIRCUIT

In a **parallel circuit**, energy flows along different paths, in **parallel**. Different components are connected on different wires. In this type of circuit, each light bulb receives the full power from the battery source. If one path is broken, energy will continue to flow along the other, so only the light on the broken path will go out. A battery power source will only last half as long as in a series circuit because it is putting out twice as much power to keep two lights glowing brightly.

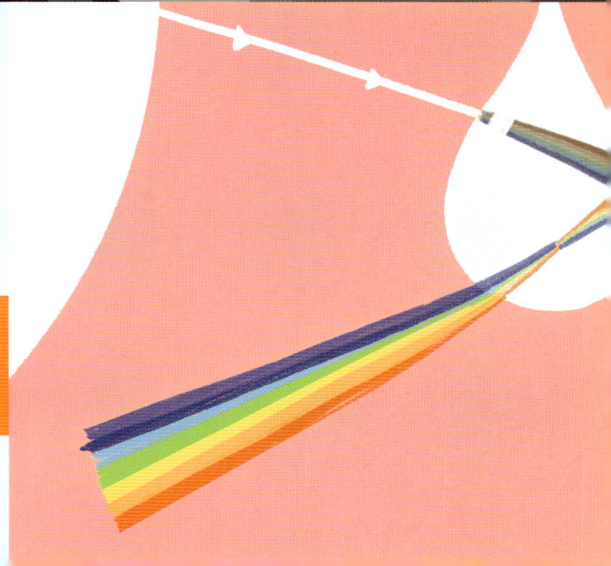

CHAPTER 14

OPTICS & ACOUSTICS: LIGHTWAVES & SOUNDWAVES

Optics is the study of light and sight—what light is made of, how it behaves, and how we can see. In this chapter we'll shed a light on the electromagnetic spectrum, waves, the speed of light (hint: it's the fastest thing in the Universe!), the ways of light, color, and rainbows.

Acoustics is the study of sound and its properties. How can a sound be loud or quiet? High or low? How fast is sound? How do echoes work? And what about sounds that are out of range of our hearing? Listen closely to the world around you as you make your way through this noisy chapter.

WAVES OF ENERGY

Before we can understand how light works, we need to know how it fits into the greater spectrum of our world.

ALONG THE SPECTRUM

The **electromagnetic spectrum** is a range of types of radiation. **Electromagnetic radiation** is tiny packets of energy, called photons, that travel in a wave-like pattern. Light and sound are good examples of this.

All waves have a **wavelength**—the distance from one peak to the next. When energy travels in waves, the wavelength can vary. The shorter the wavelength, the more energy it has. As you go along the electromagnetic spectrum, the wavelength decreases from long to short, and the energy increases.

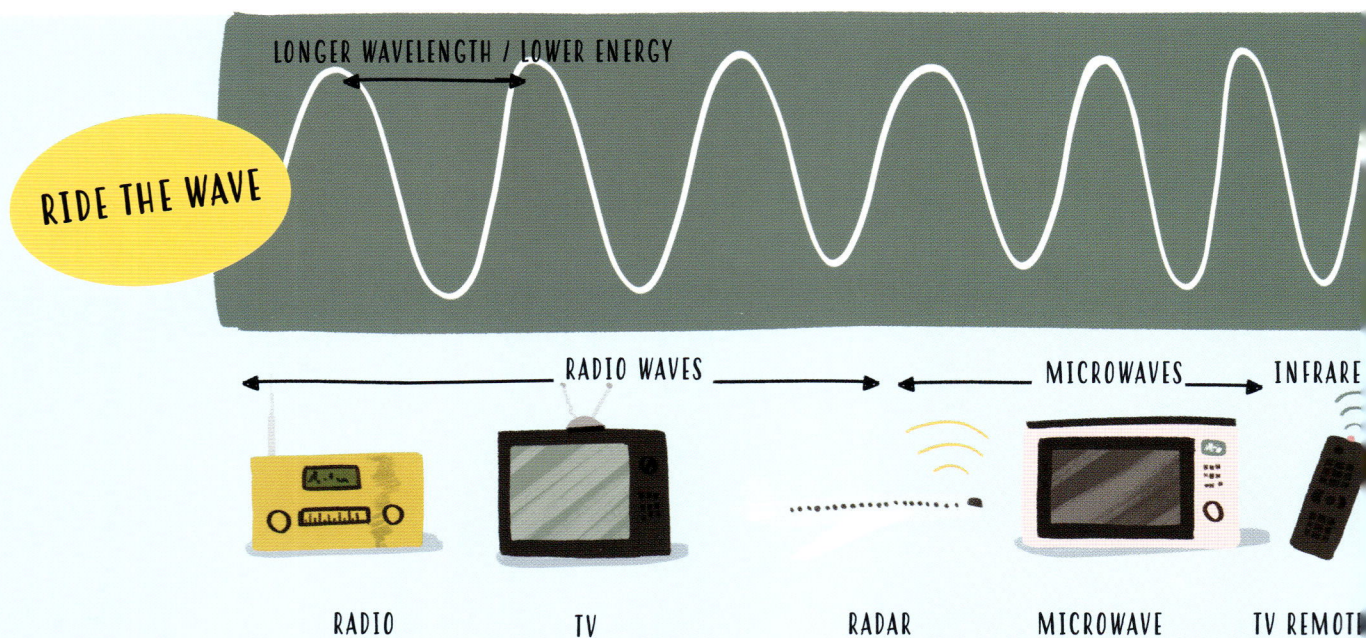

LONGER WAVELENGTH / LOWER ENERGY

RIDE THE WAVE

RADIO WAVES   MICROWAVES   INFRARE

RADIO   TV   RADAR   MICROWAVE   TV REMOTE

Radio waves have the longest wavelength —around 0.6 mi (1 km). They are emitted from stars and gas in space. You also know them in your own home. They travel long distances and bring sound to the radios in our homes and cars, as well as pictures to TV. They allow us to communicate.

Microwaves have a shorter wavelength than radio waves. They are also used for communication, such as by satellites and telephones. You'll also recognize them as the waves used in your microwave oven, although microwave ovens use a shorter wavelength than cell phones. Microwaves have enough energy to heat or defrost food.

Infrared: Infrared radiation is radiating heat. If you use special goggles or cameras at night, you can see an image that shows the varying intensity of infrared radiation coming from an object, detected by heat. These waves are used by remote controls, to send signals to a device such as a TV.

Visible light: This small section of the electromagnetic spectrum is the light that we see. It has its own spectrum, ranging from red light to orange to yellow to green to blue to indigo and to violet. Lightbulbs, screens, stars, and even fireflies **emit** light that our eyes can detect.

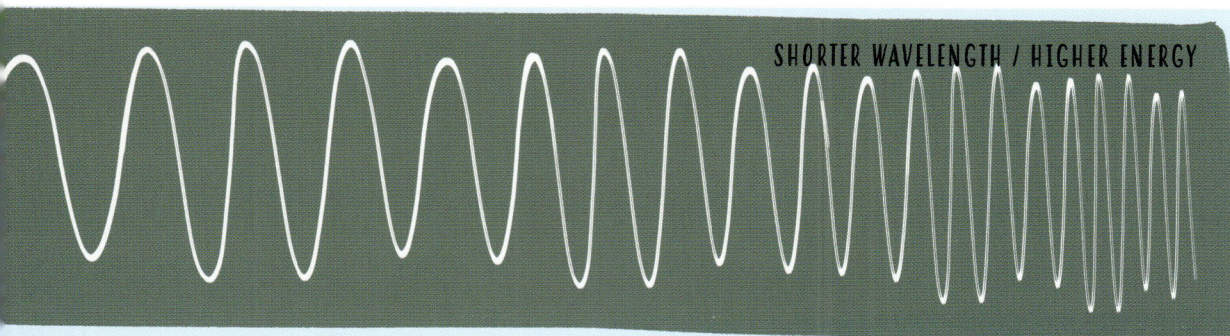

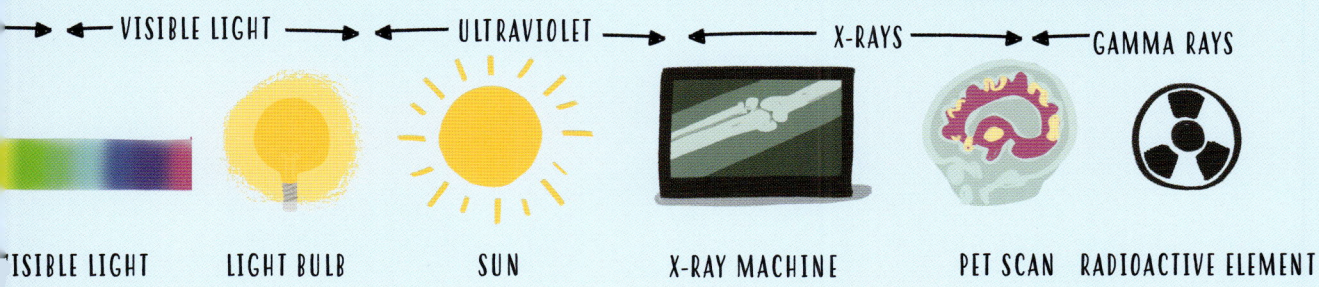

SHORTER WAVELENGTH / HIGHER ENERGY

← VISIBLE LIGHT → ← ULTRAVIOLET → ← X-RAYS → ← GAMMA RAYS

VISIBLE LIGHT   LIGHT BULB   SUN   X-RAY MACHINE   PET SCAN   RADIOACTIVE ELEMENT

Ultraviolet radiation is emitted by the sun—it is what can burn us! Other objects in space can also emit these waves. Some animals, such as bees, can see ultraviolet light.

X-rays can pass through many materials that light can't. They are used by dentists to take pictures of your teeth, and by scanners at the airport to check inside bags.

Gamma rays have the most energy of all. They are produced when the nuclei of radioactive materials break down. They can be used in medicine, such as to kill cancerous cells in the body.

✳ THE WAYS OF LIGHT ✳

We know that light travels in waves. We also know that these waves move as rays, in straight lines. Light only changes course if it can bounce off an object and scatter in new directions.

✳ LIGHT OR DARK

Objects look bright to us when they bounce light into our eyes. Shiny, smooth objects, such as a mirror, **reflect** most of the light they receive. Dark, solid objects **absorb** most of the light that reaches them, and so they look darker.

✳ MIRROR IMAGE

A mirror is so smooth and shiny that the light reflects with hardly any **distortion**. This means that the reflection of an image is very clear. A pond is another reflective surface, but the ripples of water cause the light to reflect in different directions and **scatter**. Your reflection in a pond will be much more distorted and wobbly than in a mirror because of the movement of the water's surface.

❋ REFLECTION

When light **reflects** off a smooth surface, it travels out at the same angle that it struck the object. The light ray shown here, for example, travels in a straight line until it hits the smooth, flat mirror. The ray bounces back and out at the same but opposite angle.

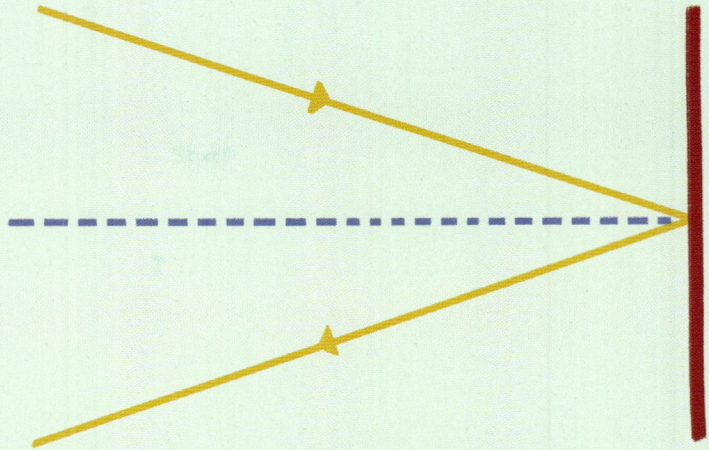

❋ REFRACTION

When light moves from one material to another, it can look as if the light bends. This is due to **refraction**. Just as you run slower through water than you do through the air, light travels at different speeds through different materials. Think about a straw or pencil in water. The top of the pencil, out of the water, looks normal. This is because light bounces off it and into our eyes as usual. But when the light reaches the pencil in the water, the light slows down, and the bottom of the pencil looks to be in a different place.

❋ JUST A MIRAGE

People wandering in the desert sometimes see a **mirage**. They think they see water where there isn't any! This is a trick that the light plays on their eyes. In the desert, there is a layer of very hot air just above the ground. This hot air refracts the Sun's rays, bending them back upward and creating a reflection of the sky on the sand. The brain assumes what it's seeing is water!

THE SPEED OF LIGHT

Light waves travel a million times faster through the air than sound waves. A flash of lightning reaches your eyes before the boom of thunder reaches your ears. You see the burst of fireworks before you hear the pop and sizzle. In fact, light is the fastest thing in the Universe.

TOP SPEED

If light moved only in a **vacuum**—empty space with nothing to slow it down—it would travel at nearly 300 million m/s (186,000 mi/s). This is the **speed of light**. How fast is that? It means that light rays from the Sun, which is about 150 million km (93 million miles) away from Earth, can reach us in just over eight minutes. Put another way, if you ran at the speed of light, you could run around Earth 7.5 times in just one second.

SPEEDY LIGHT

OUT OF CURIOSITY

Measuring things in space uses HUGE numbers. So scientists came up with using light as a measure of distance. One light year is the distance that light travels in one year. In these terms, the Sun is only 8 light-minutes away from us.

SPACE SHUTTLE

LIGHT

CAR

WHO WOULD WIN IN A RACE?

Spoiler alert—in a vacuum, light will always win! It is quicker than a race car, zippier than a rocket, and even faster than a speeding bullet. It travels 40,000 times faster than space shuttles, which reached speeds of 28,000 km/h (17,500 mph) to stay in orbit around Earth. It travels 10 MILLION times faster than a car on a highway.

IT'S ALL RELATIVE

RELATIVELY SPEAKING...

Because light travels so fast, it acts in strange and unusual ways. Albert Einstein published his **theories of relativity** in the early 1900s to help explain how light behaves. **Relativity** says that how things look depends on how you are moving relative to them. When you stand on Earth, light travels in an expected way and everything looks normal. But if you could travel nearly as fast as light, time would slow down. Beyond that, if you could travel faster than light (which you can't!), time should in theory go backward.

CREATING COLOR

Light isn't only about the bright glow that we see from the Sun.
It includes a full range of shades, which give color to our world.

WAVES OF COLOR

Visible light is part of the electromagnetic spectrum. It is made up of many colors, and each color has its own **wavelength**. Colors at the red end of the spectrum have a longer wavelength, and colors at the violet end have a shorter wavelength. The rest of the colors that we know fall somewhere in between.

INFRARED

ULTRAVIOLET

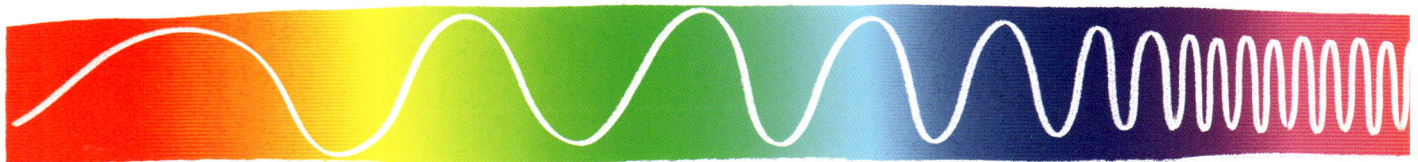

WHERE COLOR COMES FROM

We see color because of the way light is reflected off objects. A white object reflects all the light that hits it. The colored waves combine to form the white that we see. White light is all the colors mixed together. A black object, on the other hand, absorbs the light and doesn't reflect any colors. Meanwhile, a yellow object absorbs all colors apart from yellow, which it reflects back into our eyes. Some colors mix together to form different shades.

CHASE THE RAINBOW

The white light of the Sun is made of every color of the rainbow. When it hits droplets of rain, the waves bend—but not all in the same way. The light reflects off the back of the raindrop and bends again as it passes back out through the front, spreading the colors out into the sky. Blue and violet wavelengths are shorter, meaning these waves have more energy, and reflect at a shallower angle than the longer wavelength colors. As the colors all reflect at their own angle, we see a rainbow form in the sky.

SUN

WHITE LIGHT

RAINDROP

OUT OF CURIOSITY

The colors of a rainbow always appear in the same order (red, orange, yellow, green, blue, indigo, violet) because of their different wavelengths.

WHY IS THE SKY BLUE?

As the Sun's rays reach Earth's atmosphere, they hit gas and dust particles. These particles reflect and scatter the different shades of the light. The shades with short wavelengths and high energy, such as blue and violet, are scattered the most and reflected into our eyes. Our eyes are more sensitive to blue than to violet, so we see a blue sky. As the Sun sets in the sky, we can see shades from the other end of the spectrum, such as red, orange, and yellow, because the rays are going through even more particles of dust and air. The blue is scattered further, allowing the other shades to shine through.

Chapter 14

217

ᨒᨒᨒᨒ WAVES OF SOUND ᨒᨒᨒᨒ

If you shout in space, no one can hear you. But if you scream
on Earth, you'll wake your whole house! It's all down to how sound travels.

ᨒᨒᨒ WHAT IS SOUND?

Sound is energy that comes from **vibrations**—when things shake back and forth. When a
sound is made, the vibrating object makes the air around it vibrate. This is a **sound wave**.
The wave shows the pattern of changes in air pressure. Sound waves travel through the air
all the way into your ear and to the **eardrum**. The eardrum vibrates and sends a message to
your brain to **hear** the sound.

A sound wave showing
the pattern of changes
in air pressure

When a musician strums a guitar, the
strings vibrate. These vibrations cause
the air next to them to vibrate, and the
sound waves travel to your ears. Your
brain then recognizes these as music!

Sound waves lose energy as they travel,
and the sound gets quieter along the
way. Sometimes we can see the source
of the sound vibrating, such as the
guitar string quivering, but a lot of
the time we don't see the vibrations
at all. We only HEAR them.

ROCK ON!

MODE OF TRANSPORT

Sound waves need to travel through some sort of **medium**, with particles that they can cause to vibrate. They can travel through gases (such as air), liquids (such as water), and solids (such as wood or metal) . . . but not in a vacuum, where there is no matter at all, such as space. In space, there are no air particles, so there is nothing for the sound to vibrate or travel on.

SOUND

ECHO

ECHO, ECHO

Just like light, sound waves can be **reflected** or **absorbed**. If a sound wave hits a soft surface, such as a cushion, it will be absorbed and the sound will disappear. But if a sound wave hits a hard, smooth object, some of it will bounce back. This is an **echo**. The sound wave reflects off the surface and carries the sound back in the opposite direction, bringing a repeat of the sound to your ears, a few moments after the original occurred. If there is another hard surface, such as in a tunnel, the sound wave will reflect again. Echo, echo! Echoes can most easily be heard where there are lots of hard surfaces, such as in caves and mountains.

VARYING VOLUME

There is a whole range of sound, from so quiet you can barely hear it to so LOUD you need to cover your ears! Sound can vary this much because of **energy**.

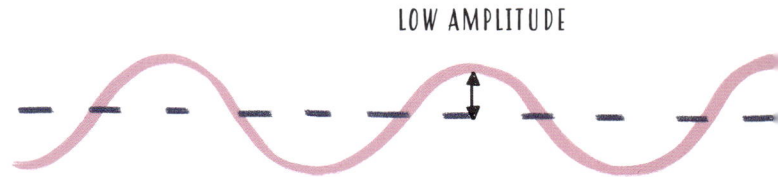

LOW AMPLITUDE

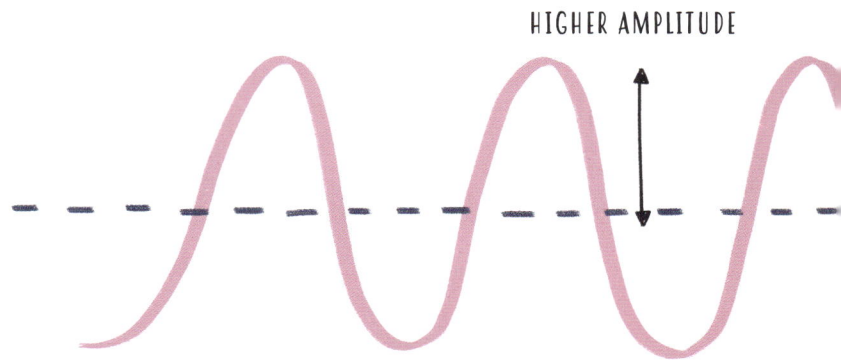

HIGHER AMPLITUDE

WHAT IS VOLUME?

Volume is whether something is loud or quiet. We know that sound is energy that travels in waves of vibrations, disturbing the air. The bigger and stronger the vibration, the more energy it has, and the louder sound that is produced. Bigger waves push harder against your eardrums. Smaller, weaker waves have less energy and produce quieter sounds. They don't push as hard when they enter your ear. When you whisper to a friend, you produce a quiet sound. But when you shout, the vibrations are much stronger, with more energy, and the sound is heard as loud!

RUSTLE OF LEAVES

NORMAL CHATTING

HAIRDRYE

| 0 | 10 | 20 | 30 | 40 | 50 | 60 | 70 |

🔊 AMP IT UP

The height of a wave is called **amplitude**. It is measured from the middle up to the highest point in the sound wave. If you look at the wave with high amplitude, you can see it has higher peaks (the tops of the waves) and lower troughs (the dips) than the wave with low amplitude. Sounds with more energy produce more amplitude. The taller the wave, the higher the amplitude, and the louder the sound.

🔊 DISCOVERING DECIBELS

The energy of sound is measured in **decibels**. The higher the decibel level, the louder the noise. Some noises are so loud that they can damage your ears and hearing. Near the top of the decibel scale, 150 dB is the absolute limit that our ears can take, but even before that could be damaging, depending on how close you are to the source of the sound, and how long you're exposed to it.

We can use special devices to measure decibel levels and determine how safe a sound is. These could determine whether a rock concert is too loud for its audience, or even what volume is safe to listen to in your earphones.

❓ OUT OF CURIOSITY

One of the loudest sounds ever recorded on Earth was the eruption of the Krakatoa volcano in 1883. It is estimated to have been 180 dB and could be heard 5,000 km (3,100 mi) away.

FIREWORKS OR EXPLOSION CLOSE BY

JET ENGINE

TRUCKS IN TRAFFIC

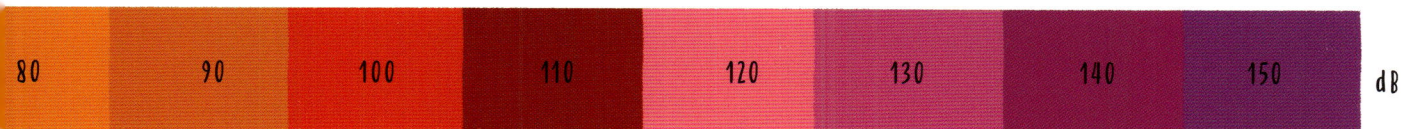

| 80 | 90 | 100 | 110 | 120 | 130 | 140 | 150 | dB |

PITCH PERFECT

Sound doesn't vary only by volume. It can also range in pitch.
A sound's pitch can be so high or low that our ears can't even detect it.

WHAT IS PITCH?

Pitch is how high or low a sound is. When an object vibrates and makes a sound, it can vibrate at different speeds. If an object vibrates quickly, it makes a high-pitched sound. If an object vibrates slowly, the pitch of the sound is much lower.

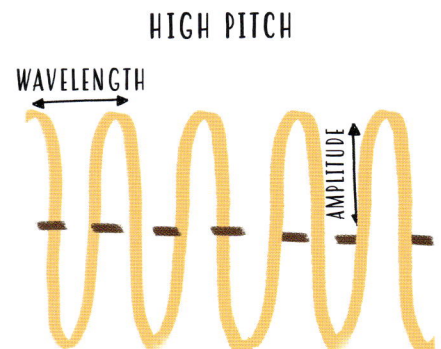

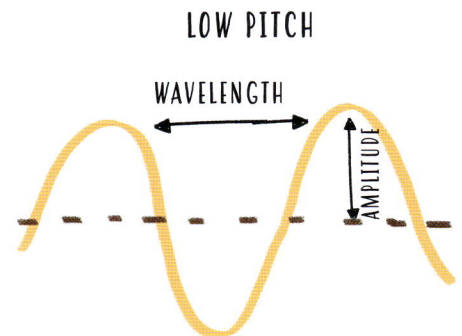

TWEET, TWEET!

HIGH PITCH

WAVELENGTH

AMPLITUDE

LOW PITCH

WAVELENGTH

AMPLITUDE

ON ANOTHER WAVELENGTH

Each sound wave has its own **wavelength**. This is the distance between the crests of two waves. The wavelengths of a high-pitched sound are short, and the waves are close together. A low-pitched sound has longer wavelengths, and the peaks are more spread out. When a bird tweets, it produces a sound that vibrates quickly. The wavelengths are close together, and the sound comes out as a high pitch. But when a truck honks its horn, the sound waves are much slower. The crests and peaks of the waves are farther apart, the wavelength is longer, and the sound comes out slow and low. Hoooonk!

◎ FINDING FREQUENCY

Pitch is measured as **frequency**. This is the number of sound waves produced by the sound each second. It is measured in Hertz (Hz). When the waves are close together, more waves are produced in the same amount of time than when the waves are further apart. So, sounds with a short wavelength have a **high frequency** and pitch. Sounds with a longer wavelength have a **low frequency** and pitch.

A radio makes use of frequency to provide different stations. Each station has a different frequency, such as 93.9 or 100.1, which is its **waveband**. It broadcasts signals using this frequency for you to tune into.

TUNE IN!

◎ OUT OF RANGE

Some sounds are too high or too low for our ears to detect. Sounds that are too high for our ears are called **ultrasound**. Sounds that are too low for us to hear are called **infrasound**. Some animals are able to hear sounds that we can't. A dog, for example, has ears that are more sensitive to higher frequencies. Special dog whistles can make a dog come running, while the owner can't hear the sound of the whistle at all!

GOING SUPERSONIC

Some objects can travel faster than sound in air. When they do, they can create incredible shock waves and sounds.

FASTER THAN THE SPEED OF SOUND

The speed that sound particles travel through normal air—340 m (1,120 ft) per second—is known as **Mach 1**. If something travels faster than Mach 1, it is called **supersonic**. It is faster than the speed of sound.

BOOM!

SONIC BOOM

As a jet plane flies, its engines make sound waves that spread out in all directions. The jet plane eventually moves faster than the sound particles and passes in front of them. As the plane catches up with its own sound waves, it squashes these waves together. This creates a huge sound called a **sonic boom.** On the ground, you might hear this as a loud sound a bit like thunder sweeping past you.

SHOCK WAVE

A **shock wave** is a sharp change in pressure that occurs when something passes the speed of sound. We can see this as a cone-shaped cloud. As a plane nears supersonic speeds, it squashes the air particles in front of it closer together. Behind the aircraft, the particles of air spread out, and the temperature cools. With the cooler temperature, any water in the atmosphere condenses into droplets. Behind the jet, this water vapor spreads out into a cone shape. Eventually, it disappears as the air particles return to normal.

TOO LOUD!

Aircrafts that travel faster than the speed of sound are normally fighter jets. Most commercial planes that you take to travel from place to place don't reach these speeds, so you won't hear a sonic boom. However, private jets are getting faster and faster—but they are limited by the sound of reaching Mach 1. A sonic boom can be considered too much noise impact for the environment, and so scientists and **engineers** are working hard to find ways to muffle the sound.

? OUT OF CURIOSITY

Concorde was the first passenger-carrying commercial plane to fly at supersonic speeds. It could reach a speed over Mach 2—twice as fast as the speed of sound. It operated from the 1970s until 2003, when it went out of service due to the high costs of running it, and the noise.

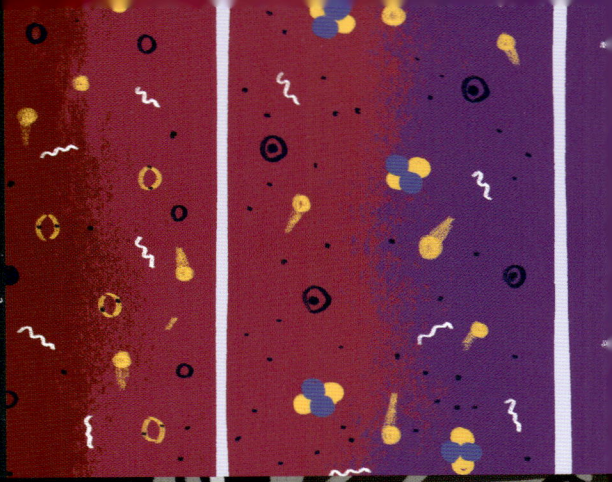

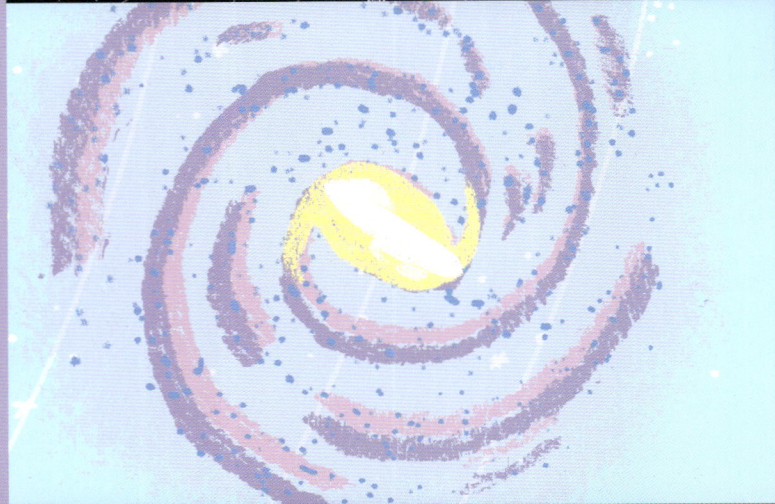

CHAPTER 15

ASTROPHYSICS: JOURNEY INTO SPACE

We know that space is full of stars, planets, the Sun, the Moon…
But how? Where did the Universe begin, and how does our
Solar System stay in place? In this chapter, we
will look at the PHYSICS of space.

Astrophysics is the study of the stars and other objects in
space, and how the laws and theories of physics can explain
our Universe. This includes orbits, tides, seasons, and even
space travel. Strap in, and prepare for an out-of-this-world ride.

IT BEGAN WITH A BANG

It all started with a bang—the Big Bang that created the Universe itself. From there, energy, matter, stars, planets, and the world that we know eventually came to be.

MAGICAL MOMENT

In a fraction of a second, 13.7 billion years ago, the Universe was created by what we call the **Big Bang**. Space-time burst into existence and expanded incredibly rapidly. A tiny point exploded, and it has continued to expand ever since. That moment created all the energy and matter that exists in our Universe.

TIMELINE OF THE UNIVERSE

In the beginning, the Universe was very dense and very hot.

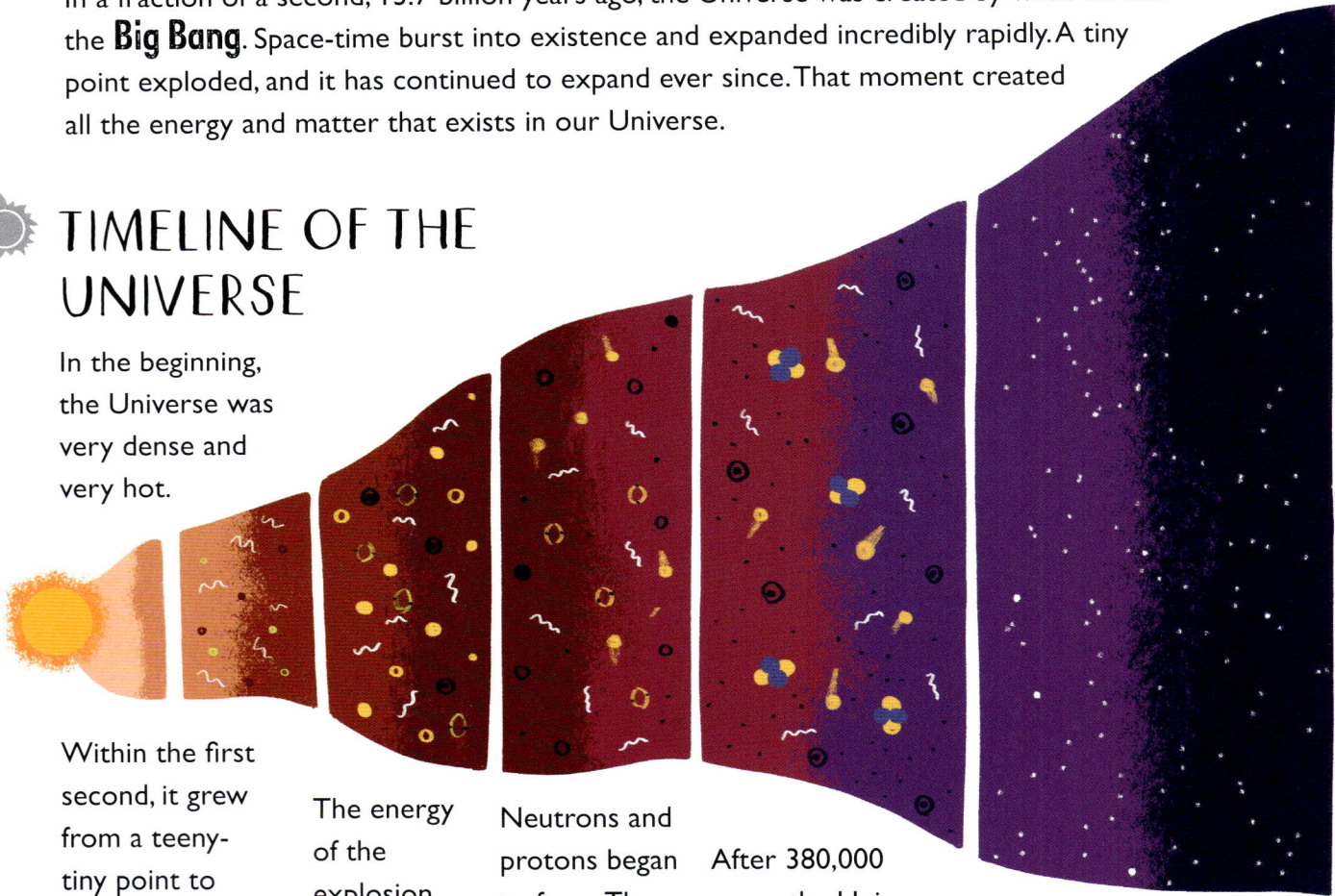

Within the first second, it grew from a teeny-tiny point to bigger than the size of a city. It then continued to expand, but at a slower rate.

The energy of the explosion created **matter**.

Neutrons and protons began to form. The Universe was still too hot for atoms to exist, but some of their pieces were there.

After 380,000 years, the Universe cooled down enough for **atoms** to form. Protons and neutrons were joined by electrons. The Universe became a swirling cloud of gases.

After about 100 to 150 million years, the first **stars** formed. The force of gravity pulled together gas in especially dense areas.

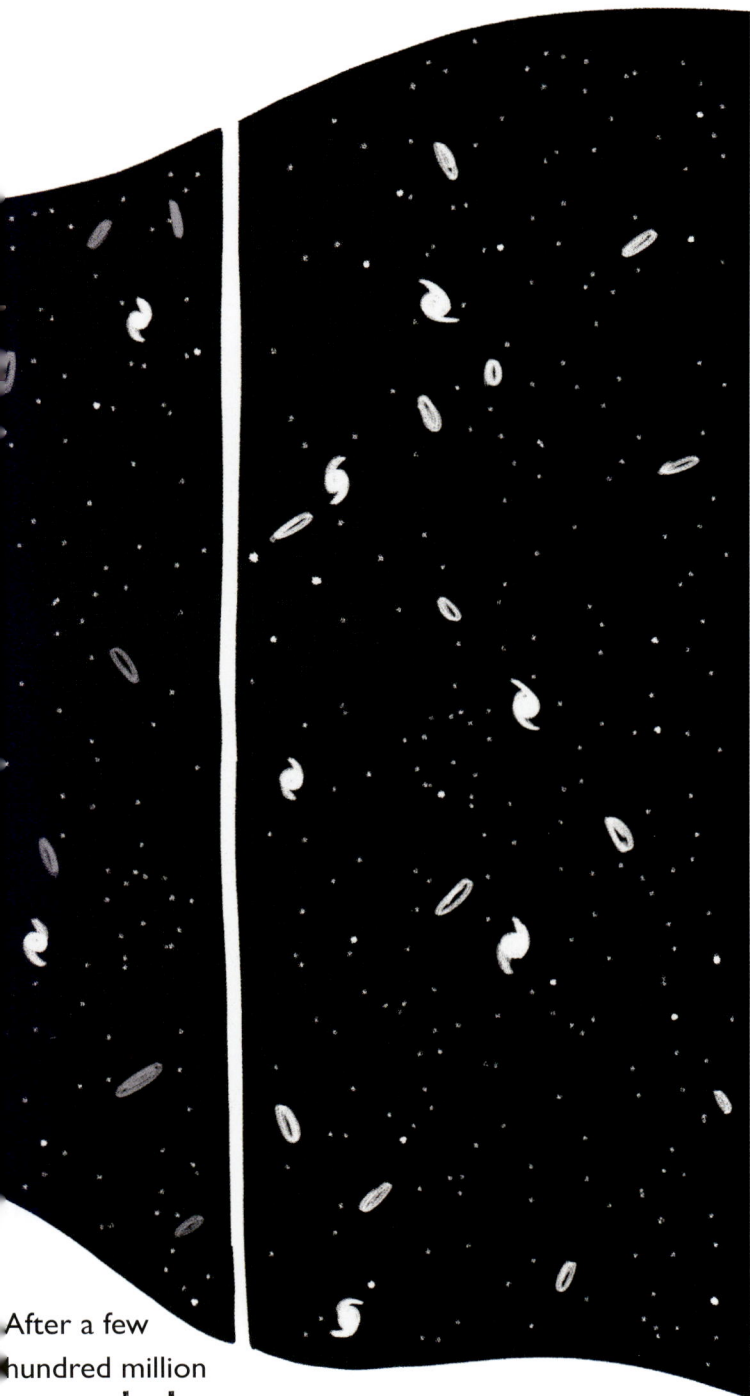

After a few hundred million years, **galaxies** formed. Gravity pulled groups of stars together into spinning clusters.

Today, the Universe has stars, galaxies, planets, moons—and living things like us. It is still expanding and seems to have no outer limits.

LEMAITRE AND HUBBLE

The first person to suggest the Big Bang was Belgian astronomer Georges Lemaître. In 1927, he proposed that the Universe was expanding. Four years later, he went on to suggest that the Universe had begun with a tiny point, which he called the "cosmic egg." In 1929, American astronomer Edward Hubble discovered that galaxies were moving farther away. This supported Lemaître's expansion theory. There was plenty of resistance to these ideas, but after several decades their theories were accepted as being correct.

LINGERING EVIDENCE

Radiation from the Big Bang still exists in our Universe today. Using special telescopes, scientists can see this cosmic microwave background radiation (CMBR), which is yet more evidence of the journey of the Universe from hot to cool and tiny to huge.

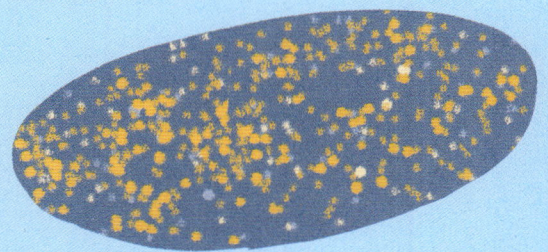

? OUT OF CURIOSITY

The name "Big Bang" was given to this event not by someone who supported the theory—but by someone who opposed it! In 1949, astronomer Fred Hoyle said, "This big bang idea seemed to me to be unsatisfactory…" And the name stuck!

OUR PLACE IN SPACE

The Solar System is the group of planets and other objects that travel around a central star—our Sun. It has been around for BILLIONS of years.

THE BIRTH OF THE SOLAR SYSTEM

The **Solar System** began to form about 4.6 billion years ago from a cloud of gas and dust. Gravity pulled the gas and dust together into a star, creating a dense core. As atoms of gas were forced closer and closer together, the temperature and pressure increased until the nuclei of hydrogen atoms crushed together and **fused**. This process created helium and continues to do so in the Sun today, releasing a whole lot of energy and keeping it hot.

Over 10 million years, this star became our Sun. Matter that wasn't drawn in to the Sun came together through the pull of gravity and formed planets, asteroids, or comets.

ASTEROID BELT

MERCURY VENUS EARTH MARS

SUN

THE PULL OF THE SUN

The Sun is the largest object in our Solar System. It has such a strong gravitational pull that it draws all the other objects toward it. Each of these objects **orbits** around the Sun, at its own distance.

PLANET POWER

While planets orbit the Sun, they also have their own **gravitational pull.** This holds them in a sphere shape. It also pulls objects around the planets in to orbit, such as moons.

There are eight planets in our Solar System. The four planets closest to the Sun—Mercury, Venus, Earth, and Mars—are called **rocky planets** because they are made up of mainly rock and metal. They are denser than the outer planets.

The outer planets are less dense and much bigger. They are made mainly of gas and liquid around a smaller rocky core. These four outer planets—Jupiter, Saturn, Uranus, and Neptune—are called the **gas planets**. Jupiter and Saturn are called **gas giants**. Uranus and Neptune are the farthest planets from the Sun. They are cold **ice giants**.

JUPITER

SATURN

URANUS

NEPTUNE

MILKY WAY

YOU ARE HERE

GALAXY QUEST

The Universe is full of billions, or possibly even trillions, of galaxies. Each galaxy is a group of stars held together by gravity. Our Solar System lives in the **Milky Way**. The Milky Way is a **spiral galaxy**. All the stars, planets, and dust swirl around a central nucleus—a supermassive black hole. It takes about 250 million years for our Solar System to travel all the way around.

BURNING BRIGHT

When you look outside on a clear night, you can see twinkling stars filling the sky. In fact, the Universe is full of stars of different types and ages.

⭐ WHAT IS A STAR?

A **star** is a giant ball of hot gas. It is made of mainly helium and hydrogen, pulled and held together by the force of gravity. Just like the Sun (which is also a star), stars burn and shine through the process of **nuclear fusion**. This process releases a whole lot of heat and light energy.

⭐ THE LIFE OF A STAR

Most stars are born inside dense clouds of gas and dust called **nebulas**. When something disturbs a nebula, it begins to collapse inward under gravity. Areas in the cloud pull in matter, and the nebula collapses around these points. Each of these draws into a ball shape and continues to shrink and heat up. When the core reaches about 10 million °C (18 million °F), nuclear fusion occurs and we have a star.

Main sequence stars: Most of the stars in the Universe are main sequence stars. These are the stars that are changing hydrogen into helium and releasing energy. This includes our Sun. Some of them are bigger, brighter, or hotter than others. These stars stay in shape due to a perfect balance of forces. The force of gravity pulls inward, while the force created by the energy of fusion pushes outward.

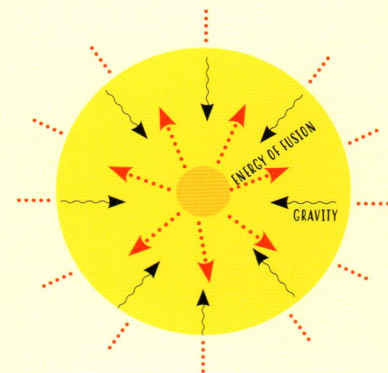

ENERGY OF FUSION

GRAVITY

MAIN SEQUENCE STARS

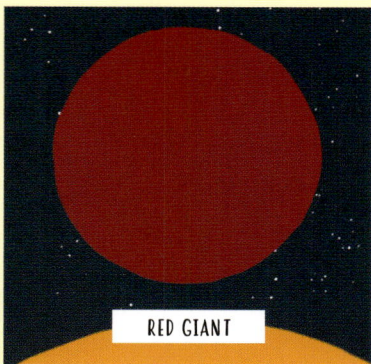

Red giant: When a star with a similar mass to our Sun begins to run out of hydrogen in its core, it becomes a red giant. These stars aren't releasing the same heat energy as before, so they are cooler than main sequence stars, giving them a red shade.

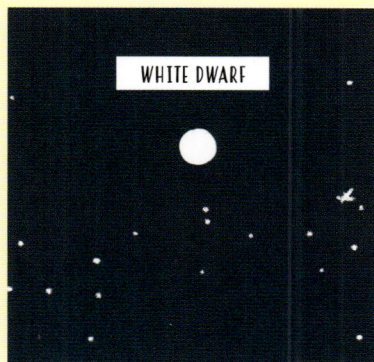

RED GIANT

WHITE DWARF

White dwarf: Eventually, the red giant stops nuclear fusion. The core collapses, and the star is left as a tiny, hot, dense spot with a faint glow that lasts for billions of years.

Supergiant: A supergiant is the largest type of star in the Universe. Supergiants burn through their hydrogen quickly and can give off a million times more energy than the Sun. They burn out quickly in star terms, within just a few million years.

SUPERGIANT

SUPERNOVA

Supernova: Instead of shrinking quietly into a white dwarf, when a supergiant runs out of fuel, it explodes! The core of the star collapses suddenly and heats up. This creates an explosion that blasts the outer layers of the star into space. The inner core then becomes a small neutron star or a black hole.

★ WHY DO STARS TWINKLE?

Stars emit light rays that travel outward. They are so far away that the beams reaching Earth are very thin. When they hit Earth's atmosphere, which is full of moving air, they bend. We see this as the star twinkling—even though it isn't. Planets are much closer to Earth, so they shine more steadily. You can pick them out in the night sky as the dots that don't twinkle.

SPREADING SUNSHINE

Without the Sun, our Solar System would not exist. It keeps all the other planets in place, and it heats Earth to just the right temperature for living things to make a home.

WHAT IS THE SUN?

The **Sun** is a main sequence star. It is a spinning ball of hot, glowing gas, continuously burning through the process of **nuclear fusion**. This process releases energy in the form of heat and light. The Sun's energy reaches all eight planets in our Solar System. By the time it reaches the outer planets, it is much weaker, so these planets are colder and darker than the inner four. The sunshine emitted is a mix of types of **electromagnetic radiation**, including visible light, infrared (which we experience as heat), and UV. Earth's atmosphere mostly protects us from any harmful radiation (and sunscreen does too!).

OUT OF CURIOSITY

The Sun's core is about 15 million °C (27 million °F). Just its surface temperature is hot enough to boil a diamond!

FORCE FROM THE SUN

The Sun is the largest object in our Solar System by far. In fact, it makes up over **99%** of the mass of the entire system. You could fit a million Earths inside it! Because it is so massive, the Sun's **gravity** is extremely strong. It holds the Sun in its ball shape, and it pulls every other object in the Solar System into orbit around it. This includes eight planets, at least five dwarf planets, thousands of asteroids, and trillions of comets and pieces of ice.

The Sun also produces a **magnetic** force. Electric currents inside it generate a magnetic field. This is carried through the Solar System on solar wind—a stream of electrically charged gas particles that blow out from the Sun in all directions. The solar wind travels extremely fast through space. Luckily, Earth has its own magnetic field surrounding it. This deflects the solar wind away from our planet.

IT'S MAGNETIC!

SUN

MOON

EARTH

ECLIPSE OF THE SUN

Earth orbits around the Sun. While doing so, our Moon orbits around Earth. Sometimes, the Moon moves directly between Earth and the Sun, and the Moon blocks the Sun's light. This casts a shadow on part of Earth. This is called a **solar eclipse**. During a total solar eclipse, the Sun's outer layer, called the **corona**, can be seen glowing around the outside. Warning! The Sun is so bright that it could damage your eyes. Never look at the Sun or an eclipse directly!

OUR HOME PLANET

Rocky planet Earth is the third closest planet to the Sun, about 150 million km (93 million miles) away. It is the only planet known to have life on it—so far.

CRUST

MANTLE

CORE

WHAT IS EARTH?

Earth was formed with the Solar System, about 4.6 billion years ago. Gas and dust were pulled together through the force of gravity, forming a ball shape. Dense materials gathered in the **core**, so tightly compacted together that they formed a hot, solid ball. The inner core is about the same temperature as the surface of the Sun. Lighter materials formed the outer rocky **crust**. The thick layer between the crust and core, called the **mantle**, is made of semi-fluid hot magma.

OUT OF CURIOSITY
All the life that we know about in the entire Universe lives only on the thin rocky crust around Earth.

IN A SPIN

Earth spins on its own **axis**—an imaginary line that runs through it from the North Pole to the South Pole. It completes a full rotation on its axis every 24 hours. This is one **day**. As Earth spins, it creates day and night. The areas facing the Sun are in daylight and daytime, while the areas turned away from the Sun have night.

IN ORBIT

While it is spinning on its axis, Earth also travels through space in **orbit** around the Sun. It completes a full journey around the Sun in just over 365 days. This is one **year**.

EARTH'S AXIS

SUMMER IN THE NORTHERN HEMISPHERE

WINTER IN THE NORTHERN HEMISPHERE

SUN

TER IN SOUTHERN ISPHERE

SUMMER IN THE SOUTHERN HEMISPHERE

ON A TILT

Earth's axis is tilted at an angle. This is what gives us **seasons**. As Earth travels around in its orbit, different areas spend more or less of each day facing the Sun. There is an invisible line around the middle of Earth called the **equator**. Above the equator is the **Northern Hemisphere**. Below the equator is the **Southern Hemisphere**. When a hemisphere is tilted toward the Sun, it receives more sunlight and heat, so it is summer. When it is tilted away, less heat energy reaches it, and it is winter. As Earth passes between these positions, it is spring or fall.

Because of the angle of the tilt, regions around the equator get the same strength of the Sun all year round, so they don't have the same changing four seasons.

237

INFLUENCE OF THE MOON

The Moon and Earth are closely connected. They each have their own gravitational pull that affects the other.

WHAT IS THE MOON?

The **Moon** is a rocky object that circles Earth. Astronomers believe it was formed about 4.5 billion years ago, when a planet about the size of Mars collided with Earth. Bits from the impact were drawn together into a ball shape, trapped by Earth's gravitational pull. Over millions of years, dense materials gathered in the ball's core, and less dense materials moved to the surface. Now, just like Earth, the Moon has a hot metal core and a solid, rocky crust.

THANK YOU, MOON

CHANGING TIDES

The Moon's gravitational pull generates a **tidal force**. The water on Earth noticeably bulges on the side closest to the Moon, being pulled toward it. Because of Earth's own gravity, the ocean also bulges on the opposite side, farthest from the Moon. These bulges are **high tide**. Earth is almost squeezed, so that two sides bulge, leaving the sections in between flatter—**low tide**. As the Earth spins on its axis, it passes under the two bulges (high tide) and the areas without bulges (low tide). Most coasts experience two high tides and two low tides every day.

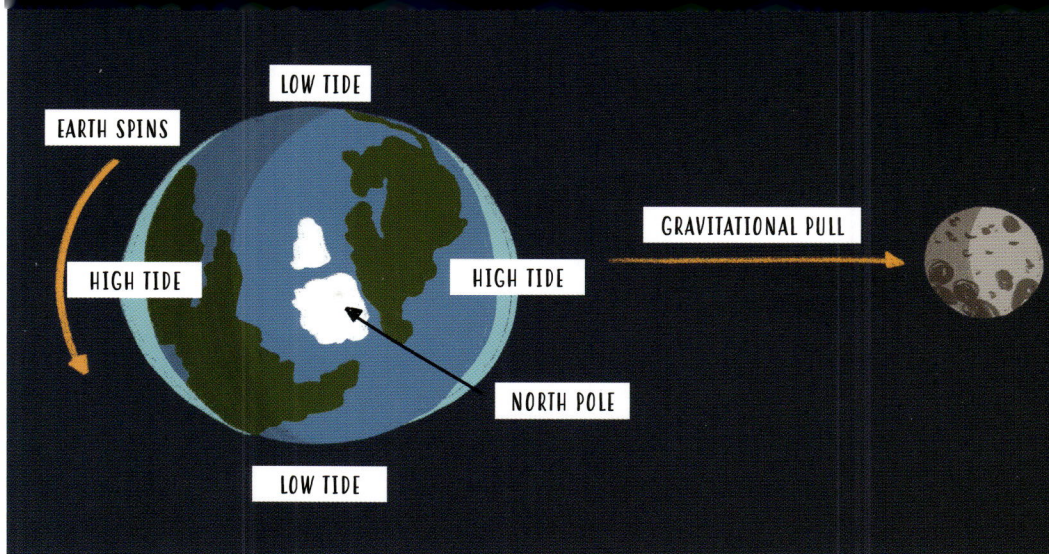

The Sun also generates a tidal force, but it isn't as strong because the Sun is so much farther away from Earth than the Moon. When the Sun, Moon, and Earth are all in a line (during a full moon or new moon—see the next page), the gravitational pull is strongest, and the tides are at their highest.

IN BALANCE

As Earth spins on its axis, it has a slight wobble—like a wobbling spinning top. The Moon's gravitational pull helps keep Earth's orbit more stable. Without it, Earth would move back and forth to a greater extent on its axis. Climates and weather would be more extreme. Even our days and seasons wouldn't be the same as we know them now. If the Moon were to disappear, sea creatures that move with the tides and lay eggs in low tides to keep them safe would also feel the effect. Without the Moon, our world could still exist, but it wouldn't be the same.

MOON LANDING

The Moon is the only other place in the Universe (apart from Earth) where human beings have set foot. Humans first stepped on the Moon in 1969. More than 100 robotic spacecraft have also been sent to the Moon to take samples and photos. Eventually, humans hope to set up permanently on the Moon.

SECTION 4: MAGNIFICENT MATHEMATICS

When you tell the time, cook, figure out change, measure things, read timetables, and more—you are using mathematics! Mathematics is used to build theme parks, in medicine, in sports, business, and space travel. Mathematics is everywhere!

We use mathematics to help us figure out money, such as how much things cost and how much change we can expect to be given when we buy things. It can also help us to work out how much more money we need when we are saving money to buy something.

We use mathematics when we measure things, such as ingredients for a recipe.

WHAT IS MATHEMATICS?

Mathematics is the science that deals with shape, quantities, patterns, and arrangements. Mathematics helps us to understand the world around us, and gives us ways to solve problems.

$$64 + 49$$

There are lots of different branches of mathematics.
These include:

ARITHMETIC

Arithmetic is about numbers. It helps us work out addition, subtraction, division, and multiplication calculations.

1 2 3 4 5
6 7 8 9 0

X = -
÷ +

ALGEBRA

Algebra allows us to use unknown quantities (often given letters) with numbers to create a formula, so we can solve problems.

GEOMETRY

Geometry is the study of shapes and their properties (such as faces, vertices, and edges).

TRIGONOMETRY

Trigonometry is the study of the relationships between the angles and sides of triangles.

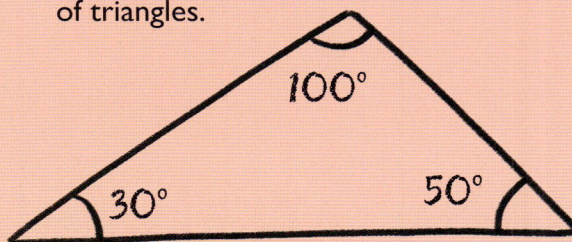

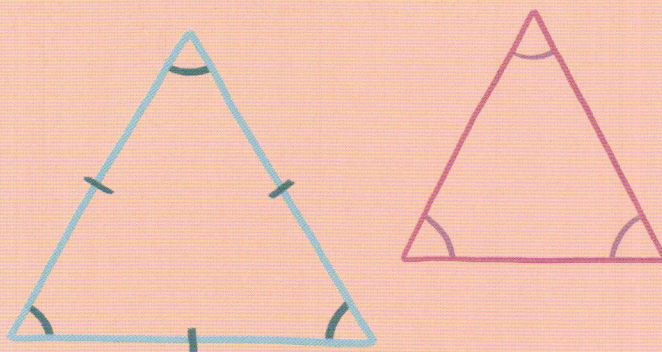

100°

30°   50°

CHAPTER 16

NUMBERS

$1_2{}^3$

People have probably always counted things—
even before they had "numbers."

TALLY STICKS

Archaeologists have found evidence of marks made on bone and stone that suggest people were counting even in prehistoric times. These are called tally sticks.

This stick is called the Lebombo bone. It was found in a cave near the border between South Africa and Eswatini. It is between 44,200 and 43,000 years old. It has 29 markings along one edge. It has been suggested the marks follow the cycle of the moon.

ROMAN NUMERALS

Roman numerals are the numbers that were used by the Roman Empire. Letters were used to represent the value of numbers.

1	2	3	4	5	6	7	8	9
I	II	III	IV	V	VI	VII	VIII	IX

10	20	30	40	50	60	70	80	90
X	XX	XXX	XL	L	LX	LXX	LXXX	XC

100	200	300	400	500	600	700	800	900
C	CC	CC	CD	D	DC	DCC	DCCC	CM

When a symbol appears after a higher-value symbol, the number is added. So 23 would be XXIII (20 + 3).

When a symbol appears before a higher-value symbol, the number is taken away. So 14 would be XIV (10+ "1 before 5").

ACROSS THE WORLD

Roman numerals were used in many parts of the world in the Roman era, because their empire covered much of Europe. Wherever the conquering armies went, they took their system of numbers with them.

I	II	III	IV	V	VI	VII
VIII	IX	X	XI	XII		
XIII	XIV	XV	XVI			
XVII	XVIII	XIX	XX			
XXI	XXII	XXIII				
XXIV	XXV	XXVI				
XXVII	XXVIII	XXIX				
XXX	XL	L	LXLXX			
LXXX	XC	C	CC			
CCC	CD	D	DC			
DCC	DCCC	CM	M			
MM	MMM	MV	VX			

ROMAN NUMERALS TODAY

We still see Roman numerals on some clocks today. For instance, take a look at Big Ben in the Clock Tower of the Palace of Westminster in London.

INDO-ARABIC NUMERALS

Indo-Arabic numbers are the numbers used across much of the world today. They originated in India by the 6th or 7th century. They spread to the West in the work of Middle Eastern scholars such as the mathematician Al-Khwarizmi.

ZERO

Zero means "no amount."

When you take 0 away from a number, nothing happens—the value is not affected.

$$7 - 0 = 7$$

In the same way, when you add 0 to a number, nothing happens—the value is not affected.

$$7 + 0 = 7$$

Each zero added after a digit increases the value tenfold.

1 (add a zero as place holder) becomes 10

10 (add a zero as place holder) becomes 100

100 (add a zero as place holder) becomes 1,000

Zero is also used as a **place holder** in place value systems, such as the decimal system.

1
10
100
1,000

ZERO IN THE ANCIENT WORLD

The ancient Egyptians, Romans, and Greeks had no symbol for zero. Ancient Americans did use a symbol for zero, however. The Olmec people flourished in the area now known as Mexico until around 400 BCE. They had a symbol for zero, which was used as a place holder.

O MAYAN AND INCAN ZERO

After the Olmecs, the Mayan civilization also used a symbol for zero. It looked like a turtle shell!

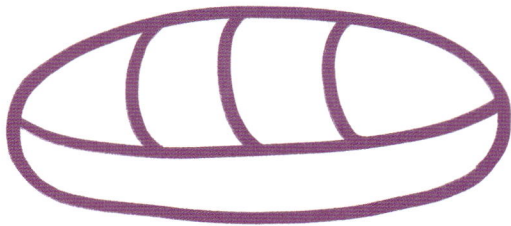

The Incas, who lived in the area now known as Peru, had a form of zero. They used a knotted device called a quipu for counting. The knots stood for different values. The absence of a knot in a particular position stood for zero.

O ZERO IN THE MIDDLE AGES

In 825 CE, the Persian mathematician Al-Khwarizmi published a book which combined ancient Greek and Indian mathematics. This book included an explanation of the use of zero. He also said that if no number appears in the place of tens in a calculation, a circle should be used to "keep the rows"—using zero as a place holder. The circle was called sifr.

O ZERO IN EUROPE

In 1202, the idea of zero came to Europe (along with the rest of the Indo-Arabic number system) largely through the work of the Italian mathematician Fibonacci. He had studied with the Moors, or Spanish Muslims. That is why the numerals in this number system, still in use today, were known as "Arabic numerals." Fibonacci helped introduce ideas about zero to the study of mathematics in Europe.

UNITY

In mathematics, unity means "one." It is our unit of counting, and the first whole number in the positive number sequence.

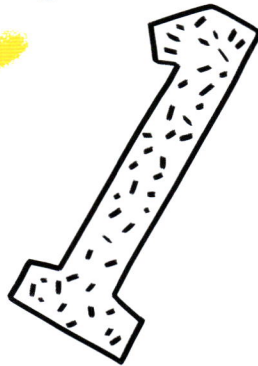

OUT OF CURIOSITY

The number 1 has several names. Apart from unity, it is also called "unit" and "identity."

SIMPLE!

Any number multiplied by 1 remains unchanged.

$3 \times 1 = 3$

$25 \times 1 = 25$

$168 \times 1 = 168$

$1,265 \times 1 = 1,265$

NO CHANGE

You can multiply 1 by itself any number of times and it is always still 1.

$1 \times 1 = 1$

Even when 1 is squared or cubed, it stays the same.

$1^2 = 1$

$1^3 = 1$

So unity squared is the same value as unity, and unity cubed is the same value as unity.

1 POSITIVELY ODD . . .

Unity is the first positive odd number. It is the first and smallest positive integer (a whole number that can be positive, negative, or zero). It is the unit of counting.

The number 1 can do a kind of mathematical magic, too—adding it to any number can change an odd number into an even number and an even number into an odd number!

1 WHERE DID 1 COME FROM?

The modern number 1 used around the world traces its beginnings back to ancient India. In the Brahmi script, 1 was just a line:

1 THE ORIGIN OF 1

A single stroke was used to mark "one" for a long time before the Indo-Arabic numeral 1 was introduced to Europe.

Do you remember the tally sticks on page 242? Each mark there stood for one event or thing being recorded. The strokes were not numerals but each stroke represented one "thing" as it was counted, such as the passing of a day.

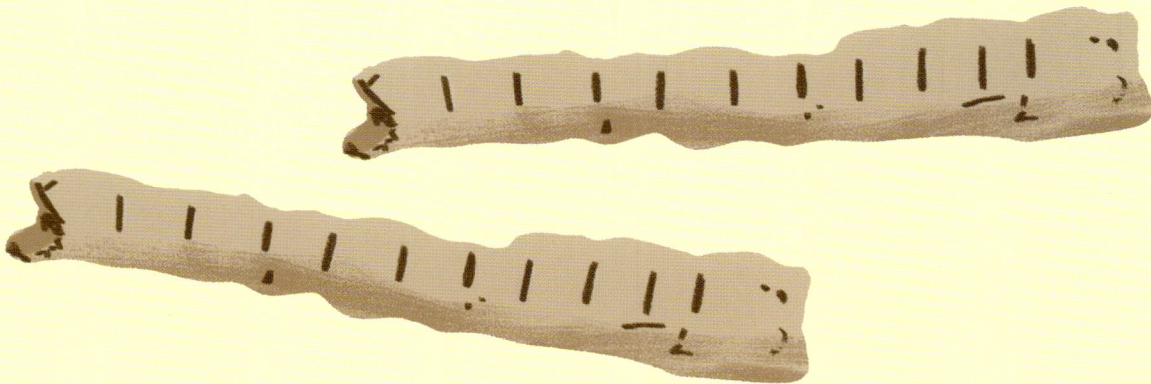

EVEN NUMBERS

Even numbers are numbers that can be divided exactly by 2, with no remainder.

0 2 4 6 8

NUMBER LINES

If you count along in 2s on a number line, starting at zero, you will see a series of even numbers. If you wrote this series down, you would be able to see a pattern.

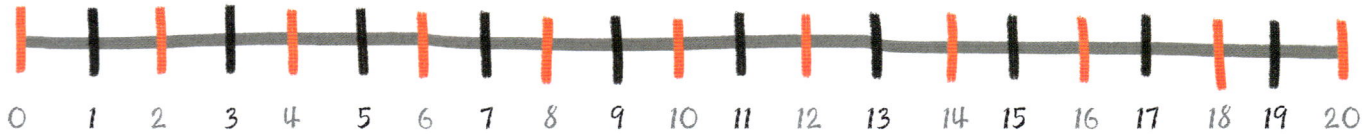

0 1 2 3 4 5 6 7 8 9 10 11 12 13 14 15 16 17 18 19 20

Can you see the pattern when you look at this number line? The pattern of even numbers is that they always end in 0, 2, 4, 6, or 8—no matter how large the value!

So, these numbers are all even:

2

16

96

112

678

1,132

11,678

You can see the pattern straight away, without having to do any calculations. If a number ends in 0, 2, 4, 6, or 8 it is an even number. You can also test the numbers to see if they are even by dividing them by 2. If they divide exactly with no remainder, they are even numbers.

0
2
4
6
8

SHARING EVEN NUMBERS

Even numbers of things are easy to share between two people. If you have an even number of grapes or cookies, you can share them exactly with a friend without having to break any in half. Remember, even numbers can always be divided exactly by 2.

TRY IT YOURSELF

Which of these numbers do you think are even?

345   766   821

654   5,432   328

? OUT OF CURIOSITY

When we add, subtract, or multiply even numbers the results are always predictable:

even + even = even

even x even = even

even – even = even

Negative numbers (see pages 260–261), such as -2 and -4, can be even, too!

ODD NUMBERS

Odd numbers are numbers that cannot be divided exactly by 2. When odd numbers are divided by 2, they always leave a remainder of 1.

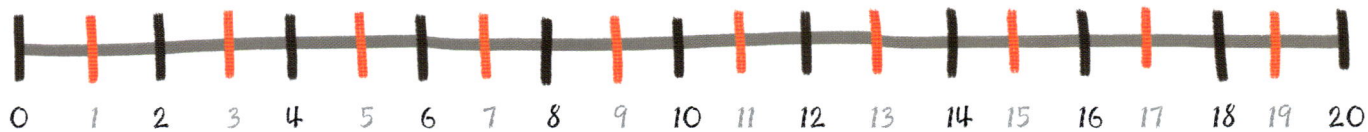

NUMBER LINES

If you count along in 2s on a number line, starting at 1, you will see a series of odd numbers. If you wrote this series down, you would be able to see a pattern.

0 1 2 3 4 5 6 7 8 9 10 11 12 13 14 15 16 17 18 19 20

Can you see the pattern when you look at this number line? The pattern of odd numbers is that they always end in 1, 3, 5, 7, or 9—no matter how large the value of the number.

So, these numbers are all odd:

5

47

169

2,135

6,121

10,893

You can see the pattern straight away, without having to do any calculations. If the number ends in 1, 3, 5, 7, or 9 it is an odd number. You can test the numbers to see if they are odd by dividing them by 2. If there is a remainder of 1, it's an odd number.

OUT OF CURIOSITY

The sum of two odd numbers is always even—try it out by adding odd numbers together and see what you find!

ODD TIMES

The **product** of two or more odd numbers is always odd. Try it out!

$$3 \ (\text{odd}) \times 5 \ (\text{odd}) \qquad 15 \ (\text{odd})$$

$$9 \ (\text{odd}) \times 7 \ (\text{odd}) \qquad 63 \ (\text{odd})$$

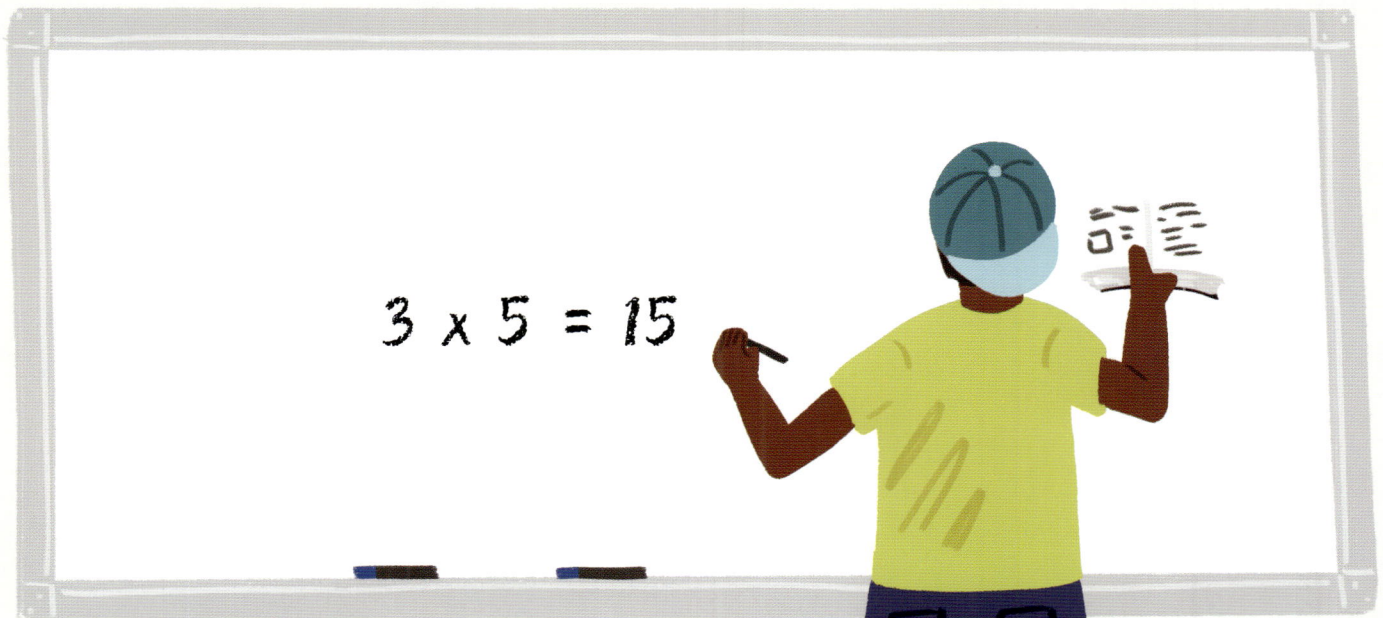

$$3 \times 5 = 15$$

PRIME NUMBERS

Prime numbers are numbers greater than 1 that can only be divided exactly by themselves and 1. They cannot be divided by any other numbers without leaving a remainder. 19 is an example of a prime number. It can only be divided by 1 and 19. If you divide by any other number there will be a remainder.

11 is a prime number because it cannot be divided exactly by any numbers except 11 and 1.

12 is NOT a prime number because it can be divided exactly by 12, 1, 2, 3, 4, and 6.

1	2	3	4	5	6	7	8	9	10
11	12	13	14	15	16	17	18	19	20
21	22	23	24	25	26	27	28	29	30

FIRST 10 PRIME NUMBERS

There are 10 prime numbers under 30. They are:

2, 3, 5, 7, 11, 13, 17, 19, 23, 29

None of these numbers can be divided exactly by anything but themselves and 1. 2 is the only even prime number.

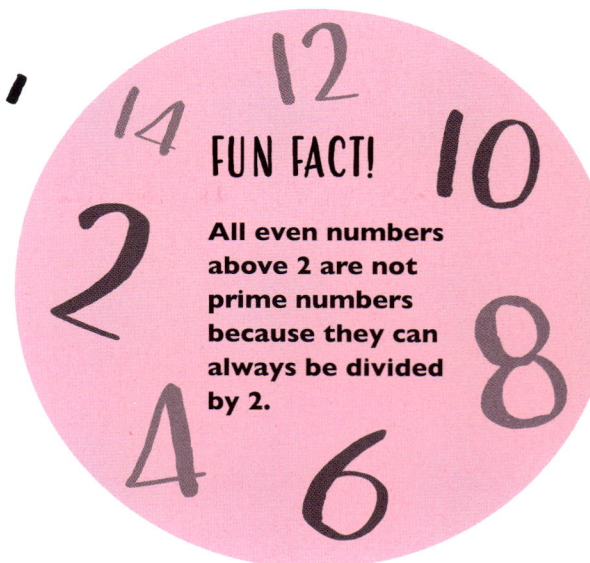

FUN FACT!

All even numbers above 2 are not prime numbers because they can always be divided by 2.

PRIME NUMBERS IN THE REAL WORLD

Prime numbers are used in cyber security—making the information we share over the Internet safer. **Software** engineers use prime numbers to **encrypt** (make hard to read and decipher) things that need to be kept secure, such as credit card details, messaging programs such as WhatsApp, and medical records. Almost every online purchase uses prime numbers to keep the transaction secure.

Software engineers use huge prime numbers and multiply them together to make really large numbers with original **factors** (the two original prime numbers) to encrypt information. Information is kept secure because it would take years to work out which original factors were used.

PRIME NUMBERS TO 100

These numbers are the prime numbers up to 100.
Can you explain why?

2	3	5	7	11	13
17	19	23	29	31	37
41	43	47	53	59	61
67	71	73	83	89	97

OUT OF CURIOSITY

The world's largest known prime number is nearly 25 million digits long!

FACTORS

A factor is a number that divides into another number exactly, with no remainder. 1 and the number itself are always factors of any given number.

POSITIVE FACTORS OF 10:

1, 2, 5, and 10

FACTORS OF 100:

1, 2, 4, 5, 10, 20, 25, 50, and 100

FINDING FACTORS

To find factors of a number, start by looking to see if it is an even number. If it is, you know 2 is a factor. Then see if the number ends in zero. If it does, 10 is a factor. Factors are whole numbers—not fractions of numbers.

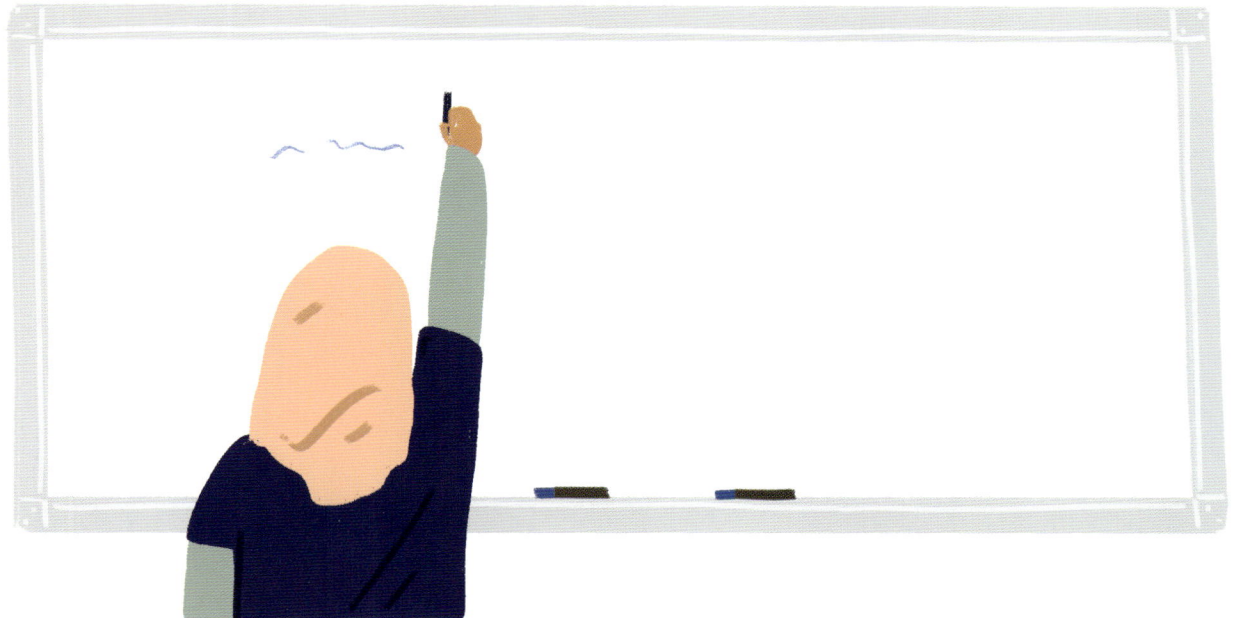

FACTOR PAIRS

Factor pairs are combinations of two factors that, when multiplied together, equal a given number. The factor pairs of 100 are:

POSITIVE FACTORS:

$$1 \times 100 = 100$$

$$2 \times 50 = 100$$

$$4 \times 25 = 100$$

$$5 \times 20 = 100$$

$$10 \times 10 = 100$$

$$20 \times 5 = 100$$

$$25 \times 4 = 100$$

$$50 \times 2 = 100$$

$$100 \times 1 = 100$$

FACTORING

Factoring is the process of breaking numbers down into all of their factors (the numbers that can divide into the number exactly). Take a number and factorize it.

LEARN YOUR TIMES TABLES

Your times tables are really useful for helping you to work out the factors of numbers.

You know that $3 \times 7 = 21$, so you know that 3 and 7 are both factors of 21.

FRACTIONS AND DECIMALS

A fraction is a part of a whole. Think about what happens when you slice a pizza into parts. If those parts are equal, they can tell us about fractions.

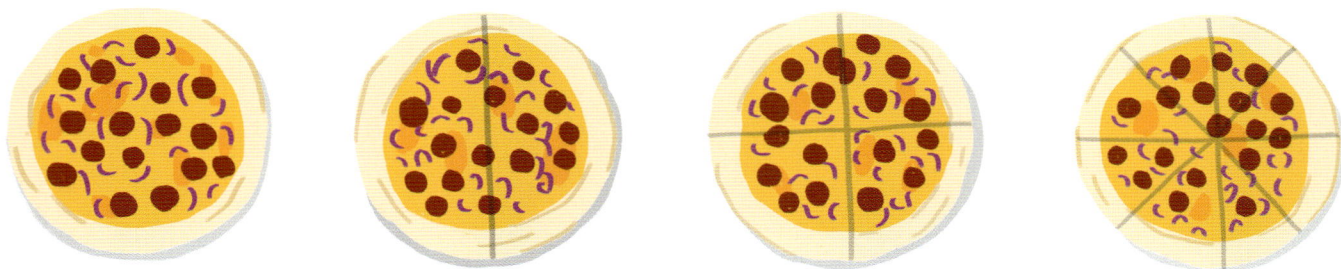

NUMERATOR AND DENOMINATOR

Fractions have a numerator and a denominator. The numerator is the number on the top of a fraction. The denominator is the number on the bottom. The numerator gives us information about how many parts of the "whole" we have. The denominator tells us how many parts the "whole" was divided into.

$$\frac{\text{NUMERATOR}}{\text{DENOMINATOR}}$$

¼ means 1 part of a whole that has been divided into 4 parts.

⅞ means 7 parts of a whole that has been divided into 8 parts.

PROPER FRACTIONS

A "proper fraction" is a fraction where the numerator is less than the denominator. Proper fractions are always less than 1 whole.

$\frac{1}{2}$ = 1 part of a whole cut into 2 parts

$\frac{9}{10}$ = 9 part of a whole cut into 10 parts

$\frac{3}{4}$ = 3 part of a whole cut into 4 parts

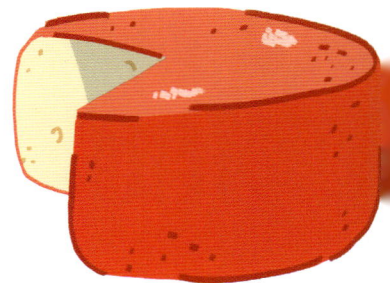

IMPROPER FRACTIONS

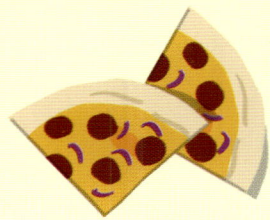

Improper fractions are fractions where the numerator is larger than the denominator. Improper fractions are greater than 1 whole. They are "top-heavy."

$3/2$ = 3 parts of a whole divided into 2 parts = 3 halves = $1\frac{1}{2}$

$5/4$ = 5 parts of a whole divided into 4 parts = 5 quarters = $1\frac{1}{4}$

$8/3$ = 8 parts of a whole divided into 3 parts = 8 thirds = $2\frac{2}{3}$

MIXED FRACTIONS

Mixed fractions have both a "whole number" and a fraction of a whole number. Here are some examples of mixed fractions:

$1\frac{1}{2}$

$8\frac{3}{4}$

$4\frac{5}{6}$

WHAT ARE DECIMALS?

When decimal points are used in numbers, the number to the right of the decimal point is a kind of fraction.

1.1 is the same as $1\frac{1}{10}$

1.01 is the same as 1 and $\frac{1}{100}$

1.001 is the same as $1\frac{1}{1000}$

WHAT IS THE RELATIONSHIP BETWEEN FRACTIONS AND DECIMALS?

Fractions and decimals can give us the same information:

0.25 is the same as $\frac{1}{4}$ 0.5 is the same as $\frac{1}{2}$

0.3 is the same as $\frac{3}{10}$ 0.75 is the same as $\frac{3}{4}$

We can change fractions into decimal equivalents by seeing the line that divides the numerator from the denominator as a division sign ÷. To convert a fraction to a decimal, we divide the numerator by the denominator.

$\frac{1}{2}$ is the same as $1 \div 2 = 0.5$

INFINITY

Infinity means "without end." We say that things are infinite
when they go on forever, like space or numbers.

Infinity means an endless number of the things being described. Infinity is not a real number;
it is an idea. It is something that never ends. It cannot be measured.

∞ INFINITY AND THE ANCIENT WORLD

The ancient Greeks called infinity apeiron. It meant boundless and formless. One of the
earliest discussions of infinity in mathematics was about the **ratio** between the diagonal and
side of a square. Aristotle (384–322 BCE) rejected "actual" infinity, but he did recognize the
potential infinity of being able to count and never stop counting.

∞ BOUNDLESS SPACE

It's not just numbers that are infinite! Space might be infinite if it carries on forever. We don't know if space has an end (**finite**), and often call it "infinite."

∞ SYMBOL FOR INFINITY

We can use a symbol to stand for infinity. It looks like an 8 lying on its side and was created by the mathematician John Wallis in 1665.

∞ ENDLESS NUMBERS

You could count forever—numbers have no end as you could always add another one. Mathematicians call the endlessness of numbers "infinity."

10
20 30 40
50 60 70 80
90 100 110 120 130
140 150 160 170 180 190
200 210 220 230 240 250
260 270 280 290 300 310
320 330 340 350 360 370

∞ ON AND ON

Even a computer couldn't count to infinity. If we could have set a computer counting one number a second at the time of the dinosaurs it would still be going and continue forever!

1234567891011121314151617
1819202122232425262728
82930313233343536373839
39404142434445464748
4950515253545556575...

NEGATIVE NUMBERS

A negative number is a real number that is less than zero. When you count backward from zero, you start counting in negative numbers. The numbers that are more than zero are called positive numbers. Zero is neither negative nor positive.

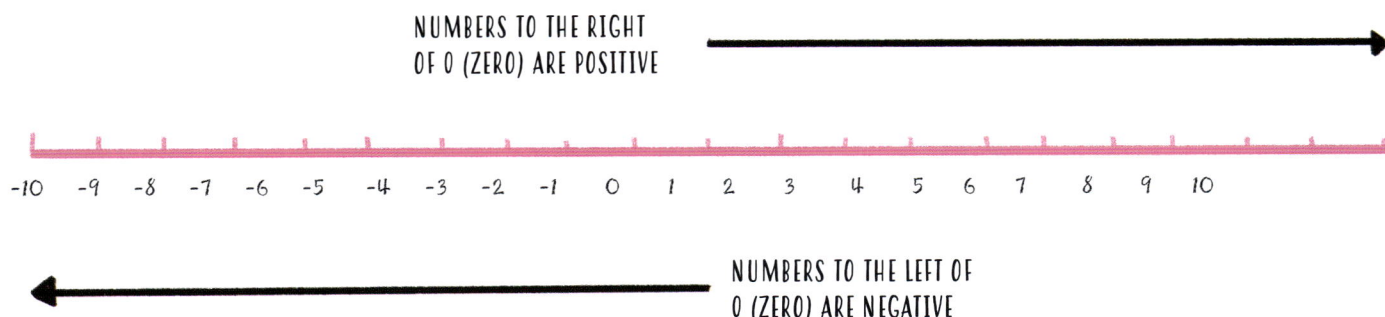

NUMBERS TO THE RIGHT OF 0 (ZERO) ARE POSITIVE

-10 -9 -8 -7 -6 -5 -4 -3 -2 -1 0 1 2 3 4 5 6 7 8 9 10

NUMBERS TO THE LEFT OF 0 (ZERO) ARE NEGATIVE

● NEGATIVE NUMBERS IN HISTORY

The use of negative numbers dates from the Chinese Han Dynasty (202 BCE–220 CE). In the 7th century, the Indian scholar Brahmagupta wrote about the use of negative numbers.

Islamic mathematicians continued working on negative numbers and developed rules about the way they behaved. For instance, negative numbers were used in early accounting, where debts were recorded as negative amounts of money.

NEGATIVE NUMBERS IN SCIENCE

Science uses negative numbers in lots of ways.

TEMPERATURE
COLDER THAN
ZERO

Negative numbers can be used for measurements on a scale that can go below zero. One example is temperature. The Celsius scale sets zero degrees as the freezing point of water, but temperatures can go much lower than that. In Antarctica, it can reach nearly -148°F (-100°C)!

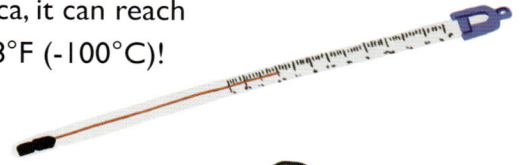

In geography, negative numbers are used to show the measurements of the Earth's surface when it falls below sea level.

NEGATIVE NUMBERS IN EVERYDAY LIFE

You can see negative numbers everywhere if you look closely!

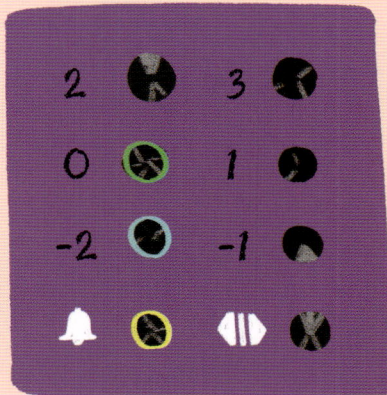

The buttons in elevators use negative numbers to show floors below ground, such as the basement.

In video games, negative numbers are used to show damage, loss of "lives," or using up of a resource.

0:10   -2:01

When playing an audio file, negative numbers are sometimes used to show the time left to play.

Really large numbers can be hard to understand. It can be confusing when numbers have a whole string of zeros. In order to get a clear picture in your head, it helps if you think about everyday things, and what a million or perhaps billion of them would look like.

000 MILLIONS

A million is written as 1 followed by 6 zeros.

$$1,000,000$$

It can be easier to understand if you think of how the value relates to a number you understand. A million is "worth" 1,000 lots of 1,000.

1,000 lots of 1,000 = 1 million

1,000 x 1,000 = 1,000,000

000 WHAT IS COUNTED IN MILLIONS?

Populations of cities and countries are counted in millions. The world's biggest city is Tokyo in Japan, with around 14 million people living there. Find out how many million people live in your country.

OUT OF CURIOSITY

There are 1 million seconds in 11.5 days and 1 million minutes in around 2 years.

000 BILLIONS

A billion is the equivalent of a thousand million. It is written as the numeral 1 followed by 9 zeros.

1,000,000,000

1,000 lots of 1,000,000 = 1 billion

1,000 x 1,000,000 = 1,000,000,000

000 WHAT IS COUNTED IN BILLIONS?

The population of the world is counted in billions. By November 2021, the population of the world stood at around 7,900,000,000.

OUT OF CURIOSITY

If you counted non-stop, one number per second, it would take you nearly 32 years to count up to 1 billion!

7,900,000,000

HUGE NUMBERS

Some numbers have such large values that they are not often used outside of mathematics or astronomy.

We have:

Trillion (twelve zeros)
1,000,000,000,000

Quadrillion (fifteen zeros)
1,000,000,000,000,000

Quintillion (eighteen zeros)
1,000,000,000,000,000,000

Sextillion (twenty-one zeros)
1,000,000,000,000,000,000,000

Septillion (twenty-four zeros)
1,000,000,000,000,000,000,000,000

Octillion (twenty-seven zeros)
1,000,000,000,000,000,000,000,000,000

Nonillion (thirty zeros)
1,000,000,000,000,000,000,000,000,000,000

Decillion (thirty-three zeros)
1,000,000,000,000,000,000,000,000,000,000,000

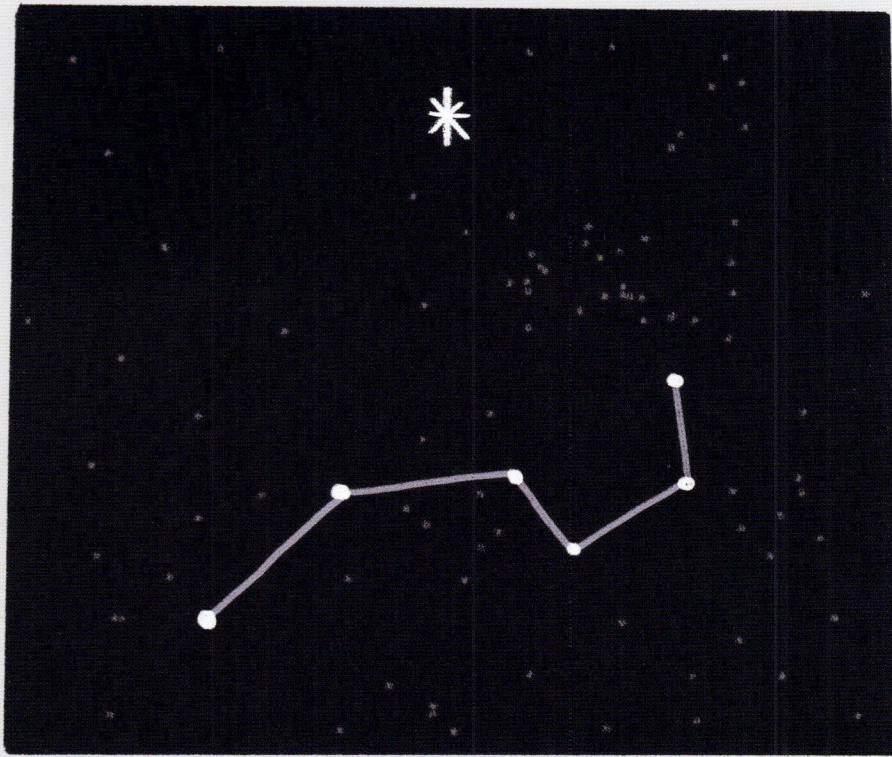

WHAT ARE THEY USED FOR?

Many of these numbers are used for the calculation of mathematical ideas. In everyday life, we do not use them very often. Scientists sometimes use large numbers. When physicists talk about the speed of light, they use trillions, for example. Light travels approximately 9.5 trillion km (5.9 trillion miles) in a year. That distance is called a "light year."

Earth is at least 320 light years from Polaris, the bright North Star.

STARRY, STARRY NIGHT...

Have you ever looked up at the sky on a clear night and seen bright, shining stars filling the sky? Counting them all would be hard! There are between 100 and 300 sextillion stars in the Universe.

PRODUCTS AND FACTORS

In mathematics, a product is the value found by multiplying two or more numbers together.

$$3 \times 6 = 18$$

18 is the product of 3 and 6

$$5 \times 4 = 20$$

20 is the product of 5 and 4

KEEP IT POSITIVE!

The product of two positive numbers is always positive. That doesn't seem too surprising. However, the product of two negative numbers is also positive.

$$-4 \times -5 = 20$$

FACTORS

A factor is the mathematical opposite of a product. It is the number you multiply with other factors to get a product.

3 and **6** are factors of **18**

A number can have just two factors or many.

FACTORING IN EVERYDAY LIFE

You may sometimes think, "When will I ever use this mathematics skill outside the classroom?" The answer is that factoring is used in many places! Factoring is basic mathematics that reverses multiplication to find the numbers that multiply together to make a bigger number.

When you divide something into equal parts, you use factoring. For example, if 6 children grew strawberry plants and the plants gave 24 strawberries, it would be fair to share them out so that each child received 4 strawberries each. Dividing 24 by 6 gives 4, so each child receives 4 strawberries.

Factoring can also be used when exchanging money for smaller coins and notes.

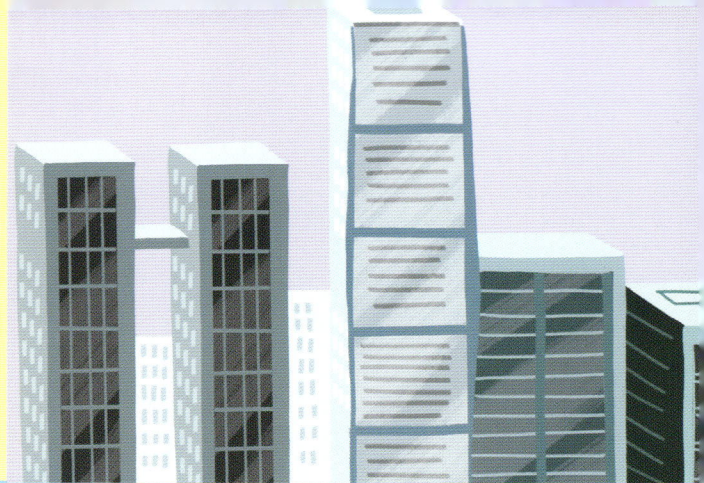

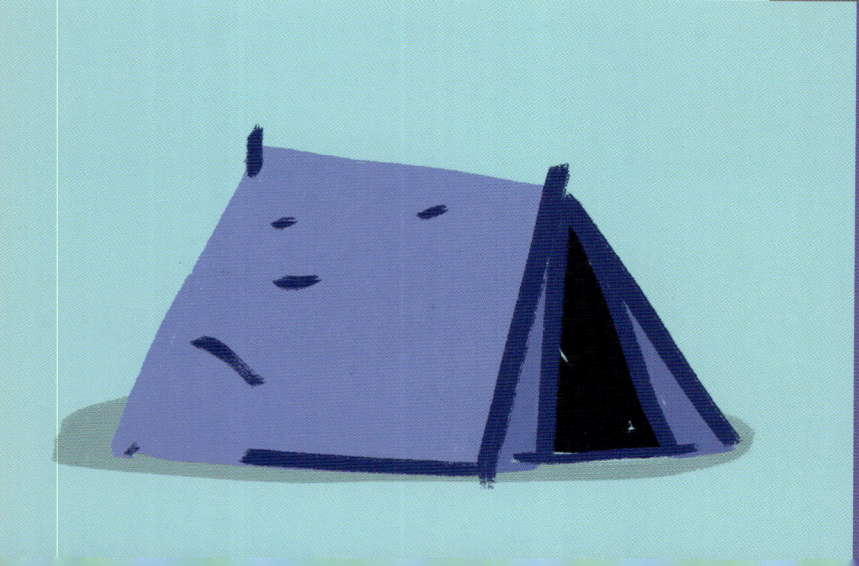

CHAPTER 17

SHAPE

Shapes are everywhere—have a look around you! Have a look around you. Everything can be broken down into shapes. The mathematics of shape is called **geometry**.

We talk about shapes in terms of **dimensions**.
In mathematics, width, length, and height are dimensions.

A line has 1 dimension. It has length but no width.

Then there are two-dimensional (2D) shapes such as circles, squares, triangles, and more. They have length and width. They are flat plane figures and do not have any depth.

There are also three-dimensional (3D) shapes such as spheres, cubes, pyramids, and more. Three-dimensional shapes have three dimensions—length, width, and height. They are solid figures, and have depth.

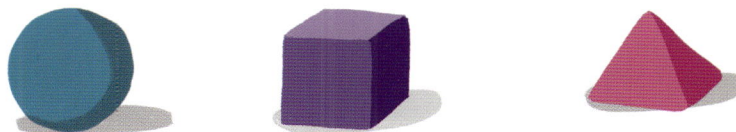

POLYGONS AND POLYHEDRONS

Polygons are 2D shapes made up of straight lines, angles, and points. The word polygon is a Greek word meaning "many" and "angle." Any shapes with curved sides are not polygons.

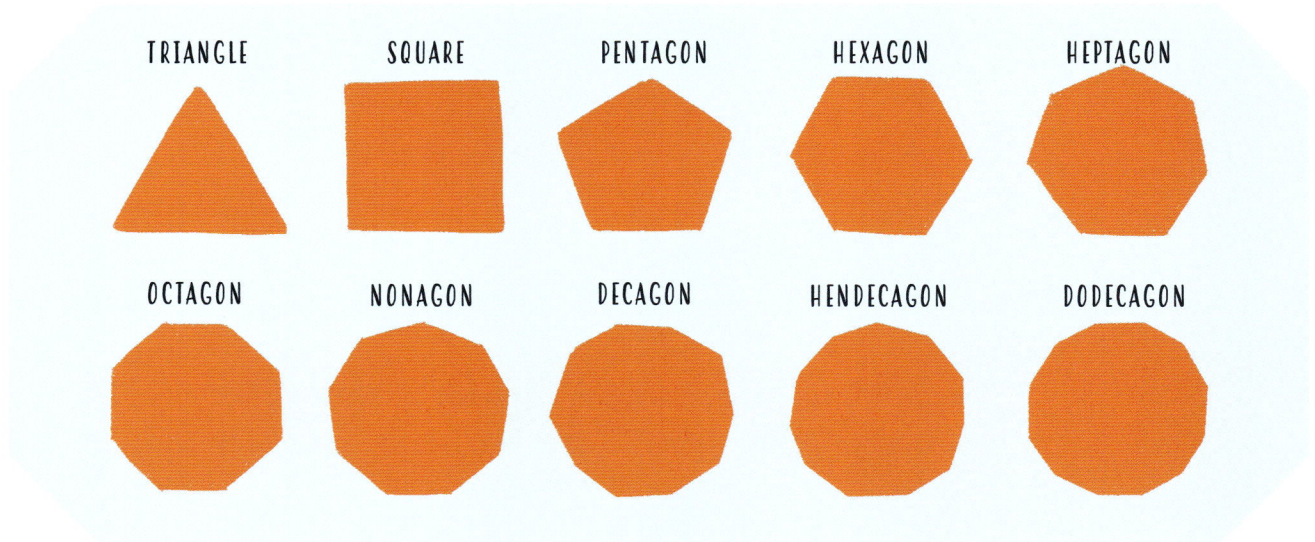

TRIANGLE	SQUARE	PENTAGON	HEXAGON	HEPTAGON

OCTAGON	NONAGON	DECAGON	HENDECAGON	DODECAGON

REGULAR POLYGONS

Regular polygons have sides that are all the same length and internal angles (angles inside the shape) that are all the same.

This is a regular heptagon, with seven straight sides.

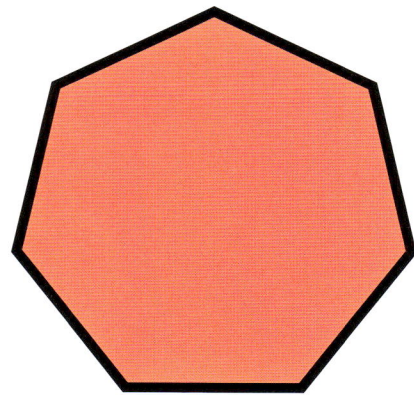

IRREGULAR POLYGONS

Irregular polygons have sides with different lengths and their interior angles may all be different.

This is an irregular heptagon because its sides are not the same length and its interior angles are not the same.

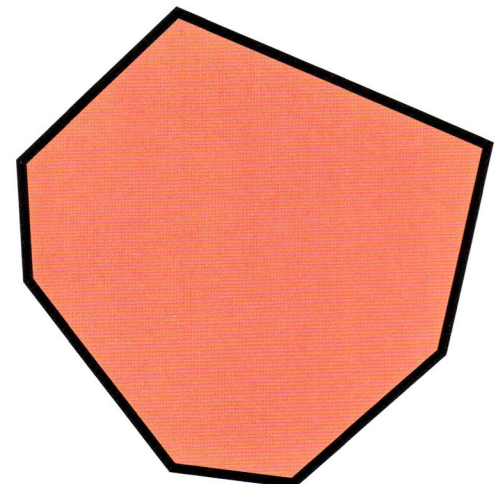

SPOT THE DIFFERENCE

Look at these triangles and **quadrilaterals**. Can you see why some are regular polygons and others are irregular polygons?

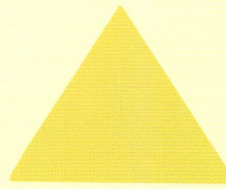

POLYGONS IN NATURE

You can see lots of polygons in the world around you. For example, honeycombs have regular polygons called hexagons, with six sides.

You can also see hexagons on snake skin.

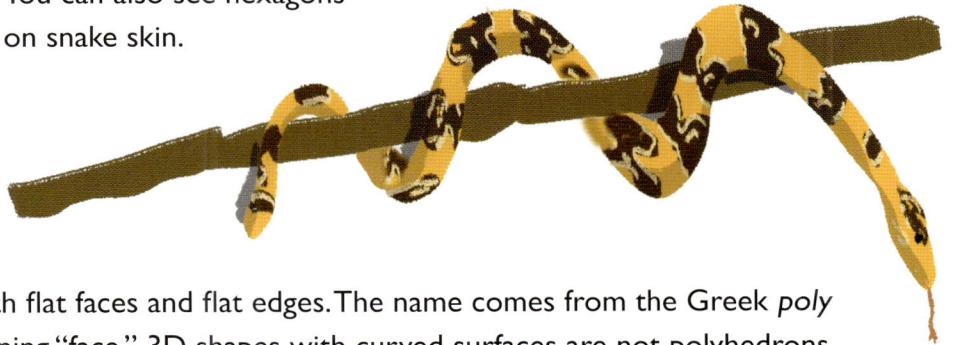

POLYHEDRONS

A **polyhedron** is a 3D shape with flat faces and flat edges. The name comes from the Greek *poly* meaning "many" and *hedron* meaning "face." 3D shapes with curved surfaces are not polyhedrons.

A cube and a pyramid are examples of polyhedrons.

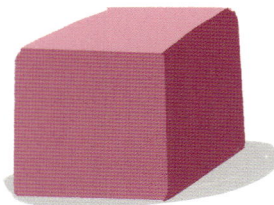

A cone and a sphere are not polyhedrons as they have curved surfaces.

SHAPES WITH CURVES

Some 2D shapes have curved edges, such as **circles** and **ellipses**. 3D shapes with curved edges include **spheres**, **cylinders**, and **cones**. If you look around you, can see shapes with curves everywhere!

CIRCLE

Circles are 2D shapes with curved edges. An example is a coin. The shape's edge is always an equal distance from the center. Circles are the most symmetrical shapes in the Universe, with nearly infinite lines of **symmetry**—wherever you draw a line that cuts a circle in two through the center, you will have a reflected image on each side of the line!

ELLIPSE

An ellipse is a 2D shape with curved edges. It has two **axes** running through the center.

The major axis is the long axis and the minor axis is the shorter one. An ellipse has **reflectional symmetry** on either side of its axes.

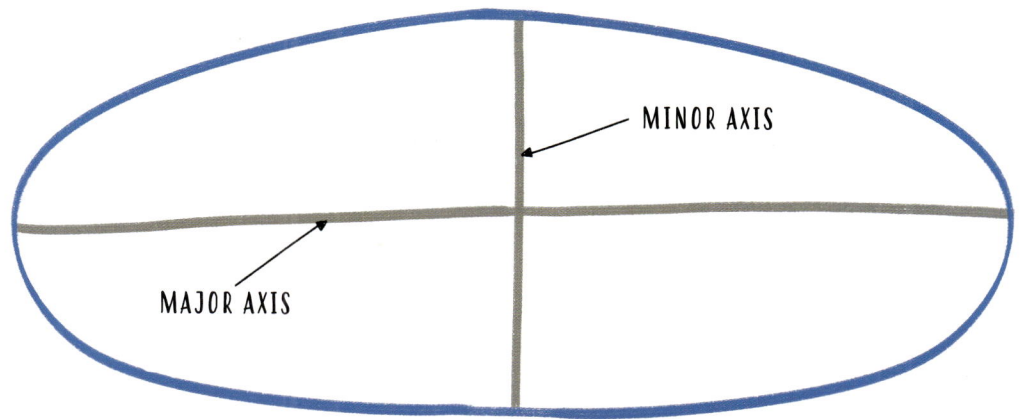

MINOR AXIS

MAJOR AXIS

SPHERE

A sphere is a 3D shape with curved sides. It is perfectly round. A ball is a sphere. Planets are roughly spheres. Every point on the surface of a sphere is an equal distance from its center.

CONE

A cone is a 3D shape—a pyramid with a circle for its base. A tasty example is an ice cream cone! You also find cones on the end of sharp things, like nails used to build things from wood. You may have used some in your shop classes at school!

CYLINDER

A cylinder is a 3D shape with curved edges. A drink can is a cylinder, and so is a wheel. Cylinders are often used for storage because they have a flat bottom so they can be stood upright and even stacked.

If you flattened a cylinder, you would see a rectangle and two circles.

CIRCUMFERENCE AND MORE

Circumference is a measure of the distance all the way around the edge, or perimeter, of a circle. An **arc** is a section of the circumference.

Mathematicians talk about a special number called **pi** (see pages 276–277), which is the circumference of a circle divided by its **diameter**.

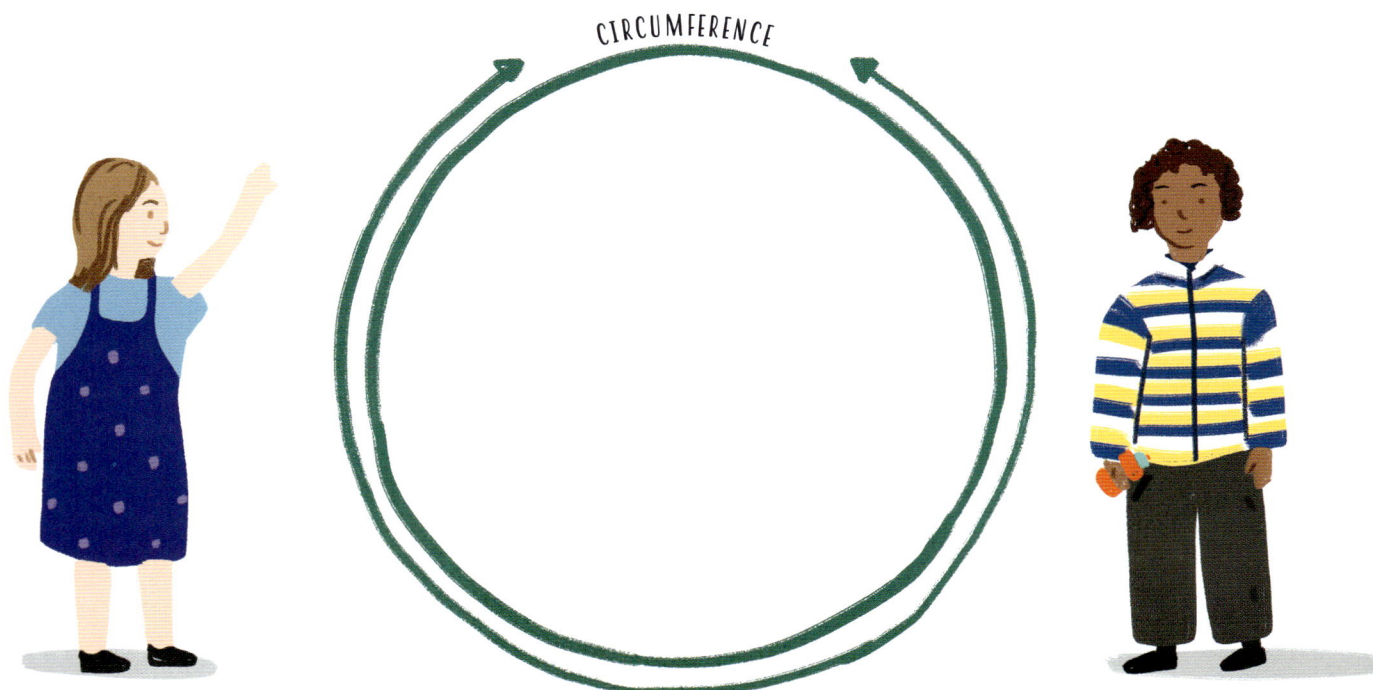

CIRCUMFERENCE

● RADIUS

The **radius** of a circle is the distance between the center of the circle and the edge, or perimeter, of the circle. The radius is half the length of the diameter. Mathematicians use **r** for the length of a circle's radius.

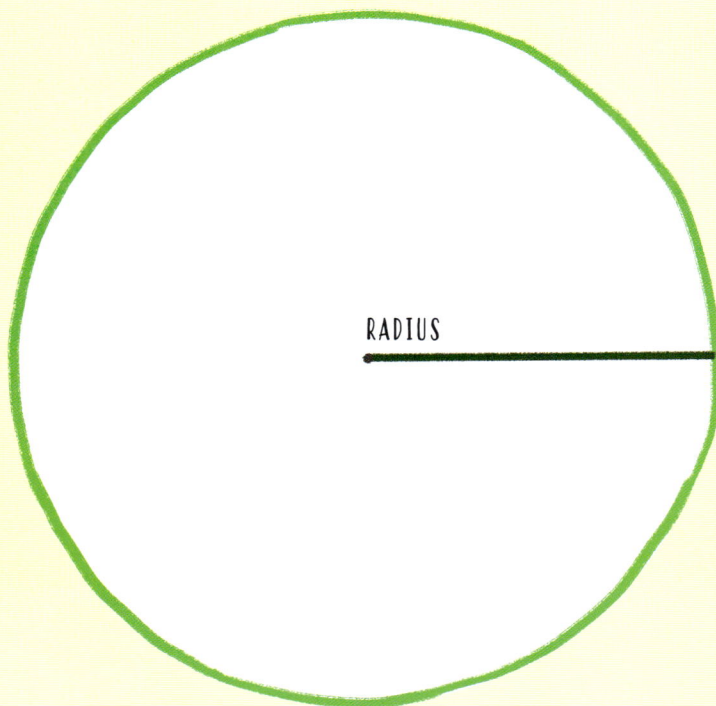

RADIUS

DIAMETER

The **diameter** of a circle is the distance running across a circle through the center, from edge to edge. The diameter is double the length of the radius.

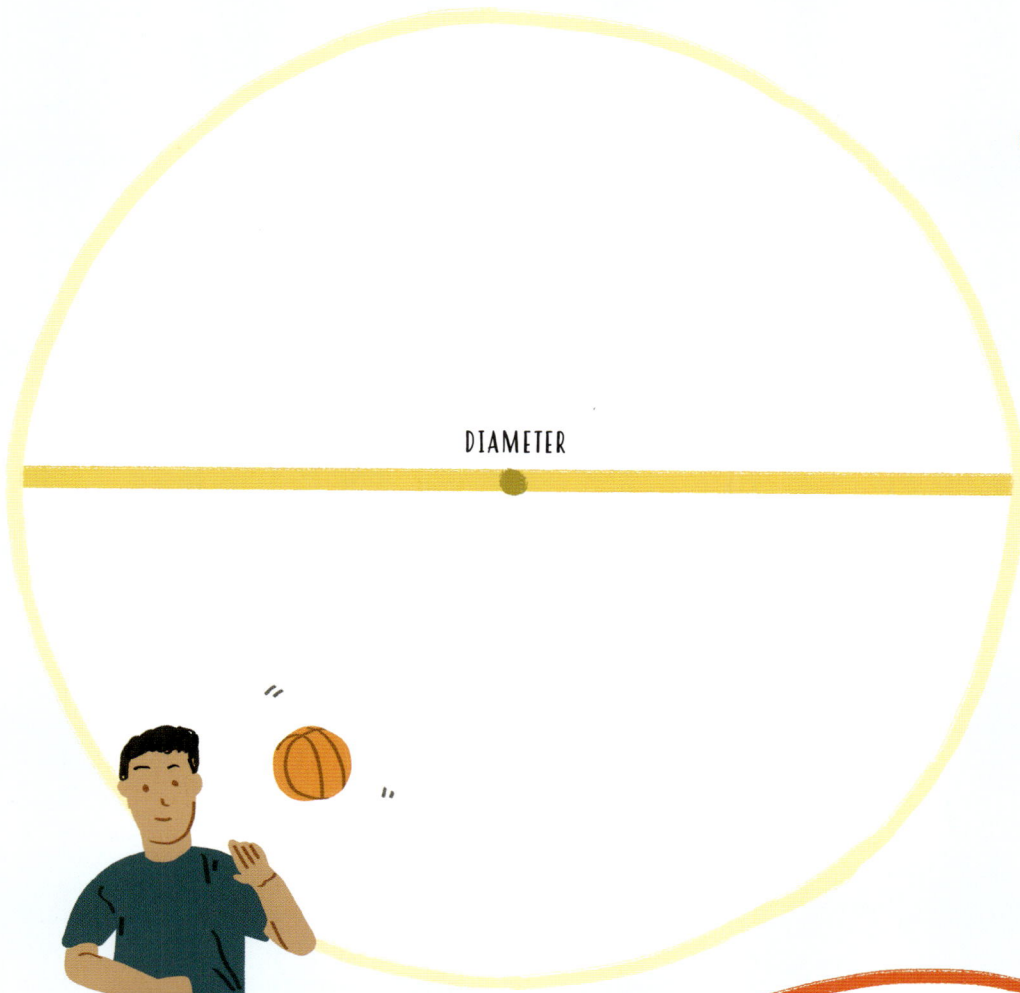

DIAMETER

CHORD

A **chord** is a straight line that joins two points on the circumference of a circle. The diameter is a special kind of chord— and it is the longest chord possible, because it goes from one edge of the circle across the center to the other side.

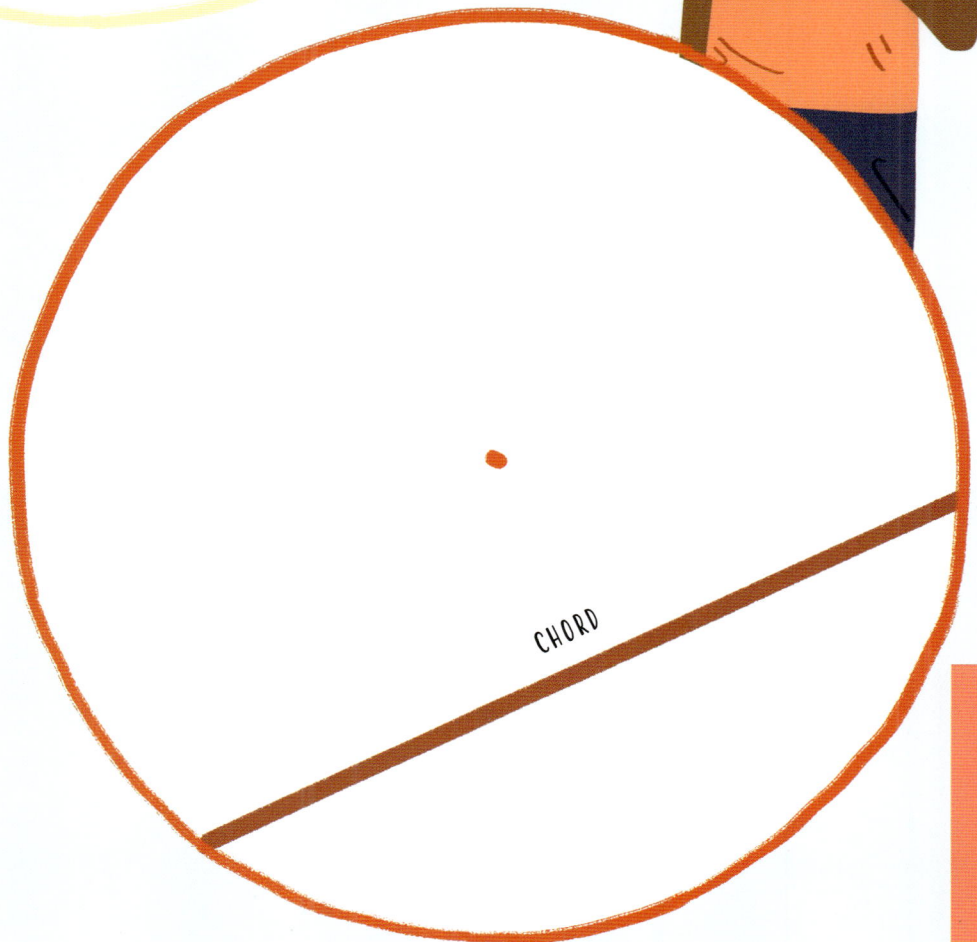

CHORD

275

Pi is a special number. It can be written using the π symbol, a letter from the Greek alphabet. The letter is the first letter of the Greek word for perimeter. Pi is the ratio of the distance around a circle—the circumference—to its diameter. It doesn't matter how big a circle is, the circumference of any circle is around 3.14 times its diameter—and that "around 3.14" is the value of pi.

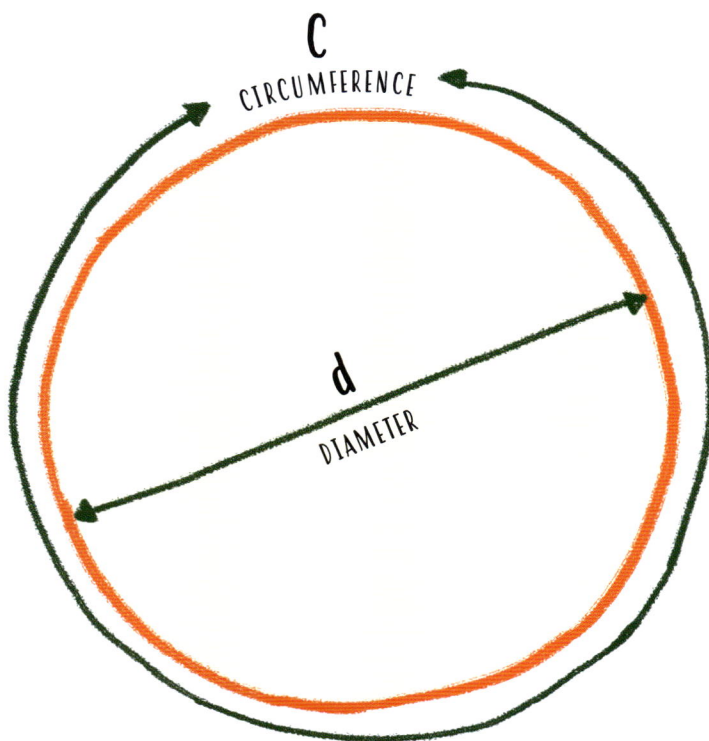

C
CIRCUMFERENCE

d
DIAMETER

π EQUATION FOR Pi

We can write this rule as an equation that means pi equals circumference divided by diameter.

$$\pi = \frac{C}{d}$$

π INFINITE NUMBER

Pi is an infinite number—the numbers after the decimal point keep going on and on. It starts 3.14159265358979323846433 and goes on forever!

3.14159265358979323846...

π THE QUEST FOR PI

In around 1550 BCE, Egyptian scholar Ahmes gave a rough value for pi in a document called the Rhind Papyrus.

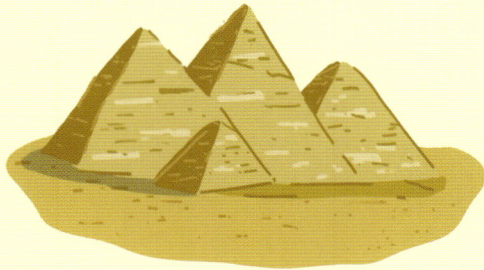

Babylonians discussed pi and explored it by making huge circles and measuring the circumference and diameter with long ropes to help their calculations.

π USING PI

Pi is used in astronomy to work out **orbits**. It is also used for calculating the **area** of circles. The area of a circle is pi times the radius squared—$A = \pi r^2$.

π ARCHIMEDES AND ON

The Greek mathematician Archimedes used a 96-sided polygon drawn inside a circle to find the value of pi in 250 BCE. The Greco-Roman scientist Ptolemy gave pi a value equivalent to 3.1416 in around 150 CE. By 500 CE, Chinese scholars including Zu Chongzhi used a 16,384-sided polygon to work out the value with even more accuracy.

π CLOSER AND CLOSER

Persian astronomer Jamshid Al-Kashi produced a value for pi accurate to the equivalent of 16 digits in 1424. By 1621, Dutch scientist Willebrord Snellius calculated pi to 34 digits. By 1630, Austrian astronomer Christoph Grienberger reached 38 digits. Today, pi can be calculated by **artificial intelligence**—but of course, it is still an infinite number!

QUADRILATERALS AND CUBOIDS

Quadrilaterals are four-sided shapes with straight edges. Quad means "four" and lateral means "sides." All of a quadrilateral's internal angles add up to 360° (see page 282). Quadrilaterals and **cuboids** are important shapes as they are fairly strong and fit together easily, so they are used often in buildings.

PARALLELOGRAM

A parallelogram is a quadrilateral that has two pairs of **parallel** sides. The opposite sides must be an equal length. Parallelograms have four edges and four **vertices** (where edges meet).

❖ SQUARE

A square is a special kind of parallelogram whose sides and angles are all equal.

A square is a 2D shape with four equal sides. Opposite sides of a square are parallel, and all sides are the same length. Each corner, or vertex, of a square is a right angle, or 90°.

❖ RECTANGLE

A rectangle is a type of parallelogram. It is a 2D shape with two pairs of equal sides.

Like a square, each corner, or vertex, is a right angle, or 90°.

❖ CUBOID

A cuboid is a 3D shape. Most boxes are cuboids. Cuboids have six rectangular faces, and all of their angles are right angles. A cuboid is also a rectangular prism, as it has the same cross-section along its length. This means that, if you cut a slice of a cuboid, you would still see the same shape.

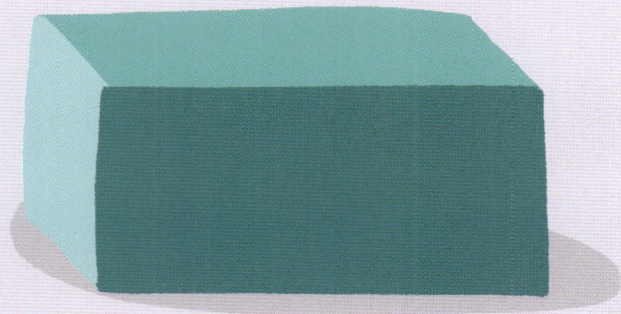

❖ CUBE

A cube is a cuboid with sides that are all the same length. Like all cuboids, cubes have six faces and 12 edges. They have eight vertices, or corners. At each vertex, three edges meet. A cube is a platonic solid. That means that all of its faces are the same regular polygon (or shape) and the same number of polygons meet at each vertex.

TRIANGULAR SHAPES

Triangular shapes are very strong and are used often in architecture and building, just like squares, cubes, and cuboids. We see triangles in roofs in particular, where their strong shape but slanted sides allow rain and snow to run off. That means water will be less likely to damage the roof, so triangles save money, too!

TRIANGLE

A triangle has three straight sides and three vertices. The angles inside a triangle all add up to 180°.

There are different types of triangles:

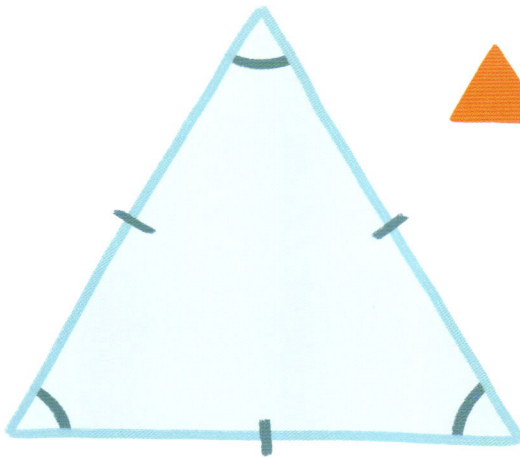

EQUILATERAL TRIANGLE

Equilateral triangles have three equal sides and three equal angles. The angles inside a triangle add up to 180°, so that means each angle is 60°.

ISOSCELES TRIANGLE

Isosceles triangles have two equal sides and two interior (inside) angles, called base angles, that are the same.

SCALENE TRIANGLE

Scalene triangles have three sides of different lengths and three different interior angles—but the angles still add up to 180°.

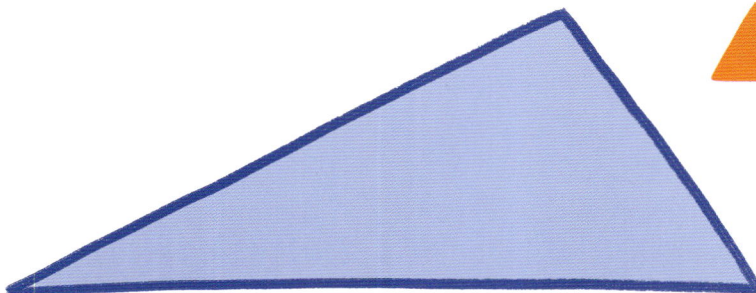

RIGHT-ANGLED TRIANGLE

In a right-angled triangle, one of the interior angles is 90°, so the other two angles add up to 90° together—because, remember, the angles in a triangle must add up to 180°.

PYRAMID

Pyramids are 3D shapes that have four triangular faces. Pyramids can be square or triangular-based. A square-based pyramid has five faces and five vertices. It has eight edges.

A triangular-based pyramid has four faces and four vertices. It has six edges.

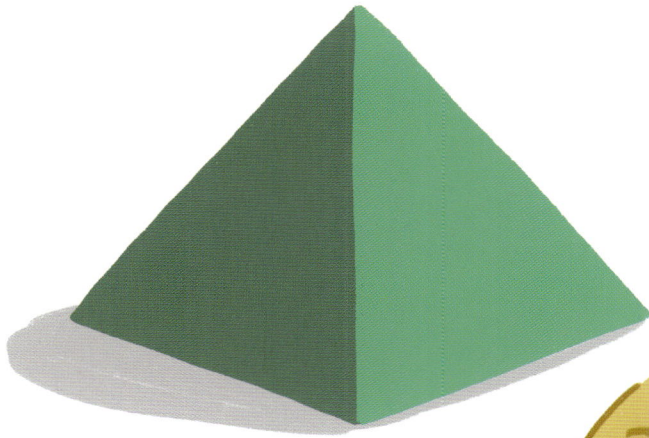

? OUT OF CURIOSITY

A triangular-based pyramid with equal sides is called a tetrahedron.

TRIANGULAR PRISM

A triangular prism is a 3D shape. Three sides are parallelograms and the opposite ends of the shape are triangles. Some tents are the shape of triangular prisms!

ANGLES

Angles are made wherever two lines meet. Angles are measured in degrees.
A complete turn (if you held out your arms and turned in a complete circle) is 360°.

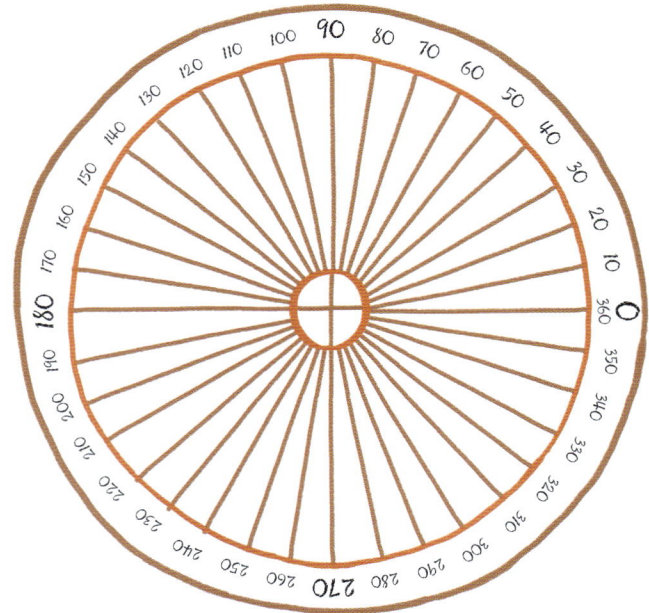

PROTRACTORS

Angles can be measured with an instrument called a protractor.
You can get 180° and 360° protractors.

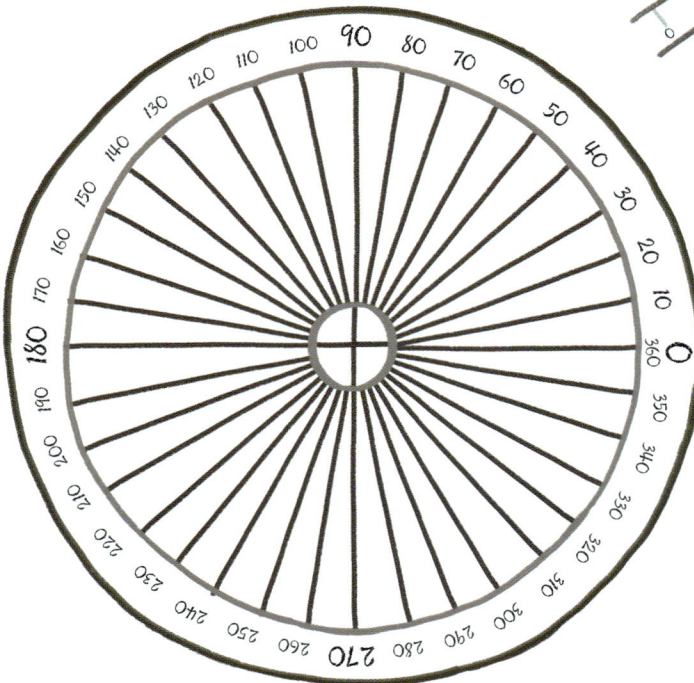

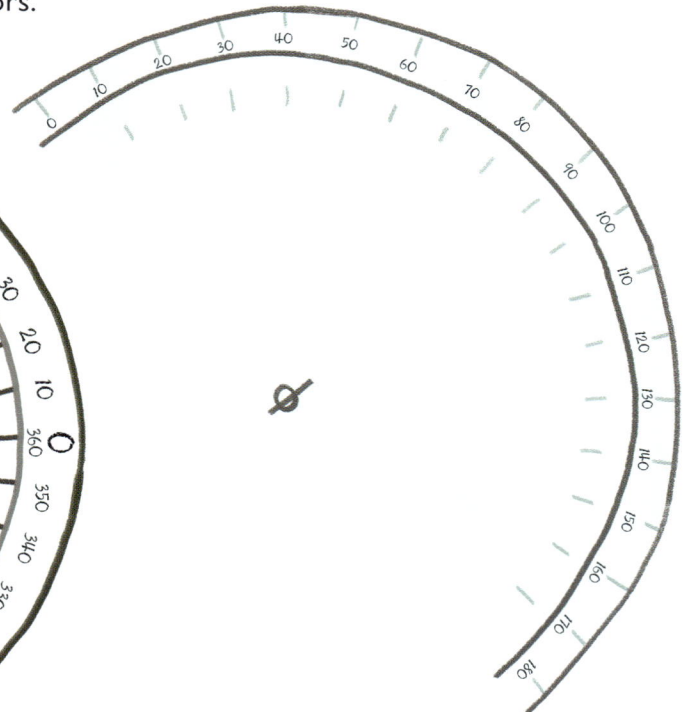

There are different types of angles:

RIGHT ANGLES

A right angle is exactly 90°. Right angles are represented in mathematical diagrams by a square, so you immediately know it is a right angle.

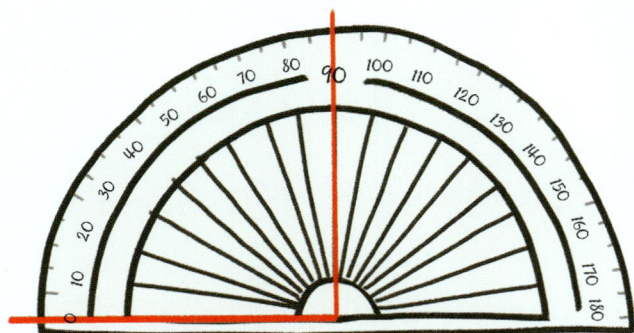

ACUTE ANGLES

Acute angles are angles of less than 90°. They are smaller than right angles.

OBTUSE ANGLES

Obtuse angles are angles of between 90° and 180°.

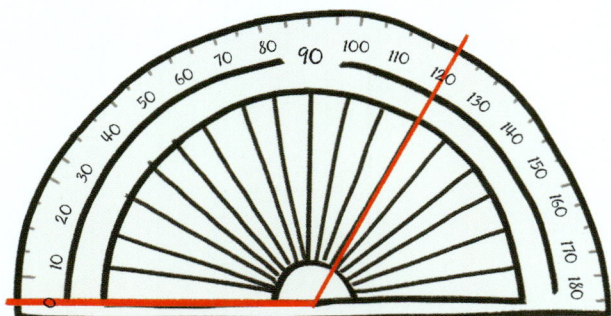

STRAIGHT ANGLES

A straight angle is exactly 180°.

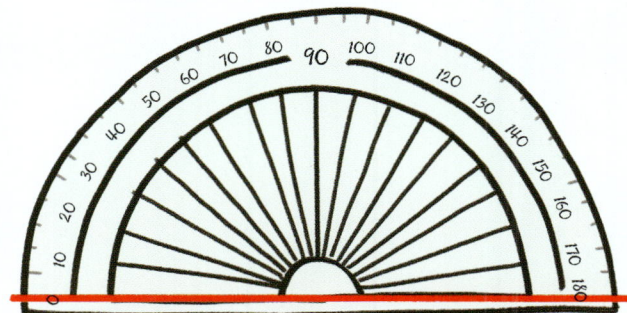

REFLEX ANGLES

A reflex angle is between 180° and 360°.

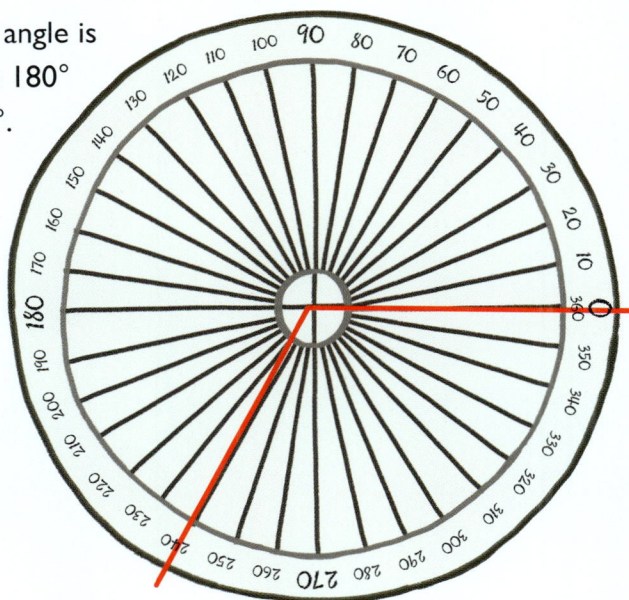

When mathematicians draw angles, they draw a curved line inside (unless it is a 90° angle, which is drawn with a square).

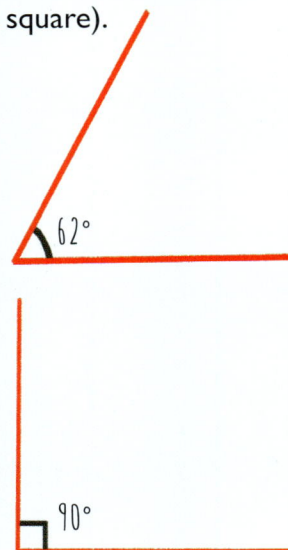

62°

90°

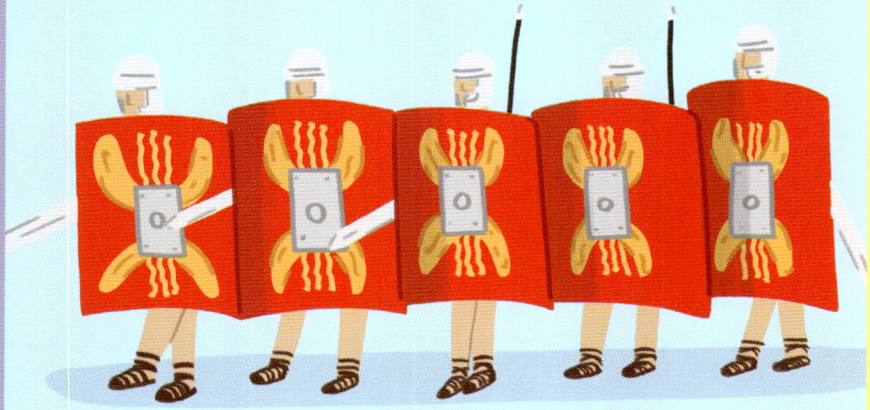

CHAPTER 18

MEASURE

We measure things to see how much they weigh, what size they are, and the passing of time. We measure things to organize our lives. We measure time using calendars and clocks.

We measure things using standard measures. If you go into a shop in Tokyo and buy a kilogram or pound of nuts, it will weigh the same as a kilogram or pound of nuts bought in London. We all know what a kilogram or pound "means."

Similarly, a day lasts 24 hours, wherever you are in the world. Although time zones are different around the world, this helps people to organize meetings together, and coordinate their plans. School days, working hours, times of buses and trains—we need to measure time to organize our lives.

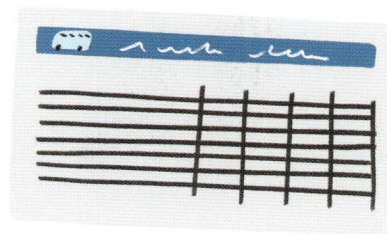

NON-STANDARD MEASURE

Non-standard measure is when things such as hand spans or pencils are used to measure with instead of rulers and scales. It gives people a rough idea of measures and allows people to compare things—but it is not very accurate!

MEASUREMENT IN EARLY HISTORY

People have been measuring things for as long as there have been people! That does not mean there were always rulers and clocks, though—at least not as we know them. There is evidence from archeological digs to suggest that early people measured things such as the passing time with tally sticks. The first recorded systems of measurement appeared in ancient civilizations such as those in Mesopotamia, Egypt, and the Indus Valley. Different regions used different measures in farming, building, and trade. There were no worldwide "standard" measurements like we have today.

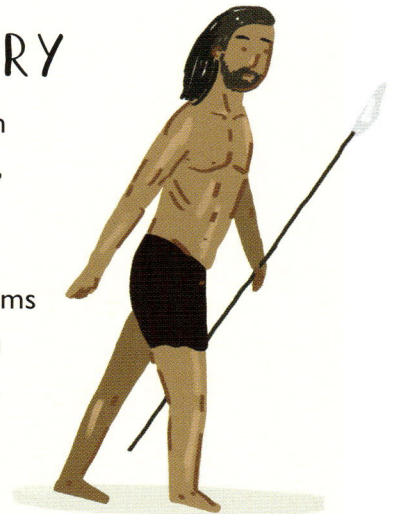

NON-STANDARD MEASURE

Even if you do not have a ruler, you can measure things. Imagine you wanted to measure a table and bench but you did not have a ruler handy. You could measure them in hand spans— or even with objects such as pencils!

You would have to place the pencils end to end to make sure there were no gaps. The table might be 10 pencils long and 6 pencils wide. If you measured the bench in the same way and it was 5 pencils long and 3 pencils wide, you would be able to compare the sizes of the two items (the bench is half as long and half as wide as the table) without actually knowing the measurements in centimeters or inches.

CUBITS AND BUSHELS

In ancient Egypt and Rome, people often measured length in cubits. These varied from place to place, but were often measured from the tip of the middle finger to the elbow, equal to two hand spans. Goods such as corn or flour were often measured by volume: the amount of seeds that fit in vessels. In medieval Europe, the measure of volume was often the bushel.

OUT OF CURIOSITY

The carat is a unit still used today for measuring gemstones. Originally, the unit of measure was the weight of a carob seed!

BODY-BASED MEASUREMENTS

King Henry 1 of England decided that a "yard" was the distance from his nose to his thumb on his outstretched arm! The thing is, not everyone has arms of the same length, so that measure is non-standard. People also used to measure things in the length of a foot and the width of a finger. If you look around at your family and friends, you will easily see how this could be a problem as not all feet and fingers are the same size.

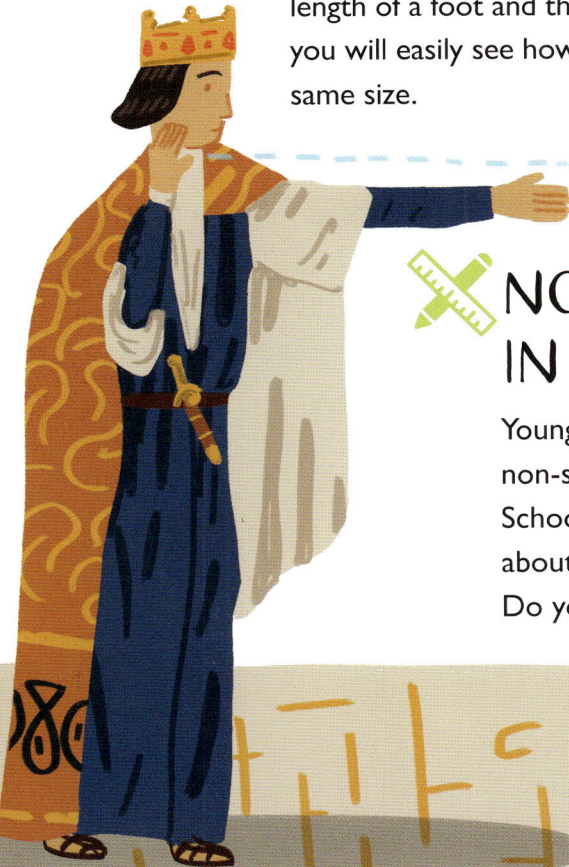

NON-STANDARD MEASUREMENT IN SCHOOLS TODAY

Young children are introduced to measuring length and weight using non-standard measurement. Measuring things accurately is hard. Schools use non-standard measurement to teach young children about ideas such as "lighter," "heavier," "longer," and "shorter." Do you remember learning about measurement in this way?

STANDARD MEASURE

A standard measure is one that is exactly the same wherever you are in the world. It never varies and is measured accurately using instruments such as rulers, scales, clocks, and thermometers.

WHY USE STANDARD MEASUREMENTS?

When people around the world started trading with each other on a regular basis, they needed measurements everyone could understand. Local or non-standard measurements were no good as people in one country needed to know weights and measures that they were talking about when they made deals with people in other countries.

EARLY "STANDARD" MEASUREMENT

The ancient Egyptians, Romans, and Greeks used a "foot" as a measure—but these were not true standard measures as they were different lengths in different places. The Romans also introduced the "mile" or *mille passus* ("thousand paces"). This Roman mile spread across Europe as their armies invaded and occupied territories, including Britannia (modern Britain). The Roman mile was 5,000 Roman feet (around 4,859 feet or 1,481 m). In the 1500s, Queen Elizabeth I changed the length of a mile in England by law to be 5,280 feet.

OUT OF CURIOSITY

Before truly standard measure was introduced, there were many different strange measurements used, such as span, finger, nail, rod, pole, and perch!

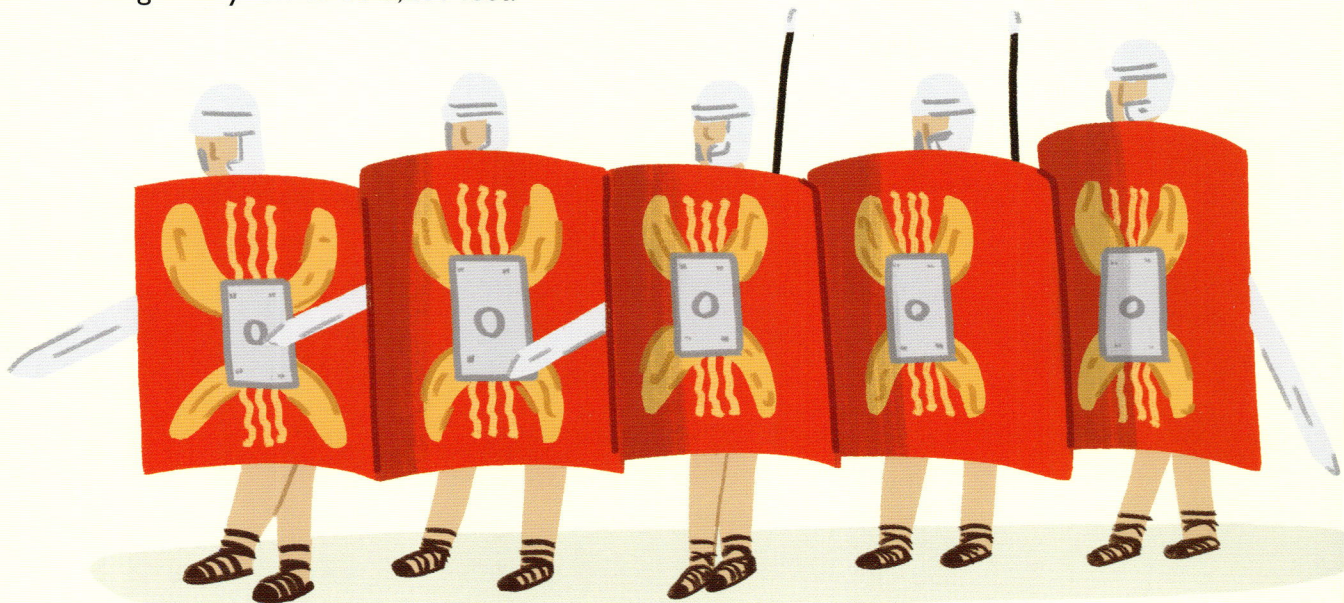

IMPERIAL AND US MEASUREMENT

Imperial measurement is a type of standard measure that was used by the British Empire. The British Weights and Measures Act 1824 introduced the measures wherever Britain held control. Imperial measures are very similar to those used in the USA, as both systems are based on medieval English measurements.

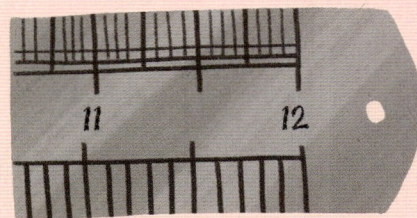

In the last century, the UK and most other countries changed to the metric system (see below). The USA still uses its own customary **units**, such as pounds and ounces.

IMPERIAL AND US UNITS

Length: inches, feet, yards, miles

Weight: ounces, pounds

Volume: fluid ounces, gills, pints, quarts, gallons

Area: acres, hectares

Temperature: degrees Fahrenheit

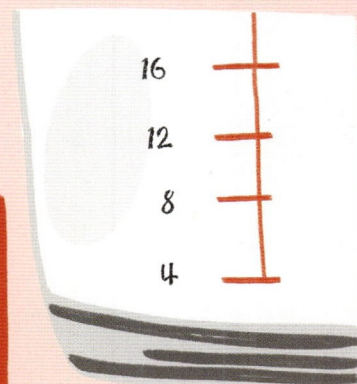

METRIC MEASUREMENT

The metric system was adopted in France in 1799. It became the dominant system across the world by the end of the 20th century. The International System of Units is the modern metric system, agreed in 1960 by the General Conference on Weights and Measures. It has been adopted across the world except for in the USA, Liberia, and Myanmar.

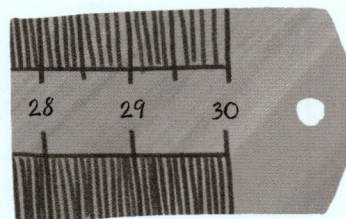

METRIC UNITS

Length: millimeters, centimeters, meters, kilometers

Weight: grams, kilograms

Volume: milliliters, liters

Area: square centimeters, square kilometers

Temperature: degrees Celsius

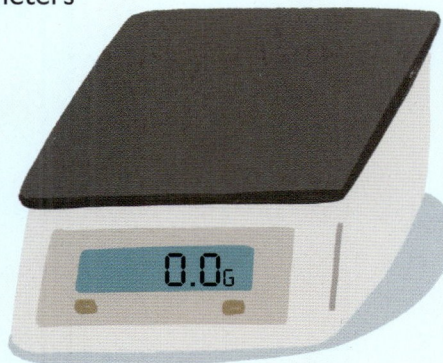

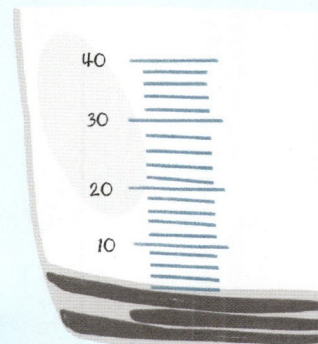

MEASURING LENGTH AND DISTANCE

We label the measurements of a two-dimensional shape in length and width, with the larger dimension usually being called length. Distance is measured between two points or objects. Length is measured as a dimension of a single object: We talk about the length of a line, for example.

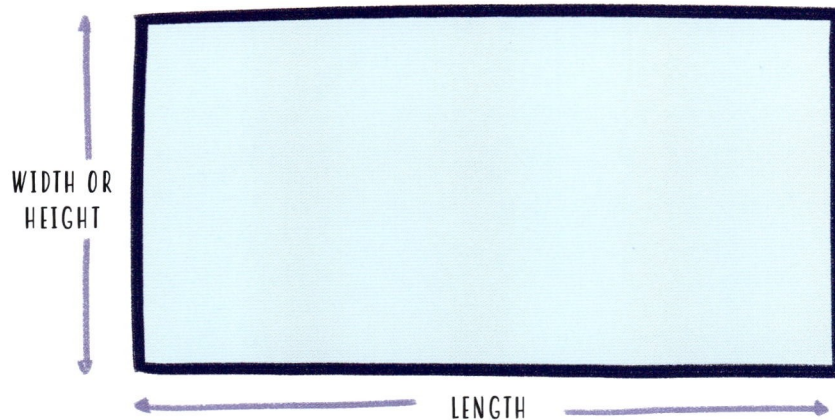

WIDTH OR HEIGHT

LENGTH

IMPERIAL AND US UNITS OF LENGTH

In the Imperial and US system, length is measured in inches (in), feet (ft), yards (yd), and miles (mi). Inches are used to measure small things, like a pencil or an eraser. Feet, yards, and miles are used to measure larger things, like the distance between two places, such as home and school.

TOOLS FOR MEASURING LENGTH

Rulers and tape measures are used for measuring smaller items.

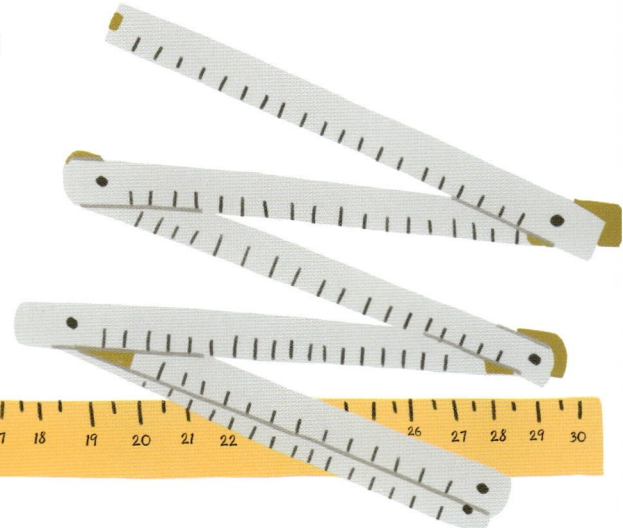

Short distances (in a garden or on a building site) may be measured with surveyor's wheels or a **laser**.

Look on the dashboard in a car to see an odometer. It shows the distance the car has driven.

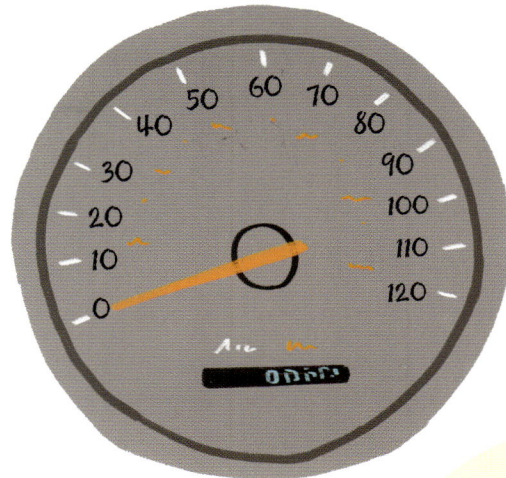

METRIC UNITS OF LENGTH

In the metric system of measure, it is easy to work out equivalent measures. One meter is the equivalent of 100 centimeters, for example. "Cent" comes from the Latin word for 100, and "centi" means "one-hundredth," which can help you to remember how many centimeters there are in a meter!

One kilometer is the equivalent of 1,000 meters. "Kilo" comes from the Greek word *kilo*, which means 1,000, which makes it easy to remember that there are 1,000 m in a km.

1 cm = 10 mm

1 m = 100 cm

1 km = 1,000 m

MAPS

A map that is drawn to **scale** helps us to work out the distance between two points. The scale tells us the ratio of a distance on the map to a distance on the ground. For example, in the metric system, a map scale of 1:50,000 means that 1 cm on the map is equal to 50,000 cm (or 500 m) on the ground. In the Imperial and US system, a scale of 1:63,360 means that 1 in on the map is equal to 63,360 in (or 1 mi) on the ground.

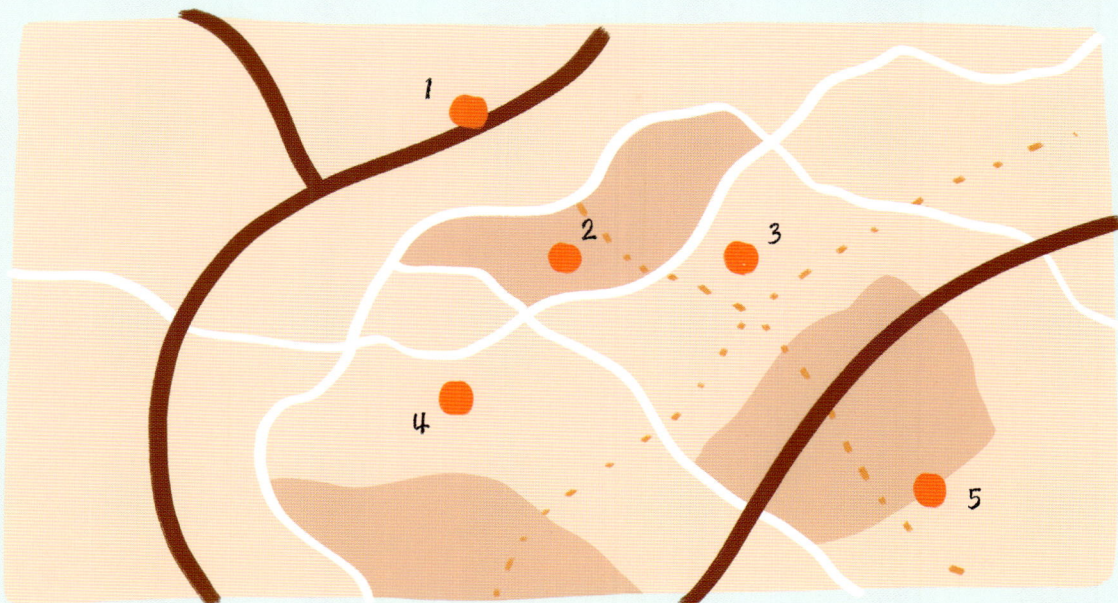

MEASURING WEIGHT

Have you ever lifted anything heavy or carried full shopping bags? Weight measures the force of **gravity** pulling down on an object. Gravity is the force that pulls objects toward each other. Earth's gravity keeps you on the ground rather than floating in the air! Gravity is the force that makes things fall to Earth when they are dropped. Gravity pulls harder on "heavy" things—and that's why they are harder to carry!

MASS

The weight of an object is a measure of the effect gravity has on its **mass**. On Earth, mass and weight are usually treated as the same and we report weight using the same units as we measure mass. A big, heavy rock has a lot of mass and a large weight. On the Moon, that rock would have the same mass but less weight, because the force of gravity on the Moon is smaller so it can't "pull" on the rock as hard.

WEIGHING THINGS UP

Scales and balances report weight in ounces (oz) and pounds (lb), or in the metric system, in grams (g) and kilograms (kg).

Milligrams (mg) are used for weighing tiny, light things, such as a feather or an ant.

Grams or ounces are used for weighing small things. A paper clip weighs around 1 g (0.035 oz).

You may buy a bag of candy that weighs around 100 g (3.5 oz).

Kilograms or pounds are used to weigh larger things, such as sacks of potatoes—or people!

Metric tons and US tons are used to weigh heavy things, such as an elephant!

TOOLS FOR MEASURING WEIGHT

Weight is measured using scales:

Kitchen scales

Bathroom scales

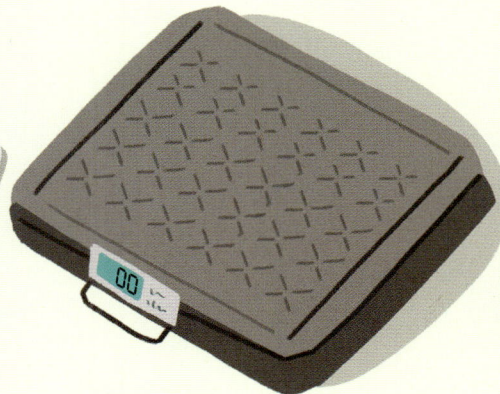

Vehicle scales

Postal scales

METRIC CONVERSIONS

A milligram is 1,000th of a gram—there are 1,000 mg in 1 g.
There are 1,000 g in 1 kg.
There are 1,000 kg in 1 metric ton (1 t).

OUT OF CURIOSITY

If you weigh 32 kg (70.5 lb) on Earth, you would weigh around 77 kg (169.8 lb) on Jupiter—that's because of the force of gravity. Your weight would change due to the planet's different mass. Jupiter is a massive planet, and it has gravity around 2.4 times Earth's gravity.

AREA

Area is measured in square units. The area is the number of these squares that will fit inside the region being measured. In mathematics, area is used to measure shapes. In a real-life setting, area is used to measure rooms in houses, carpets, plots of land, and even whole countries!

FINDING AREA

If your backyard was a rectangle 7 m long and 5 m wide (or if you live in the USA, let's say 7 yards long and 5 yards wide), you multiply the length by the width to find the area.
7 x 5 = 35, so the garden has an area of 35 m^2 (or 35 yards^2 if you're working in the USA).

7 M/7 YARDS

5 M/5 YARDS

In the metric system, area is measured in square centimeters (cm^2), square meters (m^2), and square kilometers (km^2). In the USA and Imperial systems, the measurements are in^2, ft^2, and mi^2.

15 CM/6 IN

10 CM/4 IN

FINDING THE AREA OF A RECTANGLE

To find the area, multiply the width by the height.

Area = width x height   A = w x h

The area of this rectangle is 15 cm x 10 cm = 150 cm^2 or 6 in x 4 in = 24 in^2.

FINDING THE AREA OF A SQUARE

A square is a type of rectangle, but all sides of a square are the same length. To find the area of a square, multiply the length of two sides together.

The area of this square is 5 cm x 5 cm = 25 cm^2. or 2 in x 2 in = 4 in^2.

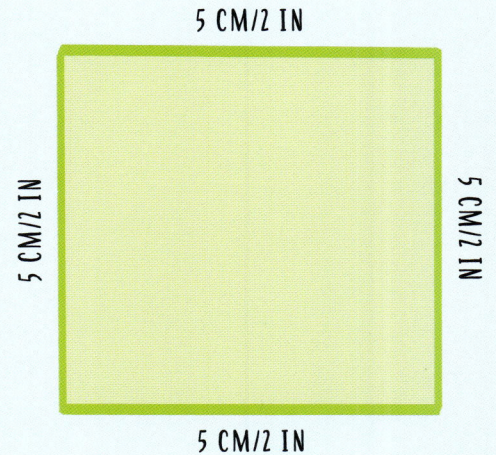

5 CM/2 IN

5 CM/2 IN

5 CM/2 IN

5 CM/2 IN

FINDING THE AREA OF A TRIANGLE

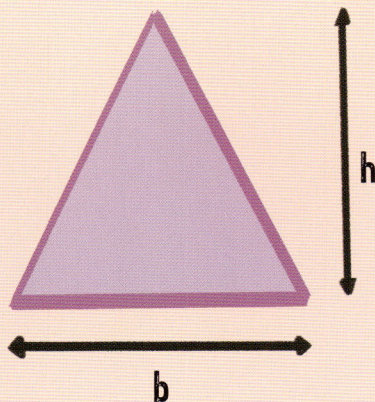

h

b

To find the area of a triangle, multiply half of the base measurement by the height measurement. If the base was 5 cm/2 in and the height was 10 cm/4 in, the area would be: 2.5 cm x 10 cm = 25 cm^2 or 1 in x 4 in = 4 in^2.

The formula is:

Area = ½ base x height   A = ½ x b x h

FINDING THE AREA OF A CIRCLE

To find the area of a circle, we multiply pi x radius x radius.

Area = pi x radius x radius   A = π x r x r

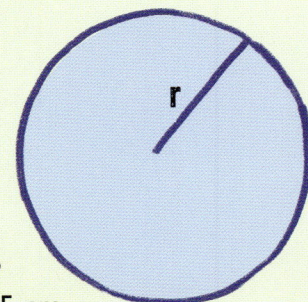

r

Pi (see page 276) is equivalent to around 3.14. Imagine you want to find the area of a circle with a radius of 5 cm/2 in. 5 cm x 5 cm = 25 cm. So, the area is 3.14 x 25 cm = 78.5 cm^2 (or 3.14 x 4 in = 12.56 in^2).

VOLUME AND CAPACITY

Volume is the amount of space an object takes up. A hollow object such as a pitcher or a box can hold a volume of something—a bottle might hold juice, for instance. The capacity of the object is the volume it can hold.

It is useful to measure volumes when you buy things like juice or milk by volume, and doctors work out the right volume of medicine to give you for your body size.

FINDING THE VOLUME OF CUBOIDS

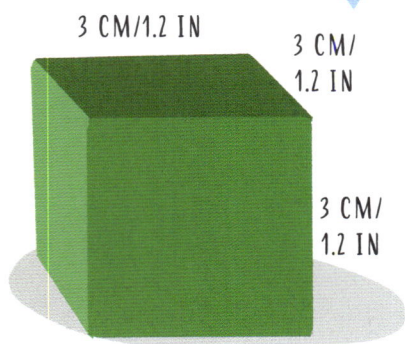

The **volume** of cuboids can be found by measuring their height, width, and depth. To find the volume of a shape, you multiply length by height by width:

3 CM/1.2 IN

3 CM/1.2 IN

3 CM/1.2 IN

V = length x height x width

V = l x h x w

The volume of this cuboid is 27 cm³.

UNITS OF MEASURING VOLUME AND CAPACITY

In metric, volume and capacity are measured in centimeters cubed (cm³), meters cubed (m³), milliliters (ml), centiliters (cl), and liters (l). In the Imperial and US system, volume and capacity are measures in fluid ounces, pints, and gallons.

OUT OF CURIOSITY

1 centimeter cubed will hold 1 milliliter of liquid.

Think about the difference between capacity and volume. Capacity is a property of a container—it is the measure of space inside the container. Volume is the amount of liquid in the container.

1l

2l

70cl

100ML

TOOLS FOR MEASURING THE VOLUME OF LIQUIDS

In a kitchen, measuring cups and measuring spoons are used to measure the volume of liquid ingredients.

In a science lab, graduated cylinders, flasks, beakers, and pipettes are used to measure the volume of liquids. Syringes may also be used.

Gas syringes may be used to measure the volume of gas produced in an experiment.

The gas (such as propane or butane) used in motorhomes for cooking is held in canisters or tanks that are measured in liters or gallons.

VOLUME OF POWDERS

In the kitchen, powders may be measured by measuring spoons or by "cups." Look at recipe books and see if you can find any recipes that call for a teaspoon of sugar or salt!

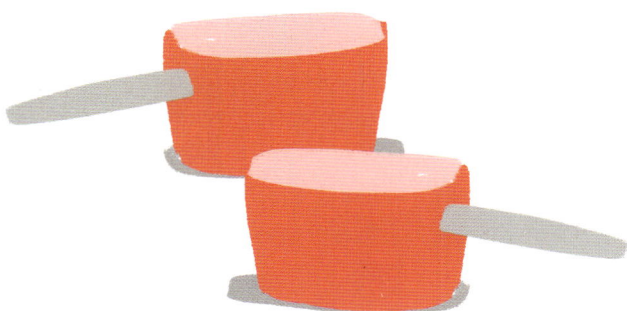

METRIC CONVERSIONS

There are 10 milliliters (ml) in a centiliter (cl) and 1,000 milliliters (ml) in a liter (l). There are 100 centiliters (cl) in a liter (l).

GLOSSARY

acceleration: How quickly an object speeds up.

acid: An acid is a chemical with a low pH. Acids have a pH lower than 7.

acoustics: Relating to sound and hearing.

adaptation: The changes a species goes through over time to be better suited to its environment.

aerodynamic: Having a shape that allows an object to pass swiftly through air, reducing air resistance.

air resistance: The force that acts on an object as it moves through air.

alchemist: A person who studied how to change basic substances such as common metals into other substances such as gold. Alchemists also studied magic and astrology.

algebra: To use unknown quantities (often given letters) with numbers to create formulas.

alkali: An alkali is any solution with a pH of more than 7. Alkali (or base) is the opposite of "acid."

amplitude: The highest point of a wave, measured from the middle.

anatomy: The branch of science that looks at the structure of a human, animal, or other organism's body.

arc: A section of the circumference of a circle.

archaea: A group of microorganisms that have been around for a very long time. Many thrive in hostile conditions.

area: The size that a surface takes up. It can be measured in cm^2 or in^2.

arithmetic: Helps us work out addition, subtraction, division, and multiplication calculations.

artificial intelligence: A computer program that is able to think and learn.

atom: The smallest particle of a chemical element that can exist.

atomic number: The number of protons in each atom. The atomic number decides the position of an element on the periodic table.

attract: To cause to draw together.

axis, axes: A real or imaginary reference line. Graphs have horizontal and vertical axes. An axis in reflectional symmetry divides an object in half

bacteria: Microscopic single-celled organisms with no nucleus. Some can be harmful and cause disease, and some can be helpful.

base: Any solution with a pH of more than 7.

biodiversity: The variety of life, either on the whole planet or in a particular place.

biologist: A person who studies or is an expert in living things.

biomass: Plant or animal matter used as fuel.

biome: A large community of life suited to a particular climate and landscape.

botanist: A person who studies or is an expert in plants.

botany: The study of plants.

breed: To mate and produce offspring.

buoyant: Able to stay afloat or rise to the surface of a liquid.

cell: Every living thing is made up of cells. A cell is the smallest, basic unit that makes up all living things and with the properties of life.

chlorophyll: A green pigment in plants that absorbs light and turns it into chemical energy, via a process called photosynthesis.

chemical bond: A force holding atoms together.

chemical reaction: A process in which one or more substances are converted to one or more different substances.

chord: A straight line that joins two points on the circumference of a circle.

chromosome: A long, tightly coiled DNA strand found in the nucleus of most eukaryotic cells, which contains part or all of the genetic information for a living thing.

circumference: A measure of the distance all the way around the edge, or perimeter, of a circle.

classification: The arrangement of organisms into groups based on their similarities.

climate: The usual weather for an area over a long period of time.

conduction: The process by which heat, electricity, or sound travels through material.

convection: The process of heat being transferred through a liquid or gas due to moving currents created by hot material rising and cold material sinking.

crystal: A solid material in which the material it is made up of fits together in a repeating pattern. Common examples are table salt and sugar.

cuboid: 3D shape. Most boxes are cuboids. Cuboids have six rectangular faces, and all of their angles are right angles.

deceleration: How quickly an object slows down.

dense: When matter is closely compacted together.

density: The space a substance takes up (its volume) in relation to the amount of matter in the substance (its mass). If a substance is small but heavy, it has high density.

diameter: The diameter of a circle is the distance running across a circle through the center, from edge to edge.

digestion: The process of breaking down food into substances the body can use.

dissolve: When a solid is mixed with a liquid and it seems to disappear, it is said to have dissolved.

distillation: A process where a mixture made up of liquids with different boiling points can be separated.

DNA (deoxyribonucleic acid): The chemical that stores genetic information in a cell.

drag: The force of resistance experienced by an object moving through a liquid or gas, such as water or air.

ductile: Can be hammered thin or stretched into wire without breaking.

ecology: The branch of biology that looks at how organisms relate to each other in their surroundings.

ecosystem: The community of interacting organisms and non-living things in a habitat.

electricity: Energy from the movement of charged particles.

electron: A negatively charged particle found in an atom.

element: A substance made of a single type of atom. An example would be iron.

ellipse: 2D shape that looks like a flattened circle.

emit: To produce and let out.

encrypt: If something is encrypted it is made hard to read and decipher.

energy: Something that can do work and make things happen.

engineer: A person who designs, builds, or maintains machines and engines.

equation: A mathematical statement that contains an "equals" sign. The sign shows that two expressions are equal.

eukaryote: An organism that has cells with a nucleus and other separate structures surrounded by membranes.

evaporation: The process of changing from a liquid or solid state into a gas (like a puddle in sunshine).

evolution: The process of living organisms changing and developing over millions of years on Earth.

exoskeleton: A hard covering that provides a rigid external skeleton.

exothermic: Describes a chemical change accompanied by a release of heat.

factor: A whole number that divides exactly into another number. A factor multiplies with another number to make a third number.

fertilization: The fusion of male and female cells to produce offspring.

filtration: The process used to separate solid particles in a liquid or gaseous fluid. A filter allows fluids to pass through, but not solid particles.

finite: Means possible to be counted; has an end.

food chain: A series of plants and animals that depend on each other for food.

force: A push or pull that can make things move, change direction or speed, or change shape.

formula: A chemical formula is the way scientists write down symbols to show the number and type of atoms present in a molecule.

fossil fuel: A fuel, such as coal or gas, made from the remains of organisms that died millions of years ago.

frequency: The number of waves of a vibration in a second.

galaxy: A group of stars, gas, and dust held together by gravity.

gas: A state of matter. A gas flows like air. It can fill any container it is put inside as the molecules can move apart freely.

gene: A section of DNA that determines a specific characteristic of an organism.

generator: A machine that can convert kinetic energy into electricity.

geometry: The study of shapes and their properties (such as faces, vertices, and edges).

gravity: A force that attracts objects toward each other.

greenhouse gas: A gas in the atmosphere (such as carbon dioxide, nitrous oxide, and methane) that traps energy from the sun.

habitat: The natural home environment of a plant, animal, or other living thing.

harness: To control and use, such as harnessing solar power to produce electricity.

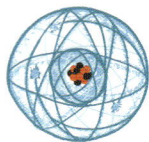

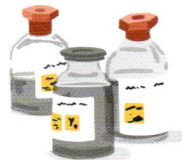

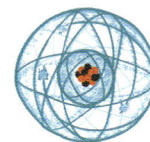

infrared radiation: A type of energy invisible to human eyes, but felt as heat.

inheritance: The passing on of characteristics to offspring from their parents.

insulation: Material used to stop electricity, heat, or sound passing from one conductor to another.

insulator: A substance that does not easily conduct heat, sound, or electricity.

invertebrate: An animal without a backbone.

ion: An atom or molecule that carries an electric charge.

isotopes: Atoms that have the same number of electrons and protons, but different numbers of neutrons—so they have different physical properties.

kinetic: Relating to motion.

laser: An instrument that can produce a powerful and narrow beam of light. A laser is sometimes used for measuring or cutting materials.

length: How long something is or the distance from one end of something to the other end.

liquid: A state of matter. Liquid molecules flow freely, like water, and take on the shape of containers they are put into.

lubricant: An oily, greasy, or slippery substance used to reduce rubbing between surfaces.

lunar: Means "to do with the Moon."

magnetism: An invisible force between some materials, causing them to attract or repel.

magnify: To make something appear larger than it is.

malleable: Bendy and able to change shape.

mass: The quantity of matter in an object.

matter: What everything in the Universe is made of. All matter is made up of atoms.

microbiology: The branch of science that looks at microorganisms.

microorganism: An organism so small that it can only be seen through a microscope, such as a bacterium.

migrate: To move daily or seasonally from one region to another.

mineral: A naturally occurring inorganic solid with a defined chemical structure.

molecule: A group of two or more atoms that form the smallest unit into which a pure substance can be divided and still keep the chemical properties of the substance.

monomer: A small molecule that reacts with another to form a larger molecule.

nanoparticle: A small particle that the human eye cannot see. Nanoparticles sometimes have very different properties from larger amounts of a substance.

nanotechnology: The science that studies nanoparticles.

natural selection: The process whereby the species best adapted to their environment survive and reproduce, while other species die out.

nebula: A cloud of gas and dust in space.

neutron: A particle with a neutral charge (neither positive nor negative), found in the nucleus of most atoms.

nuclear fusion: A reaction when nuclei join together to form a heavier nucleus, releasing energy in the process.

nucleus: The central part of a eukaryotic cell, made up of protons and neutrons, which controls the cell's function and stores its DNA.

nutrient: A substance that provides nourishment to grow and maintain an organism.

optics: The study of sight and how light behaves.

orbit: To move around a star or planet in a regular, repeated path.

orbital: The place around the nucleus of an atom where electrons move around in a wave.

organ: A group of tissues that work together to do a specific and important job. Major organs include the heart and brain.

organism: A living thing, including plants, animals, fungi, and single-celled life forms.

oxidize: Any chemical reaction that involves the movement of electrons. The substance that loses electrons is said to be oxidized.

parallel: If lines are parallel, they are the same distance apart and do not touch.

particle: A basic unit of matter, such as an atom or molecule, that makes up substances.

periodic table: The system used by scientists to arrange chemical elements.

photon: A tiny packet of energy, such as a particle of light.

photosynthesis: The process of plants using sunlight to create sugars out of water and carbon dioxide.

pi: A term used by mathematicians to describe a value which is the circumference of a circle divided by its diameter.

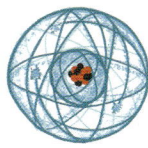

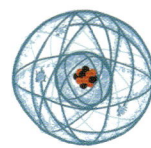

pitch: The highness or lowness of a sound.

pollination: The transfer of pollen so that plants can reproduce.

polygon: A 2A D shape made up of straight lines, angles, and points.

polyhedron: A 3D shape with flat faces and flat edges.

predator: An animal that feeds on other animals.

pressure: The amount of pushing force acting over an area.

prey: An animal that is hunted and eaten by other animals.

product: The result when two numbers are multiplied.

prokaryote: A microscopic single-celled organism with no distinct nucleus or cell membrane, such as bacteria and archaea.

protein: A type of chemical essential for the growth and repair of a living organism.

proton: A particle with a positive charge, found in an atom's nucleus.

quadrilateral: A polygon with four sides and four angles.

radiation: Energy that travels as electromagnetic rays.

radius: The radius of a circle is the distance between the center of the circle and the edge or perimeter of the circle.

ratio: The comparison of two values of the same kind.

reflect: To bounce back without absorbing.

reflectional symmetry: If a shape or an object can be divided in half by a line, and the two halves match exactly, the shape or object has reflectional (or mirror) symmetry.

refract: When a ray of light bends as it passes from one substance to another.

repel: To force apart.

rotational symmetry: A shape has rotational symmetry if, when it is turned around its central point, it matches its original outline one or more times.

scale (*map*)**:** The scale on a map tells us the ratio of a distance on the map to a distance on the ground.

software (*computers*)**:** The operating system and programs on a computer.

solar: Means "to do with the Sun."

species: A group of similar-looking organisms that can reproduce together.

streamlined: Having a shape that reduces air or water resistance.

symmetry: Symmetry in an object or shape means either side of the line of symmetry is a mirror image of the other half. There may be one or many lines of symmetry (*see also: rotational symmetry and reflectional symmetry.*)

temperature: How hot or cold something is.

thrust: A forward push, such as from a jet or rocket engine.

tide: The rise and fall of the ocean.

tissue: A collection of similar cells.

trigonometry: The study of the relationships between the angles and sides of triangles.

upthrust: The upward force that a liquid or gas exerts on an object.

vacuum: A space without any matter.

variation: The differences in characteristics between individuals of the same species.

velocity: How fast something moves in a specific direction.

vertebrate: An animal with a backbone.

vertices: The points in shapes where edges meet.

vibration: A back and forth shaking of an object, substance, or wave.

virus: An infectious biological agent that needs to take over a living cell to make copies of itself. Viruses can cause disease.

volume: The space occupied by an object.

water resistance: The force that acts on an object as it moves through water.

wavelength: The distance between one crest of a wave and the crest next to it.

weight: The force that acts on an object's mass due to gravity; how heavy something is.

zoology: The study of animals and animal life.

INDEX

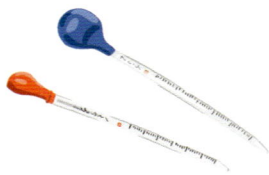

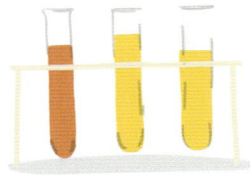

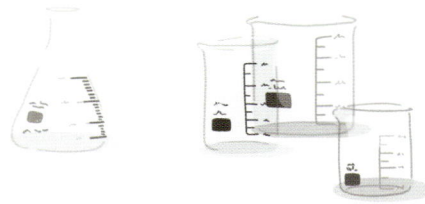

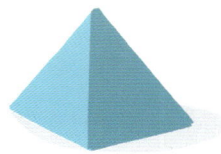